HOLT McDOUGAL

Modern World History

PATTERNS OF INTERACTION

Guided Reading Workbook

HOLT McDOUGAL
a division of Houghton Mifflin Harcourt

Printed in the U.S.A.

ISBN 978-0-547-52082-7

11 0928 16

4500590433 B C D E F G

Contents

How to Use This Book

The purpose of this *Guided Reading Workbook* is to help you read and understand your history textbook, *Modern World History: Patterns of Interaction*. You can use this *Guided Reading Workbook* in two ways.

1. **Use the *Guided Reading Workbook* side-by-side with your history book.**
   - Turn to the section that you are going to read in the textbook. Then, next to the book, put the pages from the *Guided Reading Workbook* that accompany that section. All of the heads in the *Guided Reading Workbook* match the heads in the textbook.
   - Use the *Guided Reading Workbook* to help you read and organize the information in the textbook.
2. **Use the *Guided Reading Workbook* to study the material that will appear in the chapter tests.**
   - Reread the summary of every chapter.
   - Review the definitions of the **Terms and Names** in the *Guided Reading Workbook*.
   - Review the graphic organizer that you created as you read the summaries.
   - Review your answers to questions.

Strategy: Read the **Terms and Names** and the definition of each. The **Terms and Names** are in dark type in the section.

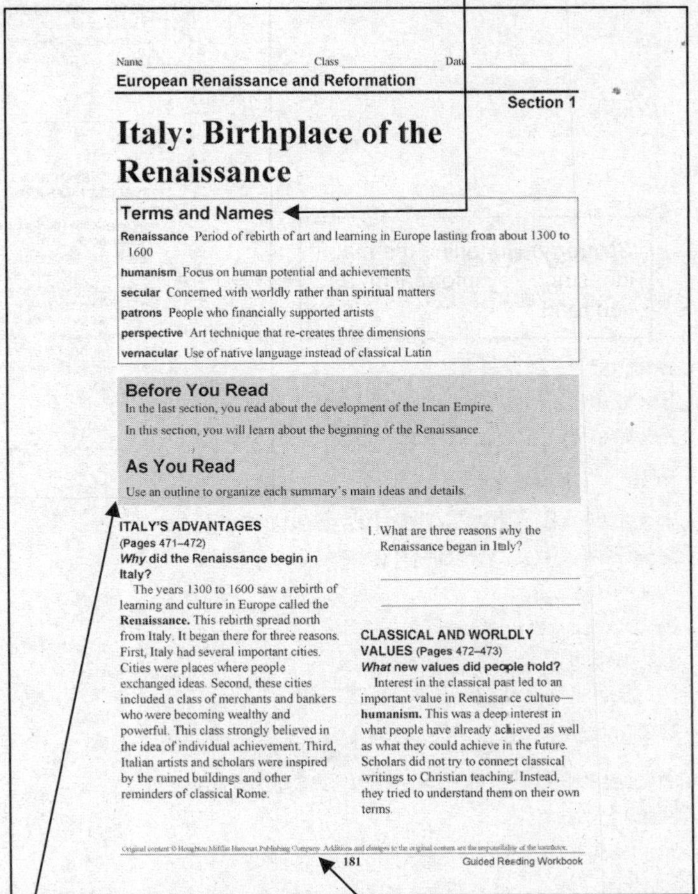

Name ______ Class ______ Date ______

European Renaissance and Reformation

Section 1

Italy: Birthplace of the Renaissance

Terms and Names

Renaissance Period of rebirth of art and learning in Europe lasting from about 1300 to 1600

humanism Focus on human potential and achievements

secular Concerned with worldly rather than spiritual matters

patrons People who financially supported artists

perspective Art technique that re-creates three dimensions

vernacular Use of native language instead of classical Latin

Before You Read

In the last section, you read about the development of the Incan Empire.

In this section, you will learn about the beginning of the Renaissance.

As You Read

Use an outline to organize each summary's main ideas and details.

ITALY'S ADVANTAGES (Pages 471–472)

***Why* did the Renaissance begin in Italy?**

The years 1300 to 1600 saw a rebirth of learning and culture in Europe called the **Renaissance.** This rebirth spread north from Italy. It began there for three reasons. First, Italy had several important cities. Cities were places where people exchanged ideas. Second, these cities included a class of merchants and bankers who were becoming wealthy and powerful. This class strongly believed in the idea of individual achievement. Third, Italian artists and scholars were inspired by the ruined buildings and other reminders of classical Rome.

1. What are three reasons why the Renaissance began in Italy?

CLASSICAL AND WORLDLY VALUES (Pages 472–473)

***What* new values did people hold?**

Interest in the classical past led to an important value in Renaissance culture—**humanism.** This was a deep interest in what people have already achieved as well as what they could achieve in the future. Scholars did not try to connect classical writings to Christian teaching. Instead, they tried to understand them on their own terms.

Original content © Houghton Mifflin Harcourt Publishing Company. Additions and changes to the original content are the responsibility of the instructor.

181 Guided Reading Workbook

Strategy: Use a graphic organizer to help you organize information in the section.

Strategy: Read the summary. It contains the main ideas and the key information under the head.

Name ______________ Class ______________ Date ______________

Section 1, *continued*

In the Middle Ages, the emphasis had been mostly on spiritual values. Renaissance thinkers stressed **secular** ideas. These ideas centered on the things of the world. One way that powerful or wealthy people showed this interest in worldly things was by paying artists, writers, and musicians to create beautiful works of art. Wealthy people who supported artists were known as **patrons.**

People tried to show that they could master many fields of study or work. Someone who succeeded in many fields was admired greatly. The artist Leonardo da Vinci was an example of this ideal. He was a painter, a scientist, and an inventor. Men were expected to be charming, witty, well educated, well mannered, athletic, and self-controlled. Women were expected to have many accomplishments, too. But women were not to show them in public.

2. What are secular ideas?

____

____

____

THE RENAISSANCE REVOLUTIONIZES ART (Pages 474–475)

How did art change during the Renaissance?

Renaissance artists sometimes used new methods. Sculptors made figures more realistic than those from the Middle Ages. Painters used **perspective** to create the illusion that their paintings were three-dimensional. The subject of artwork changed also. Art in the Middle Ages was mostly religious. Renaissance artists reproduced other views of life. Michelangelo showed great skill as an architect, a sculptor, and a painter.

3. How did the methods and subjects in art change?

____

____

____

RENAISSANCE WRITERS CHANGE LITERATURE (Pages 475–477)

How did literature change during the Renaissance?

Renaissance writers also achieved greatness. Several wrote in the **vernacular.** This means they wrote in their native languages. It was a change from the Middle Ages, when most writing was done in Latin. Writers also changed their subject matter. They began to express their own thoughts and feelings. Sometimes they gave a detailed look at an individual. Dante and others wrote poetry, letters, and stories that were more realistic. Niccolò Machiavelli took a new approach to understanding government. He focused on telling rulers how to expand their power. He believed rulers should do what was politically effective, even if it was not morally right.

4. What did Renaissance writers write about?

____

____

____

Strategy: Underline the main ideas and key information as you read.

Strategy: Answer the question at the end of each part.

The last page of each section of the *Guided Reading Workbook* ends with a graphic organizer that will help you better understand the information in the section. Use the graphic organizer to take notes as you read. The notes can help you to prepare for the section quiz and chapter tests.

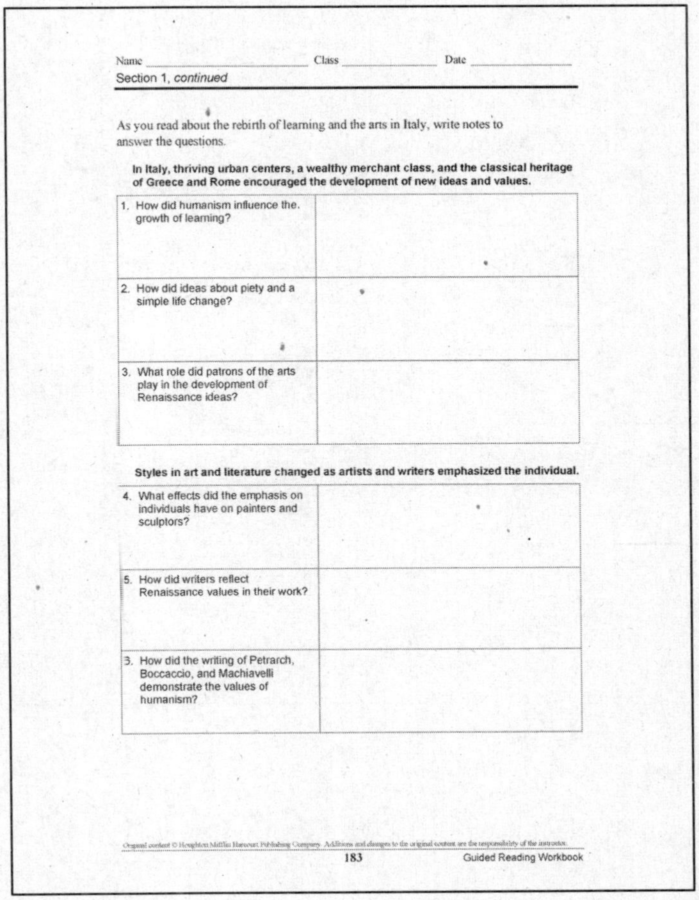

Name ______________ Class ______________ Date ______________

Section 1, *continued*

As you read about the rebirth of learning and the arts in Italy, write notes to answer the questions.

In Italy, thriving urban centers, a wealthy merchant class, and the classical heritage of Greece and Rome encouraged the development of new ideas and values.

1. How did humanism influence the growth of learning?	
2. How did ideas about piety and a simple life change?	
3. What role did patrons of the arts play in the development of Renaissance ideas?	

Styles in art and literature changed as artists and writers emphasized the individual.

4. What effects did the emphasis on individuals have on painters and sculptors?	
5. How did writers reflect Renaissance values in their work?	
3. How did the writing of Petrarch, Boccaccio, and Machiavelli demonstrate the values of humanism?	

Original content © Houghton Mifflin Harcourt Publishing Company. Additions and changes to the original content are the responsibility of the instructor.

183 Guided Reading Workbook

Name ____________________ Class ______________ Date ______________

The Legacy of Ancient Greece and Rome

Terms and Names

government System for exercising authority

monarchy Government controlled by one person

aristocracy State ruled by the noble class

oligarchy A government ruled by a few powerful people

democracy Idea that people can govern themselves

direct democracy Government in which citizens rule directly and not through representatives

republic Government in which citizens elect the leaders who make government decisions

Senate Aristocratic branch of Rome's government

Before You Read

In this section, you will learn how democracy started in Greece and Rome.

As You Read

Use a web diagram to record the contributions of Greece and Rome to democracy.

ATHENS BUILDS A LIMITED DEMOCRACY (Pages 5–7)

How did democracy develop?

Throughout history, people have known the need for a **government**, or a system for exercising authority. For most of history, people have lived under single rulers, such as kings. This type of rule is called a **monarchy**. These rulers had total power. Other governments that developed included **aristocracy**, which is a state ruled by the noble class. Later as trade expanded, a class of wealthy merchants often ruled a land. This was known as an **oligarchy**. The idea of **democracy**—that people can govern themselves—grew slowly. Many people contributed to that idea over the centuries.

Greek civilization began about 2000 B.C. Ancient Greece was made up of city-states. Each city-state had its own government. The first democracy developed in the city-state of Athens.

Athens had a king at first. Then it became an aristocracy. Each year an assembly of citizens elected three nobles to rule Athens. Citizens were adult male residents given certain rights and responsibilities.

A statesman called Solon created four new kinds of citizenship in the sixth century B.C. All free adult males were citizens. All citizens were able to vote in the assembly. But only citizens of the three higher classes could hold public office.

Democracy in Athens was limited. Only about one-tenth of the population were citizens. Women, slaves, and foreign residents could not be citizens. Slaves made up about one-third of the Athenian population at that time.

About a hundred years after Solon, a leader named Cleisthenes increased the power of the assembly. He allowed all citizens to present laws for debate and passage. He also created a council whose members were chosen by lot, or at random. The council suggested laws and advised the assembly.

1. How did Cleisthenes help to increase democracy in Athens?

____

GREEK DEMOCRACY CHANGES

(Pages 7–9)

What **changes occurred in Greek democracy?**

In the fifth century B.C., armies of the Persian Empire invaded Greece. But the Persians were defeated by the Greek city-states in 479 B.C. Athens then became the leader of the city-states. A wise leader, Pericles, ruled Athens.

Pericles strengthened democracy. He increased the number of paid public officials. This allowed poorer citizens to serve in government. He also introduced the idea of **direct democracy**. This allowed citizens to participate directly in government.

Tensions between the city-states led to fighting among them. Then Greece was defeated by armies from the kingdom of Macedonia. This defeat ended democracy in Greece.

During this troubled time, several philosophers appeared. Socrates, Plato, and Aristotle set forth their ideas on government and society.

Greek ideas had lasting influence on government and philosophy. The Greeks did not rely on traditional explanations of the world. Instead they used reason to find patterns that they called natural laws. They developed direct democracy and the three branches of government.

2. How did Pericles change democracy in Athens?

____

ROME DEVELOPS A REPUBLIC

(Page 10)

How **was the Roman government organized?**

Rome began to rise as Greece fell. By 509 B.C., Rome was a republic. A **republic** is a form of government in which citizens have the right to vote and to select their leaders. In Rome, as in Athens, citizenship with voting rights belonged only to males who were not born slaves or foreigners.

Rome's republican government had separate branches. Two officials called consuls directed the government. The legislative branch was made up of the **Senate** and two assemblies. The Senate was the aristocratic branch of government. The assemblies were more democratic. They included other classes of citizens. In times of trouble, the republic gave vast powers to a ruler called a dictator.

Rome gradually increased its territory through conquest. It then became an empire under the rule of a powerful emperor.

3. How was the Roman legislative branch organized?

______

ROMAN LAW (Page 11)
Why did Romans create a system of laws?

The Romans created a system of laws that they could use throughout their empire. Rome's laws have influenced democracy. Some of the most important principles of Roman law were: equal treatment under the law; innocent until proven guilty; the burden of proof rests with the accuser; and unreasonable or unfair laws could be set aside.

In 451 B.C., the Romans created the Twelve Tables, the first written collection of Roman laws. They gave citizens the right to be protected by the laws. About 1,000 years later, all Roman laws were put together in the Code of Justinian. It later was used as a guide on law throughout western Europe. The Code established the idea of "a government of laws, not of men." Under this idea, even rulers and other powerful persons could be held accountable for their actions.

4. Why were the Twelve Tables important?

______

As you read this section, fill in the chart below by naming each person's contribution to the development of democracy in ancient Greece.

Greek Leader	Role in Developing Democracy
1. Solon	
2. Cleisthenes	
3. Pericles	

Use the diagram to give examples and to explain how Roman laws influenced the development of democracy.

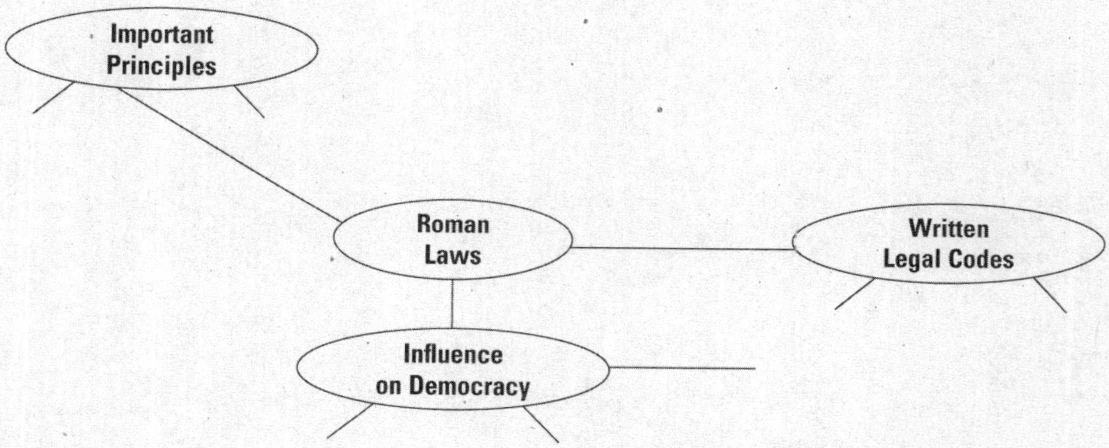

Judeo-Christian Tradition

Terms and Names

Judaism Religion of the Israelites and Jews

Ten Commandments written code of laws

Christianity Religion founded by Jesus

Roman Catholic Church Church that developed from Christianity

Renaissance Cultural movement that started in Italy in the 1300s and spread throughout Europe

Reformation Religious reform movement that began in the 16th century

Before You Read

In the last section, you read about the development of democracy in Greece and Rome.

In this section, you will learn about the teachings of Judaism and Christianity.

As You Read

Use a chart to list one contribution to democracy from Judaism, Christianity, the Renaissance, and the Reformation.

JUDAISM (Pages 12–13)

What is Judaism?

The Israelites were the ancient people who developed **Judaism**. People are the children of God according to the Hebrew Bible. (The Hebrew Bible closely resembles the Old Testament in Christianity.) Unlike other groups of people around them, Israelites believed in one God. Israelites also believed that God gave people the freedom to choose between good and evil. Therefore, each person was responsible for the choices he or she made. These beliefs led to a new emphasis on the worth of the individual.

The Israelites came to be known as the Jews. They developed a written code of laws that includes the **Ten Commandments**. The Bible says that God gave these laws to Moses on Mount Sinai. These laws focused more on morality and ethics than they did on politics.

The Israelites believed in acting responsibly toward others. They thought that the community should help the less fortunate. The prophets of Judaism hoped for a world without poverty or injustice. Prophets were leaders and teachers believed by the Jews to be messengers from God.

1. What are two beliefs of Judaism?

____

CHRISTIANITY (Pages 14–15)

How did Christianity start?

Jesus was born around 6 to 4 B.C. At this time, the Romans ruled Judea, the homeland of the Jews. Jesus began to preach at the age of 30. His preaching contained many ideas from Jewish tradition, including the Ten Commandments. He also stressed the importance of people's love for God, their neighbors, their enemies, and themselves. When Jesus and his teachings seemed to threaten the power of the Roman authorities, they put him to death.

In the first century after Jesus' death, his followers started a new religion based on his messages. It was called **Christianity**. The apostle Paul was important in spreading this religion. He preached that all human beings were equal.

The Romans opposed both Judaism and Christianity. But these religions spread throughout the Roman Empire. When the Jews rebelled against the Romans, they were forced from their homeland. The Jews then fled to many parts of the world. They carried their beliefs with them. As Christianity expanded, it became a powerful religion within the empire. By 380, it had become the empire's official religion.

Several beliefs of these religions helped to shape democratic ideas. These beliefs included:

- the duty of individuals and the community to help oppressed people
- the worth of the individual
- the equality of people before God

2. How did Judaism and Christianity spread throughout the world?

____

RENAISSANCE AND REFORMATION (Pages 16–17)

How did the Renaissance and Reformation help democracy?

The **Roman Catholic Church** was the church that developed from early Christianity. By the Middle Ages, it was the most powerful institution in Europe. It influenced all parts of life.

In the 1300s, a cultural movement called the **Renaissance** spread through Europe. This movement led to an interest in the works of the Greeks and the Romans. Renaissance thinkers were concerned about earthly life. They did not think about it as a preparation for life after death. The Renaissance also focused on the importance of the individual. Artists focused on capturing individual character. Explorers went out to find new lands. Merchants took many risks to gain huge wealth.

The Renaissance also led people to question the Church. This questioning caused the **Reformation**. The Reformation was a protest movement against the power of the Church. It started out as a call for reform. It ended up producing a new division of Christianity—Protestantism.

The Reformation began in Germany. Martin Luther criticized the Church for selling pardons for sins. He also disagreed with the Church in its teaching that people were saved by grace and good works. Luther said people could be saved only through faith in God. Soon, many new Protestant faiths sprang up.

Protestant ideas strengthened the belief in the importance of the individual. In Protestant faiths, the clergy did not have special powers. People could find their own way to God. They could read and interpret the Bible for themselves.

The Reformation broke apart the religious unity of Europe. It challenged the authority of Catholic monarchs and popes. It contributed to the growth of democracy.

3. How did the Reformation contribute to the growth of democracy?
____

As you read about religious traditions and reactions to them, fill in the chart to identify the democratic ideas that arose from each..

	Influence on the Rise of Democratic Ideas
1. Judaism	
2. Christianity	
3. Renaissance	
4. Reformation	

Name ______________________ Class ______________ Date ______________

Democratic Developments in England

Terms and Names

common law Body of English law that reflected customs and principles established over time

Magna Carta Document drawn up by nobles in 1215 guaranteeing basic political rights in England

due process of law Administration of law in known, orderly ways to protect people's rights

Parliament Lawmaking body of England

divine right Theory that a monarch's power came from God

Glorious Revolution Bloodless overthrow of King James II of England and his replacement by William and Mary

constitutional monarchy Monarchy in which the ruler's power is limited by law

bill of rights List of rights and freedoms considered essential to the people

Before You Read

In the last section, you read about the ideas of Judaism, Christianity, and Islam.

In this section, you will learn how democracy developed in England.

As You Read

Use a time line to show the main events in the development of democracy in England.

REFORMS IN MEDIEVAL ENGLAND (Pages 18–20)

***How* did democracy develop in England?**

In 1066, William of Normandy, a French duke, invaded England. He claimed the English throne. This conquest gradually led to the end of feudalism in England. Feudalism was the political and economic system of the Middle Ages. The conquest also set in motion events that led to the development of democracy in England.

An early development in English democracy was a form of trial by jury. It began in the 12th century. Unlike modern juries, these early juries did not decide whether someone was guilty or innocent. Instead, they were asked by a judge to answer questions about the facts of a case.

Another way that democracy developed in England was through **common law**. Common law was not like Roman law, which included things the ruler wanted.

Common law was made up of customs and principles established over time. It became the basis of the legal systems in many English-speaking countries, including the United States.

In 1215, King John became involved in a conflict with the English nobles. They presented their demands to him in the **Magna Carta**. This document contained important principles that placed limits on the power of the English monarch.

One of the Magna Carta's 63 clauses said that the king could not demand taxes. He had to ask for consent from the people. Another clause had to do with an accused person. The accused had a right to a jury trial and to the protection of the law. This right has come to be called **due process of law**. Over time, the clause that said the king could not tax people without their consent was interpreted to mean without the consent of **Parliament**. Parliament was England's lawmaking body.

In 1295, King Edward I needed money to pay for a war. He called together all the lords, plus some knights and leading citizens from the towns. They helped Edward make decisions. This gathering has come to be known as the Model Parliament.

1. How did the Magna Carta change the way people were taxed?

____

____

____

PARLIAMENT GROWS STRONGER
(**Pages** 20–21)

***How* did Parliament increase its power?**

Over the centuries, Parliament had begun to see itself as a partner to the monarch in governing. Its power had grown. It voted on taxes, passed laws, and advised on royal policies.

In the 17th century, European monarchs began to claim greater authority. They insisted their power came from God. It was their **divine right**. Conflicts soon arose. In England, Parliament clashed with James I over the rights of the people. When James's son, Charles, became king, Parliament tried to limit royal power. In 1628 they tried to force him to accept the Petition of Right.

The Petition was very important in constitutional history. It demanded an end to:

- taxing without consent
- imprisoning citizens illegally
- housing troops in citizens' homes
- military government in peacetime

Charles signed the petition. Later, he ignored the promises he made. Conflicts between those who supported Charles and those who supported Parliament eventually caused civil war in 1642. Several years of fighting followed. The king's opponents, led by Oliver Cromwell, won control of the government. Charles was executed in 1649.

2. Why did Parliament force the monarch to sign the Petition of Right?

____

____

____

ESTABLISHMENT OF CONSTITUTIONAL MONARCHY

(**Pages** 22–23)

What was the Glorious Revolution?

Oliver Cromwell ruled briefly. Then, a new parliament restored the monarchy. Charles's son became king as Charles II. Things had changed, however. The monarch could not tax without Parliament's consent. Also, Parliament passed the Habeas Corpus Amendment Act, which kept authorities from wrongly arresting or holding a person.

Charles II was followed by his brother, who ruled as James II. James was a believer in the divine right of kings. Within a few years, Parliament withdrew its support of James. Instead, it offered the throne to James's daughter, Mary, and her husband, William of Orange, ruler of the Netherlands. This change in rulers was called the **Glorious Revolution**. It showed that Parliament had the right to limit a monarch's power. And it had the right to control who would succeed to the throne. As a result, England became a **constitutional monarchy**. In a constitutional monarchy, a ruler's powers are controlled by a constitution and the laws of the country.

In 1689, William and Mary accepted a **bill of rights** from Parliament. It listed the rights and liberties essential to the people and limited the power of the monarchy. Democratic protections included free speech in Parliament, and no taxation without the consent of Parliament.

3. What event led to England's becoming a constitutional monarchy?

____

____

____

As you read about democratic developments in England, identify how events led to effects that promoted democracy.

Historical Event	Resulting Action or Document	Effect on Democracy
1. King John tried to raise taxes on the nobles.		
2. Edward needed money to pay for war in France.		
3. Sixteenth-century monarchs claim more power.		
4. The Glorious Revolution takes place.		

The Enlightenment and Democratic Revolutions

Terms and Names

Enlightenment Intellectual movement that started in Europe

social contract Agreement between citizens and the government

natural rights Rights all people have

separation of powers Division of government into separate branches

American Revolution Americans' fight for independence from Britain

representative government Government in which citizens elect representatives to make laws

federal system Government in which powers are divided between federal and state governments

French Revolution French people's fight for democratic freedoms

United Nations International organization established in 1945

Before You Read

In the last section, you read about the development of democracy in England.

In this section, you will learn how new ways of thinking about the rights of people led to the American and French revolutions.

As You Read

Use an outline to organize the main ideas and details in the section.

ENLIGHTENMENT THINKERS AND IDEAS (Pages 24-25)

What was the Enlightenment?

The **Enlightenment** was an intellectual movement that developed in Europe in the 17th and 18th centuries. Thinkers of this movement had been influenced by the Scientific Revolution. They hoped to use reasoning instead of traditional beliefs to discover natural laws that govern society.

One Enlightenment thinker was Thomas Hobbes. He believed that the best form of government was absolute monarchy. He said people should form a type of **social contract**, or agreement, with a ruler. They would submit to a ruler to prevent disorder.

John Locke took a different view. He said all people had **natural rights**. These were the rights to life, liberty, and property. He said people form governments to protect these natural rights. He also said people have a right to rebel against a government that does not protect their rights.

French Enlightenment thinkers included Voltaire, Jean-Jacques Rousseau, and Baron de Montesquieu. Voltaire fought for tolerance, freedom of religion, and free speech. Rousseau said the only legitimate government was one in which the people chose what was best for the community.

Montesquieu believed that government should be kept under control to protect people's freedoms. He believed that could best be done through a **separation of powers**. This meant dividing the government into branches that would include a lawmaking body, an executive branch to carry out the laws, and courts to interpret laws.

1. According to Locke, why are governments formed?

____

THE BEGINNINGS OF DEMOCRACY IN AMERICA (Pages 25-27)

Why did Americans fight for independence?

Enlightenment ideas had a strong impact on the colonists in Britain's North American colonies. The colonists helped Britain defeat France in the French and Indian War. The victory gave Britain all of North America east of the Mississippi River. To help pay for the war, the British Parliament placed taxes on the colonists. The colonists opposed these taxes because they were not represented in Parliament. This was just one of a series of measures that the colonists thought violated their rights.

The colonists fought for independence in the **American Revolution**. They issued a Declaration of Independence on July 4, 1776. After years of war, the British army surrendered in 1781.

In 1787, a group of American leaders met in Philadelphia. They met to set up a new plan for governing the nation. Enlightenment ideas helped shape this plan. The U.S. Constitution included a **representative government**, as advocated by Rousseau. This is a government in which citizens elect representatives to make laws for them. The Constitution created a **federal system**. In this system, the powers of government are divided between the federal government and state governments. The Constitution also included a separation of powers between branches in the federal government. This was based on the ideas of Montesquieu.

2. What kind of government did Americans create?

____

THE FRENCH REVOLUTION (Pages 27-28)

Why did the French revolt?

In the late 1780s, there was great unrest in France. The middle class was dissatisfied with Louis XVI's weak leadership. The Enlightenment raised questions about people's rights. The economy was failing, and the peasants were hungry and restless.

In 1789 the common people formed the National Assembly. They felt that they were not represented in their government. Soon people from other classes joined them. Peasants in Paris began an uprising to win democratic freedoms. This fight is known as the **French Revolution**.

The National Assembly made many reforms. It adopted the Declaration of the Rights of Man and of the Citizen. This document guaranteed certain rights to all French people. The Assembly also ended the feudal system and drafted a constitution that made France a limited monarchy.

The work of the Assembly did not last long, however. A radical lawmaking body took charge. Soon, a Reign of Terror took place. Many who opposed the revolution were killed for their beliefs. In 1799, a military leader, Napoleon Bonaparte, took control and created a dictatorship. Democracy in France did not develop until the mid-1800s.

3. What was the French Revolution?

____

THE STRUGGLE FOR DEMOCRACY CONTINUES (Pages 28-29)

How does the United Nations promote democracy?

It took centuries for democracy to develop throughout the world. Today, most people look upon it as the best form of government.

An international organization called the **United Nations** (UN) was established in 1945. Its goal is to keep world peace and to make people's lives better. In 1948 the UN adopted the Universal Declaration of Human Rights. This document includes such democratic ideas as the right to life, liberty, and security. It also includes rights to equal protection under the law and to the freedom to assemble.

There are many places in the world today where people do not have these rights. Recent struggles for democracy have taken place in a number of nations, including the republics of the former Soviet Union, South Africa, and East Timor.

4. What is the Universal Declaration of Human Rights?

____

As you read about the Enlightenment, take notes to show each thinker's main ideas about government.

Enlightenment Thinker	Ideas About Government
1. John Locke	
2. Baron de Montesquieu	

As you read about democratic revolutions, take notes to fill in the Venn diagram below to compare the American Revolution to the French Revolution.

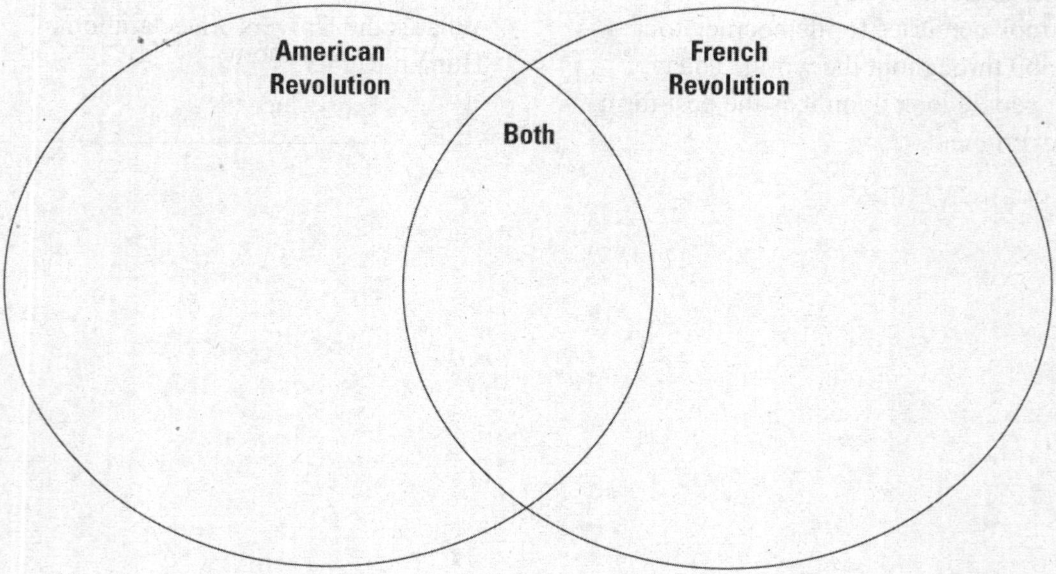

Italy: Birthplace of the Renaissance

Terms and Names

Renaissance Period of rebirth of art and learning in Europe lasting from about 1300 to 1600

humanism Focus on human potential and achievements

secular Concerned with worldly rather than spiritual matters

patrons People who financially supported artists

perspective Art technique that re-creates three dimensions

vernacular Use of native language instead of classical Latin

Before You Read

In the last section, you read about the development of the Incan Empire.

In this section, you will learn about the beginning of the Renaissance.

As You Read

Use an outline to organize each summary's main ideas and details.

ITALY'S ADVANTAGES (Pages 37–38)

***Why* did the Renaissance begin in Italy?**

The years 1300 to 1600 saw a rebirth of learning and culture in Europe called the **Renaissance.** This rebirth spread north from Italy. It began there for three reasons. First, Italy had several important cities. Cities were places where people exchanged ideas. Second, these cities included a class of merchants and bankers who were becoming wealthy and powerful. This class strongly believed in the idea of individual achievement. Third, Italian artists and scholars were inspired by the ruined buildings and other reminders of classical Rome.

1. What are three reasons why the Renaissance began in Italy?

____

____

CLASSICAL AND WORLDLY VALUES (Pages 38–39)

***What* new values did people hold?**

Interest in the classical past led to an important value in Renaissance culture—**humanism.** This was a deep interest in what people have already achieved as well as what they could achieve in the future. Scholars did not try to connect classical writings to Christian teaching. Instead, they tried to understand them on their own terms.

In the Middle Ages, the emphasis had been mostly on spiritual values. Renaissance thinkers stressed **secular** ideas. These ideas centered on the things of the world. One way that powerful or wealthy people showed this interest in worldly things was by paying artists, writers, and musicians to create beautiful works of art. Wealthy people who supported artists were known as **patrons.**

People tried to show that they could master many fields of study or work. Someone who succeeded in many fields was admired greatly. The artist Leonardo da Vinci was an example of this ideal. He was a painter, a scientist, and an inventor. Men were expected to be charming, witty, well educated, well mannered, athletic, and self-controlled. Women were expected to have many accomplishments, too. But women were not to show them in public.

2. What are secular ideas?

____

____

____

THE RENAISSANCE REVOLUTIONIZES ART (Pages 40–41)

How did art change during the Renaissance?

Renaissance artists sometimes used new methods. Sculptors made figures more realistic than those from the Middle Ages. Painters used **perspective** to create the illusion that their paintings were three-dimensional. The subject of artwork changed also. Art in the Middle Ages was mostly religious. Renaissance artists reproduced other views of life. Michelangelo showed great skill as an architect, a sculptor, and a painter.

3. How did the methods and subjects in art change?

____

____

____

RENAISSANCE WRITERS CHANGE LITERATURE (Pages 41–42)

How did literature change during the Renaissance?

Renaissance writers also achieved greatness. Several wrote in the **vernacular.** This means they wrote in their native languages. It was a change from the Middle Ages, when most writing was done in Latin. Writers also changed their subject matter. They began to express their own thoughts and feelings. Sometimes they gave a detailed look at an individual. Dante and others wrote poetry, letters, and stories that were more realistic. Niccoló Machiavelli took a new approach to understanding government. He focused on telling rulers how to expand their power. He believed rulers should do what was politically effective, even if it was not morally right.

4. What did Renaissance writers write about?

____

____

____

As you read about the rebirth of learning and the arts in Italy, write notes to answer the questions.

In Italy, thriving urban centers, a wealthy merchant class, and the classical heritage of Greece and Rome encouraged the development of new ideas and values.

1. How did humanism influence the growth of learning?	
2. How did ideas about piety and a simple life change?	
3. What role did patrons of the arts play in the development of Renaissance ideas?	

Styles in art and literature changed as artists and writers emphasized the individual.

4. What effects did the emphasis on individuals have on painters and sculptors?	
5. How did writers reflect Renaissance values in their work?	
6. How did the writing of Petrarch, Boccaccio, and Machiavelli demonstrate the values of humanism?	

Name ______________________ Class ______________ Date ______________

Section 2

The Northern Renaissance

Terms and Names

Utopia An ideal place

William Shakespeare Famous Renaissance writer

Johann Gutenberg German craftsman who developed the printing press

Before You Read

In the last section, you read how the Renaissance began in Italy.

In this section, you will learn how Renaissance ideas spread in northern Europe.

As You Read

Use a time line to note important events of the northern Renaissance.

THE NORTHERN RENAISSANCE BEGINS (Page 46)

***Why* was the time right for the northern Renaissance to begin?**

By 1450, the bubonic plague had ended in northern Europe. Also, the Hundred Years' War between France and England was ending. This allowed new ideas from Italy to spread to northern Europe. They were quickly adopted. Here, too, rulers and merchants used their money to sponsor artists. But the northern Renaissance had a difference. Educated people combined classical learning with interest in religious ideas.

1. How was the northern Renaissance different from the Renaissance in Italy?

____

____

ARTISTIC IDEAS SPREAD (Pages 46–47)

***What* ideas about art developed in northern Europe?**

The new ideas of Italian art moved to the north, where artists began to use them. Major artists appeared in parts of Germany, France, Belgium, and the Netherlands. Dürer painted religious subjects and realistic landscapes. Holbein, Van Eyck, and Bruegel painted lifelike portraits and scenes of peasant life. They revealed much about the times. They began to use oil-based paints. Oils became very popular, and their use spread to Italy.

2. What did northern European artists paint?

____

____

____

NORTHERN WRITERS TRY TO REFORM SOCIETY; THE ELIZABETHAN AGE (Pages 48–49)

What did northern writers write?

Writers of the northern Renaissance combined humanism with a deep Christian faith. They urged reforms in the Church. They tried to make people more devoted to God. They also wanted society to be more fair. In England, Thomas More wrote a book about **Utopia,** an imaginary ideal society where greed, war, and conflict do not exist.

William Shakespeare is often called the greatest playwright of all time. His plays showed a brilliant command of the English language. They also show a deep understanding of people and how they interact with one another.

3. Who were two of the most famous writers of the northern Renaissance?

____

____

____

PRINTING SPREADS RENAISSANCE IDEAS; THE LEGACY OF THE RENAISSANCE (Pages 50–51)

Why was the printing press such an important development?

One reason that learning spread so rapidly during the Renaissance was the invention of movable type. The Chinese had invented the process of carving characters onto wooden blocks. They then arranged them in words, inked the blocks, and pressed them against paper to print pages.

In 1440, a German, **Johann Gutenberg,** used this same practice to invent his printing press. He produced his first book—the Gutenberg Bible—in 1455 on this press. The technology then spread rapidly. By 1500, presses in Europe had printed nearly 10 million books.

Printing made it easier to make many copies of a book. As a result, written works became available far and wide. Books were printed in English, French, Spanish, Italian, or German. More people began to read. The Bible was a popular book. After reading the Bible, some people formed new ideas about Christianity. These ideas were different from the official teachings of the Church.

The Renaissance prompted changes in both art and society. Artists and writers portrayed people in more realistic ways and celebrated individual achievement. In a larger sense, the Renaissance opened up a world of new ideas to people and led them to examine and question things more closely.

4. What effects did the printing press have on northern European life?

____

____

____

As you read about the ways that northern Europeans adapted the ideas of the Renaissance, take notes to answer each question.

1. What factors led to the beginning of the Renaissance in northern Europe?
2. How did the invention of the printing press help spread learning and Renaissance ideas?

Describe briefly how each of the following showed Renaissance influences in his work.

3. Albrecht Dürer
4. Jan van Eyck
5. Pieter Bruegel the Elder
6. Desiderius Erasmus
7. Thomas More
8. William Shakespeare

Name ______________________ Class ______________ Date ______________

Luther Leads the Reformation

Terms and Names

indulgence Release from punishments due for a sin

Reformation 16th-century movement for religious reform, leading to the founding of new Christian churches

Lutheran Member of a Protestant church founded on the teachings of Martin Luther

Protestant Member of a Christian church founded on the principles of the Reformation

Peace of Augsburg Agreement in 1555 declaring that the religion of each German state would be decided by its ruler

annul Cancel or put an end to

Anglican Relating to the Church of England

Before You Read

In the last section, you saw how the Renaissance spread to northern Europe.

In this section, you will see how Renaissance ideas helped bring about the Reformation.

As You Read

Use a chart to identify the effects of Martin Luther's protests.

CAUSES OF THE REFORMATION (Pages 54–55)

Why was the Church criticized?

By 1500, the influence of the Church on the lives of people had weakened. Some people resented paying taxes to support the Church in Rome. Others sharply criticized the Church for some of its practices. Popes seemed more concerned with luxury and political power than with spiritual matters. Many local priests lacked education and were not able to teach people. Some lived immoral lives.

Reformers urged the Church to change its ways to become more spiritual and humble. Christian humanists such as Erasmus and Thomas More added their voices to calls for change. In the early 1500s, the calls grew louder.

1. What kinds of changes did Church critics want to make?

____

____

LUTHER CHALLENGES THE CHURCH (Page 55)

How did the Reformation begin?

In 1517, a German monk named Martin Luther protested against a Church official who was selling **indulgences.** An indulgence was a kind of forgiveness. By paying money to the Church, people thought they could win salvation.

Luther challenged this practice and others. He posted a protest on the door of a castle church. His words were printed and spread throughout Germany. This was the beginning of the **Reformation**, a movement for reform that led to the founding of new Christian churches.

2. What role did Martin Luther play in the Reformation?

____

____

THE RESPONSE TO LUTHER (Pages 56–58)

What effects did Luther's protest have?

Pope Leo X punished Luther for his views, but he refused to change them. Holy Roman Emperor Charles V, a strong Catholic, called Luther an outlaw. Luther's books were burned. But it was too late. Many of his ideas were already being practiced. The **Lutheran** Church started around 1522.

In 1524, peasants in Germany hoped to use Luther's ideas about Christian freedom to change society. They demanded an end to serfdom—a condition like slavery. When it was not granted, they revolted. Luther disagreed with this revolt. German princes killed thousands in putting the revolt down.

Some nobles supported Luther's ideas. They saw a chance to weaken the emperor's power over them. Other German princes joined forces against Luther's supporters. They signed an agreement to remain loyal to the pope and the emperor. Supporters of Luther's ideas protested this agreement. They were called the Protestants. Eventually, the term **Protestant** meant Christians who belonged to non-Catholic churches.

War broke out between Catholic and Protestant forces in Germany. It finally ended in 1555 with the **Peace of Augsburg.** This treaty granted each prince the right to decide whether his subjects would be Catholic or Protestant.

3. Why did Luther's ideas lead to war?

____

____

ENGLAND BECOMES PROTESTANT (Page 58–60)

How did England become Protestant?

The Catholic Church faced another challenge in England. Henry VIII, the king, was married to a Spanish princess. She gave birth to a daughter. England had never had a female ruler. Henry feared a civil war would start if he had no son. He believed his wife was too old to have another child. He tried to get the pope to **annul**, or put an end to, the marriage so he could remarry. The pope refused.

To remarry, Henry had to get out of the Catholic church. In 1534, Henry had Parliament pass laws that created the Church of England. These laws made the king or queen, not the pope, head of the Church. Henry no longer had to obey the pope. Henry remarried five times. His only son was from his third wife.

One of Henry's daughters, Elizabeth, became queen in 1558. She finished creating a separate English church. The new church was called **Anglican.** It had some practices that would appeal to both Protestants and Catholics. In this way, Elizabeth hoped to end religious conflict.

4. What role did Henry VIII play in creating the Church of England?

____

____

As you read this section, note some of the causes and effects of the events identified.

Causes	Event or Situation	Effects
	1. In 1517, Luther posts his 95 theses on the church door at Wittenberg.	
	2. In 1520, Luther is excommunicated. In 1521, he is declared an outlaw and a heretic.	
	3. The German peasants revolt in 1524.	
	4. The Peace of Augsburg is signed in 1555.	
	5. The English Parliament approves the Act of Supremacy in 1534.	
	6. Parliament establishes the Anglican Church in 1559.	

Section 4

The Reformation Continues

Terms and Names

predestination Doctrine that God has decided all things beforehand, including which people will be saved

Calvinism Religious teachings based on the ideas of the reformer John Calvin

theocracy Government controlled by religious leaders

Presbyterian Member of a Protestant church governed by elders and founded by John Knox

Anabaptist Member of a Protestant group during the Reformation who believed only adults should be baptized. Also believed that church and state should be separate

Catholic Reformation 16th-century Catholic reform movement in response to Protestant Reformation

Jesuits Members of the Society of Jesus, a Roman Catholic religious order founded by Ignatius of Loyola

Council of Trent Meeting of Roman Catholic leaders to rule on doctrines criticized by the Protestant reformers

Before You Read

In the last section, you read how the Reformation began.

In this section, you will learn how it developed and spread.

As You Read

Use a chart to compare the ideas of the reformers who came after Luther.

CALVIN CONTINUES THE REFORMATION (Pages 61–62)

What did Calvin teach?

Protestantism arose elsewhere in the 1530s under the leadership of John Calvin. Calvin taught that people are sinful by nature. He also taught **predestination,** the idea that God determines beforehand who will be saved. The religion based on Calvin's teachings is called **Calvinism.**

Calvin created a **theocracy** in Geneva, Switzerland. It was government run by religious leaders. It had strict rules of behavior.

A preacher named John Knox put these ideas into practice in Scotland. This was beginning of the **Presbyterian** Church. Others in Holland, France, and Switzerland adopted Calvin's ideas as well. In France, his followers were called Huguenots. Conflict between them and Catholics often turned into violence. In 1572, mobs killed about 12,000 Huguenots.

1. What is Calvinism?

____

OTHER PROTESTANT REFORMERS (Pages 62–64)

What other reformers were important during the Reformation?

Another new Protestant group was the **Anabaptists.** They preached that people should be baptized into the faith as adults. Anabaptists also taught that the church and state should be separate. In addition, they refused to fight in wars.

Many women played key roles in the Reformation. Marguerite of Navarre protected John Calvin from being killed for his beliefs. Katherina von Bora was the wife of Martin Luther. She supported an equal role for women in marriage.

2. Who were two women who played important roles in the Reformation?

____

THE CATHOLIC REFORMATION (Pages 64–65)

What was the Catholic Reformation?

Protestant churches grew all over Europe. To keep Catholic believers loyal, the Catholic Church took steps to change itself. This was called the **Catholic Reformation.**

One Catholic reformer was a Spanish noble named Ignatius. He founded a new group in the Church based on deep devotion to Jesus. Members of this group, called the **Jesuits,** started schools across Europe. They sent missionaries to convert people to Catholicism. In addition, they tried to stop the spread of Protestant faiths.

Two popes of the 1500s helped bring about changes in the Church. Pope Paul III set up a kind of court called the Inquisition. It was charged with finding, trying, and punishing people who broke the rules of the Church. He also called a meeting of church leaders, the **Council of Trent.** The council, which met in 1545, passed doctrines. These doctrines stated that the Church's interpretation of the Bible was final and that Christians needed to perform good works to win salvation. They also gave the Bible and the Church equal authority in setting out Christian beliefs and supported indulgences.

The next pope, Paul IV, put these doctrines into practice. They helped revive the Church and allowed it to survive the challenge of the Protestants.

3. What happened at the Council of Trent?

____

THE LEGACY OF THE REFORMATION (Page 66)

What was the legacy of the Reformation?

The Reformation had an enduring impact on society. In the wake of the movement, Protestant churches flourished. Meanwhile, the Catholic Church became more unified as a result of the reforms started at the Council of Trent.

The Reformation caused an overall decline in the authority of the church. As a result, individual monarchs and states gained greater power. This in turn led to the development of modern nation-states.

Women thought that their status in society might improve as a result of the Reformation. However, this did not happen. Women were still mainly limited to the concerns of home and family.

4. What was the result of the declining authority of the church?

____

As you read about new Protestant churches and reforms within the Catholic Church, take notes to answer the questions.

What were some religious or social beliefs of each new Protestant religion?	
1. Calvinism	
2. Presbyterianism	
3. Anabaptism	

4. What were the three major activities of the Jesuits?
5. Why were the effects of the work of Jesuit missionaries so long lasting?
6. What role did Popes Paul III and Paul IV play in reforming the Catholic Church?
7. What were some important effects of the Reformation?

Section 1

The Ottomans Build a Vast Empire

Terms and Names

ghazis Warriors for Islam

Osman Successful ghazi who built a small state in Anatolia

sultans Rulers of Muslim states

Timur the Lame Conqueror of Persia and Russia

Mehmed II Conqueror who made Istanbul his capital

Suleyman the Lawgiver Ruler who brought Ottoman Empire to its height

devshirme Policy for creating the sultan's army

janissary Soldier slave drawn from conquered Christian territories

Before You Read

In the last chapter, you read about changes in Europe during 1300-1600.

In this section, you will read about the rise of the Ottoman Empire during the same period.

As You Read

Use a chart to list the main rulers of the Ottoman Empire and their successes.

TURKS MOVE INTO BYZANTIUM (Pages 73–74)

***How* did the Ottoman Empire begin?**

In 1300, the world of the eastern Mediterranean was also changing. The Byzantine Empire was fading. The Seljuk Turk state had been destroyed. Anatolia, the area of modern Turkey, was now inhabited by groups of nomadic Turks. They saw themselves as **ghazis,** or Muslim warriors for Islam. They raided the lands where non-Muslims lived.

The most successful ghazi was **Osman.** Western Europeans thought his name was Othman. They called his followers Ottomans. Between 1300 and 1326, Osman built a strong but small kingdom in Anatolia. Leaders who came after Osman called themselves **sultans,** or "ones with power." They extended the kingdom by buying land. They also formed alliances with other chieftains and conquered everyone they could.

The Ottomans ruled in a kindly way. Muslims had to serve in the army but paid no taxes. Non-Muslims paid tax but did not serve in the army. Many joined Islam just to avoid the tax. Most people adjusted easily to their new rule.

One warrior did not. He was **Timur the Lame.** He conquered Russia and Persia. In 1402, he defeated the Ottoman forces.

Timur captured the sultan and took him to Samarkand in a cage.

1. Who were the Ottomans?

____

____

____

____

POWERFUL SULTANS SPUR DRAMATIC EXPANSION

(Pages 74–75)

***How* did the empire grow?**

In Anatolia, the four sons of the last sultan fought for control of the empire. Mehmed I won control. His son and the four sultans who came after him brought the Ottoman Empire to its greatest power. One of them—**Mehmed II**—took power in 1451. He built a force of 100,000 foot soldiers and 125 ships to gain control of Constantinople. In 1453, he took the city and the waterway it controlled. Mehmed made the city his capital. He renamed it Istanbul. The rebuilt city became home to people from all over the Ottoman Empire.

Other emperors used conquest to make the empire grow. After 1514, Selim the Grim took Persia, Syria, and Palestine. He then captured Arabia, took the Muslim holy cities of Medina and Mecca, and gained control of Egypt.

2. Who was Mehmed II?

____

____

____

____

SULEYMAN THE LAWGIVER; THE EMPIRE DECLINES SLOWLY

(Pages 76–77)

***Why* was Suleyman the Lawgiver a great leader?**

Suleyman I took power in 1520 and ruled for 46 years. He brought the Ottoman Empire to its greatest size and most impressive achievements. He conquered parts of southeastern Europe. He won control of the entire eastern Mediterranean Sea and took North Africa as far west as Tripoli.

Suleyman revised the laws of the empire. His people called him **Suleyman the Lawgiver.** Suleyman ruled his empire with a highly structured government. Thousands of slaves served the royal family. The policy of making people slaves was called ***devshirme.*** The **janissaries** were an enslaved group of soldiers. They were Christians taken as children and made slaves. They were trained as soldiers and fought fiercely for the sultan. Other slaves held important government jobs.

The empire allowed people to follow their own religion. Jews and Christians were not mistreated. His empire was also known for great works of art and many fine buildings.

Although the empire lasted long after Suleyman, it spent the next few hundred years in decline. That means its power slipped. None of the sultans were as accomplished as Suleyman had been.

3. What were two of Suleyman's accomplishments?

____

____

____

____

As you read this section, fill out the chart below by writing answers in the appropriate boxes.

What role did each ruler play in the building and expansion of the Ottoman Empire?	
1. Osman	
2. Murad II	
3. Mehmed II	
4. Selim the Grim	
5. Suleyman	

List the achievements of Suleyman in the boxes below.

Social Achievements	Cultural Achievements

Name ______________________ Class ______________ Date ______________

Cultural Blending

Case Study: The Safavid Empire

Terms and Names

Safavid Member of a Shi'a Muslim group that built an empire in Persia

Isma'il Safavid warrior who seized most of what is now Iran

shah Persian title meaning king

Shah Abbas Leader during the Safavid golden age

Esfahan Capital city of the Safavid Empire

Before You Read

In the last section, you read about the Ottomans.

In this section, you will learn about the development of another empire, the Safavid.

As You Read

Use a diagram to identify examples of cultural blending in the Safavid Empire.

PATTERNS OF CULTURAL BLENDING (Pages 78–79)

***What* is cultural blending?**

Throughout history, different peoples have lived together. Their cultures have influenced one another. Often these people have blended one culture with another. This can happen because of migration, trade, conquest, or pursuit of religious freedom or conversion.

Cultural blending results in changes in society. Some results of cultural blending are changes in language, religion, styles of government, or arts and architecture.

Societies that are able to benefit from cultural blending are open to new ways. They are willing to adapt and change.

1. What are the four causes of cultural blending?

____

____

THE SAFAVIDS BUILD AN EMPIRE (Pages 79–80)

***How* did the Safavids rise to power?**

Cultural blending took place in the Safavid Empire of Persia. The **Safavids** were members of the Shi'a, a branch of Islam. The major group of Muslims, the Sunnis, persecuted the Shi'a for their views. The Safavids feared the Sunni Muslims. They decided to build a strong army to protect themselves.

In 1499, a 14-year-old leader named **Isma'il** led this army to conquer Iran. He took the traditional Persian title of **shah,** or king, and made Shi'a the religion of the new empire. He destroyed Baghdad's Sunni population. Ottoman Turk rulers—who were Sunni Muslims—in turn killed all the Shi'a that they met. This conflict between the two groups of Muslims continues today.

2. Why are the Shi'a and Sunni Muslims enemies?

____

A SAFAVID GOLDEN AGE

(**Pages** 80–81)

Who was Shah Abbas?

The Safavids reached their height in the late 1500s under **Shah Abbas.** He created two armies that were loyal to him and him alone. He also gave new weapons to the army to make them better fighters. He got rid of corrupt officials in the government. He also brought gifted artists to his empire.

Shah Abbas drew on good ideas from other cultures. The main elements of that culture were the joining together of the Persian tradition of learning and sophistication with the strong faith of the Shi'a. He used Chinese artists. They helped create gorgeous artwork that decorated the rebuilt capital of **Esfahan.**

Under Shah Abbas, the Safavids enjoyed good relations with nations of Europe. The demand for Persian rugs increased greatly in Europe. In this period, rug-making, which had been a local craft in Persia, became a major industry for the country.

3. What were four reforms made by Shah Abbas?

____

THE DYNASTY DECLINES QUICKLY

(**Page** 81)

Why did the Safavids lose power?

Like the Ottoman Empire, the Safavid Empire began to decline soon after it had reached its greatest height. Shah Abbas had killed or injured his most talented sons—just as Suleyman had done. Shah Abbas feared that his sons would seize power from him. As a result, a weak and ineffective grandson became shah after him.

4. Why weren't there strong leaders after Shah Abbas?

____

____

As you read this case study, take notes to answer the questions about patterns of cultural blending.

Interaction among peoples can create a blending of cultures.

1. What activities cause cultural blending to occur?	2. Which of those activities contributed to the culture of the Ottomans?

The Safavids built a Shi'a Empire.

3. How did Isma'il help the Safavids rise to power?	4. How did Isma'il's rule affect the Islam religion?

Shah Abbas helped create a Safavid culture.

5. How did Shah Abbas promote cultural blending in his empire?	6. What was probably the most important result of Western influence on the Safavid Empire?

Name ______________________ Class ______________ Date ______________

Section 3

The Mughal Empire in India

Terms and Names

Babur Founder of the Mughal Empire

Mughal One of the nomads who invaded the Indian subcontinent and established a powerful empire there

Akbar Mughal ruler with a genius for cultural blending, military conquest, and art

Sikh Nonviolent religious group that became the enemy of the Mughals

Shah Jahan Mughal ruler who built Taj Mahal

Taj Mahal Tomb built by Shah Jahan for his wife

Aurangzeb Last important Mughal ruler

Before You Read

In the last section, you learn about how the Safavids established an empire in what is present-day Iran.

In this section, you will learn about the establishment of the Mughal Empire in what is now India.

As You Read

Use a time line to identify the Mughal emperors and their successes.

EARLY HISTORY OF THE MUGHAL EMPIRE (Page 82)

***How* did the Mughal Empire begin?**

Starting in the 600s, India went through a long, unsettled period. Nomads from central Asia invaded the area and created many small kingdoms. In the 700s, Muslims arrived on the scene. This began a long history of fighting with the Hindus who had lived in India for centuries.

After about 300 years, a group of Muslim Turks conquered a region around the city of Delhi. They set up a new empire there. They treated the Hindus in their area as conquered peoples. Their rule was brought to an end in 1398.

A little over a hundred years later, a new leader named **Babur** raised an army and began to win large parts of India. He had many talents. He was a lover of poetry and gardens. He was also an excellent general. His empire was called the **Mughal** Empire because he and his families were related to the Mongols.

1. Who was Babur?

____

THE GOLDEN AGE OF AKBAR (Pages 83–84)

***Who* was Akbar?**

Babur's grandson was **Akbar.** His name means "Greatest One." He ruled with great wisdom and fairness for almost 40 years.

Akbar was a Muslim. However, he believed strongly that people should be allowed to follow the religion they choose.

Both Hindus and Muslims worked in the government. He hired people in his government based on their ability.

Akbar ruled fairly. He ended the tax that Hindu pilgrims and all non-Muslims had to pay. To raise money, he taxed people on a percentage of the food they grew. This made it easier for peasants to pay the tax. His land policy was less wise. He gave much land to government officials. However, when they died he took it back. As a result, workers did not see any point in caring for the land.

He had a strong, well-equipped army that helped him win and keep control of more lands. His empire held about 100 million people—more than lived in all of Europe at the time.

During Akbar's reign, his policy of blending different cultures produced two new languages. One was Hindi, which is widely spoken in India today. The other was Urdu. It is now the official language of Pakistan. The empire became famous for its art, literature, and architecture. He also sponsored the building of a new capital city.

2. What are some examples of Akbar's policy of fair rule?

____

AKBAR'S SUCCESSORS (Pages 84–87)

Who ruled after Akbar?

After Akbar's death in 1605, his son Jahangir took control of the empire. During his reign, the real power was his wife, Nur Jahan. She plotted with one son to overthrow another son. She had a bitter political battle with the **Sikhs,** members of a separate, nonviolent religion, who became the target of attacks.

The next ruler was **Shah Jahan.** He too chose not to follow Akbar's policy of religious toleration. Shah Jahan was a great patron of the arts and built many beautiful buildings. One was the famous **Taj Mahal,** a tomb for his wife. His ambitious building plans required high taxes, though. People suffered under his rule.

His son **Aurangzeb** ruled for almost 50 years. He made the empire grow once again with new conquests. His rule also brought new problems. He was a devout Muslim, and he punished Hindus and destroyed their temples. This led to a rebellion that took part of his empire. At the same time, the Sikhs won control of another part of the empire.

3. How did Aurangzeb deal with Hindus?

____

THE EMPIRE'S DECLINE AND DECAY (Page 87)

How did the Mughal Empire lose its power?

Aurangzeb used up the empire's resources. People did not feel loyalty to him. As the power of the state weakened, the power of local lords grew. Soon there was only a patchwork of independent states. There continued to be a Mughal emperor, but he was only a figurehead, not a ruler with any real power. As the Mughal empire was rising and falling, Western traders were building power. They arrived in India just before Babur did. Shah Jahan let the English build a trading fort in Madras. Aurangzeb handed them the port of Bombay. This gave India's next conquerors a foothold in India.

4. How did the Mughal Empire change after Akbar?

____

As you read about the Mughal Empire, make notes in the chart to describe the outcome of each action listed.

Action		Outcome
1. Babur leads troops to victories over an army led by the sultan of Delhi and the rajput army.	→	
2. Akbar governs through a bureaucracy of officials in which natives and foreigners, both Hindus and Muslims, can rise to high office.	→	
3. Akbar prohibits inheritance of land granted to bureaucrats.	→	
4. Akbar appoints rajputs as officers in Mughal army.	→	
5. Akbar practices cultural blending.	→	
6. The Sikhs defend Khusrau in his rebellion against his father, Jahangir.	→	
7. Shah Jahan orders the building of the Taj Mahal.	→	
8. Aurangzeb strictly enforces Islamic laws and reinstates tax on non-Muslims.	→	
9. Aurangzeb dies.	→	

Section 1

Europeans Explore the East

Terms and Names

Bartolomeu Dias Portuguese explorer who rounded the tip of Africa

Prince Henry Portuguese supporter of exploration

Vasco da Gama Explorer who gave Portugal a direct sea route to India

Treaty of Tordesillas Treaty between Spain and Portugal dividing newly discovered lands between them

Dutch East India Company Dutch company that established and directed trade throughout Asia

Before You Read

In the last chapter, you read about empire building in Asia.

In this section, you will learn why and how Europeans began an age of exploration.

As You Read

Use a time line to take notes on important events in the European exploration of the East.

FOR "GOD, GLORY, AND GOLD" (Pages 95–96)

Why **did Europeans begin to explore new lands?**

For many centuries, Europeans did not have much contact with people from other lands. That changed in the 1400s. Europeans hoped to gain new sources of wealth. By exploring the seas, traders hoped to find new, faster routes to Asia—the source of spices and luxury goods. Another reason for exploration was spreading Christianity to new lands.

Bartolomeu Dias, an early Portuguese explorer, explained his motives: "to serve God and His Majesty, to give light to those who were in darkness and to grow rich as all men desire to do."

Advances in technology made these voyages possible. A new kind of ship, the caravel, was stronger than earlier ships. It had triangle-shaped sails that allowed it to sail against the wind. Ships could now travel far out into the ocean. The magnetic compass allowed sea captains to stay on course better.

1. What were the two main reasons for European exploration?

____

____

____

PORTUGAL LEADS THE WAY; SPAIN ALSO MAKES CLAIMS (Pages 96–99)

How **did Portugal lead the way in exploration?**

Portugal was the first nation to develop the caravel and magnetic compass.

Prince Henry was committed to the idea of exploring. In 1419, he started a school of navigation. Sea captains, mapmakers, and navigators met and exchanged ideas there.

Over the next few decades, Portuguese captains sailed farther and farther down the west coast of Africa. In 1488, Bartolomeu Dias reached the southern tip of Africa. Ten years later, **Vasco da Gama** led a ship around Africa, to India and back. The Portuguese had found a sea route to Asia.

The Spanish, meanwhile, had plans of their own. Christopher Columbus convinced the king and queen that he could reach Asia by sailing west. In 1492, instead of landing in Asia, Columbus touched land in the islands of the Americas. Spain and Portugal argued over which nation had the rights to the land that Columbus had claimed. In 1494, they signed the **Treaty of Tordesillas.** It divided the world into two areas. Portugal won the right to control the eastern parts—including Africa, India, and other parts of Asia. Spain got the western parts—including most of the Americas.

2. How did Spain and Portugal solve their differences over claims to new lands?

____

____

TRADING EMPIRES IN THE INDIAN OCEAN (Pages 99–101)

Who established trading empires in the Indian Ocean?

Portugal moved quickly to make the new Indian Ocean route pay off. Through military might, Portugal gained power over islands that were rich in desirable spices. They were called the Spice Islands. Spices now cost Europeans one-fifth of what they had cost before, while still making Portugal very wealthy.

Other European nations joined in this trade. In the 1600s, the English and Dutch entered the East Indies. They quickly broke Portuguese power in the area. Then both nations set up an East India Company to control Asian trade. These companies were more than businesses. They were like governments. They had the power to make money, sign treaties, and raise their own armies. The **Dutch East India Company** was richer and more powerful than England's company.

By 1700, the Dutch ruled much of Indonesia. They had trading posts in many other Asian countries and commanded the southern tip of Africa. At the same time, both England and France finally gained footholds in India.

Nevertheless, even though Europeans controlled the trade between Asia and Europe, they had little impact on most people living in these areas.

3. How did the Dutch and English become Indian Ocean trading powers?

____

____

____

As you read about the age of exploration, take notes to answer questions about events listed in the time line.

Year	Event	Question
1400		
1419	**Prince Henry starts a navigation school.**	1. What technological advances made possible the age of exploration?
1487	**Bartolomeu Dias rounds the southern tip of Africa.**	2. What were some immediate and some long-term outcomes of Columbus' voyage?
1492	**Christopher Columbus reaches the Caribbean.**	
1494	**Spain and Portugal sign the Treaty of Tordesillas.**	3. What was the most important result of this agreement?
1498	**Vasco da Gama reaches the port of Calicut on the Indian Ocean.**	4. How did Portugal benefit from his voyage?
1500		
1521	**Ferdinand Magellan leads a Spanish expedition to the Philippines.**	
1565	**Spain begins settlements in the Philippines.**	5. Why did Spain set up trading posts in Asia?
1600		
1619	**The Dutch establish a trading center on Java.**	6. How did the Dutch gain control of much of the Indian Ocean trade?
1664	**France sets up its own East India Company.**	7. How did the European battles for Indian Ocean trade affect the peoples of Asia before the nineteenth century?

Name ______________________ Class ______________ Date ______________

China Limits European Contacts

Terms and Names

Hongwu Commander of the rebel army that drove the Mongols out of China in 1368

Ming Dynasty Chinese dynasty that ruled from 1368 to 1644

Yonglo Ming ruler; son of Hongwu

Zheng He Muslim admiral who led seven voyages of exploration during the Ming Dynasty

Manchus People from Manchuria

Qing Dynasty Chinese dynasty that followed the Ming Dynasty and was begun by the Manchus

Kangxi Powerful Manchu emperor of the Qing Dynasty

Before You Read

In the last section, you read about European exploration in the East.

In this section, you will read about China's reactions to the world around it.

As You Read

Use a chart to summarize relevant facts about each emperor discussed in this section.

CHINA UNDER THE POWERFUL MING DYNASTY (Pages 102–105)

What occurred during the Ming Dynasty?

Mongol rule in China ended in 1368 when **Hongwu** led a rebel army that took control of the country. He declared himself the first emperor of the **Ming Dynasty,** which was to last for almost 300 years. Hongwu began his rule by increasing the amount of food produced and improving the government. Later he grew suspicious and untrusting. He caused the deaths of many people whom he suspected of plotting against him.

His son **Yonglo** continued his better policies. He also launched a major effort at making contact with other Asian peoples. Beginning in 1405, an admiral named **Zheng He** led several voyages to Southeast Asia, India, Arabia, and Africa. Wherever he went, he gave away gifts to show Chinese superiority.

Eventually the Chinese began to isolate themselves. China allowed Europeans to trade at only three ports, but illegal trade took place all along the coast. Europeans wanted Chinese silk and ceramics, and they paid silver for them. Manufacturing never grew very large in China, however.

The Confucian ideas that shaped Chinese thinking said that farming was a better way of life, so manufacturing was heavily taxed. Missionaries entered China at this time, bringing both Christianity and technology.

1. How was China influenced by foreigners during the Ming Dynasty?

____

____

MANCHUS FOUND THE QING DYNASTY (**Pages** 105–106)

How **did China change during the Qing Dynasty?**

The Ming Dynasty lost power because the government could not solve several problems. Manchus, people who came from a land north of China called Manchuria, took control of the country in 1644. They started the **Qing Dynasty.** Two important emperors were **Kangxi** and his grandson Qian-long. They brought China to its largest size, increased its wealth, and sponsored an increase in artistic production.

The Chinese insisted that Europeans had to follow certain rules in order to continue trading with them. These rules included trading only at special ports and paying fees. The Dutch were willing to do so, and they carried on the largest share of trade with China. The British, though, did not agree to following these rules.

At the same time, a feeling of national pride was rising in Korea, which had long been dominated by China.

2. Why was trade a problem during the Qing Dynasty?

____

____

LIFE IN MING AND QING CHINA (**Page** 107)

What **was life like in China under the Ming and Qing?**

In China, the production of rice and the long period of peace gave the people better lives. In the1600s and 1700s, the number of people in China almost doubled. The majority of these people were farmers. Because of the use of fertilizer and better irrigation, they could grow more food. The level of nutrition improved. This caused the population to grow.

In Chinese families, sons were valued over daughters. It was believed that only sons could carry out family religious duties and tend to the family farm. For that reason, many infant girls were killed, and adult women had few rights.

The invasions by the foreigners from Manchuria and the pressure from European traders bothered the Chinese. They tried to preserve their traditions and their isolation. Artists created books and paintings that showed traditional Chinese values and ideas. Plays about Chinese history and heroes were popular. They helped to unify the Chinese people.

3. Which parts of society improved during this time, and which continued to be the same?

____

____

As you read this section, take notes to answer questions about the Ming and Qing dynasties.

The rulers of the Ming Dynasty drive out the Mongols and bring peace and prosperity to China.

1. How did Hongwu bring stability to China?	→	2. What were some of his agricultural reforms?
3. Why was only the government allowed to conduct foreign trade?	→	4. How did foreign trade affect Ming China?

The Manchus invade China and begin the Qing Dynasty.

5. How did Manchu rulers gain the respect of the Chinese people?	→	6. How were traditional styles reflected in Chinese culture?
7. What restrictions did the Manchus place on foreign trade?	→	8. Why did the Chinese accept the Dutch and reject the British as trading partners?

Japan Returns to Isolation

Terms and Names

daimyo Warrior-chieftains

Oda Nobunaga Daimyo who hoped to control all of Japan and seized Kyoto

Toyotomi Hideyoshi Daimyo who took control of almost all of Japan

Tokugawa Shogunate Dynasty that ruled Japan from 1603 to 1868

kabuki Type of Japanese theater

haiku Type of Japanese poetry

Before You Read

In the last section, you saw how the Chinese reacted to foreigners.

In this section, you will read about civil war in Japan and its effects.

As You Read

Use a chart to compare the achievements of the daimyo who unified Japan.

A NEW FEUDALISM UNDER STRONG LEADERS (Pages 108–110)

***Why* were warriors fighting in Japan?**

From 1467 to 1568, Japan entered a long, dark period of civil war. Powerful warriors took control of large areas of land. They were called **daimyo.** They became the most important powers in the country. The daimyo fought each other constantly to gain more land for themselves.

In 1568, one of the daimyo, **Oda Nobunaga,** took control of Kyoto. It was the site of the emperor's capital. Another general, **Toyotomi Hideyoshi,** continued the work of bringing all of Japan under one rule. Using military conquest and clever diplomacy, he won that goal in 1590. He failed in his effort to capture Korea, however.

The work of unifying Japan was completed by Tokugawa Ieyasu. He became the shogun, or sole ruler. He moved the capital of Japan to a small fishing village named Edo. Later, it grew to become the city of Tokyo.

While all of Japan was ruled by Tokugawa, the daimyo still held much power in their lands. Tokugawa solved that problem by forcing them to follow his orders. Tokugawa died in 1616. All of the shoguns to follow him were from his family. They maintained a strong central government in Japan. This system of rule, called the **Tokugawa Shogunate,** lasted until 1867.

1. Which three leaders helped bring Japan under one rule?

____

____

LIFE IN TOKUGAWA JAPAN (Page 110)

How was Tokugawa society organized?

The new government brought about a long period of peace and prosperity for most people. Peasant farmers suffered greatly during this time, however. They worked long and hard on the farms and paid heavy taxes. Many left the countryside to move to the cities. By the mid-1700s, Edo had more than a million people. It was perhaps the largest city in the world. Women found more opportunities for work in this and other cities than they had in the country.

A traditional culture thrived, characterized by ceremonial dramas, stories of ancient warriors, and paintings of classical scenes. However, in cities, new styles emerged. Townspeople attended **kabuki,** dramas of urban life. They hung woodblock prints of city scenes in their homes. They also read **haiku,** poetry that presents images instead of expressing ideas.

2. What kinds of old and new culture were found in the cities?

____

____

CONTACT BETWEEN EUROPE AND JAPAN; THE CLOSED COUNTRY POLICY (Pages 111–113)

Who came to Japan?

In 1543, Europeans began to arrive in Japan. The Portuguese were first. In the beginning, Japanese merchants and the daimyo welcomed them. They even welcomed the Christian missionaries who came after 1549. Some missionaries scorned traditional Japanese beliefs. They also got involved in local politics. Tokugawa became worried. In 1612, he banned Christianity from the country. Christians were persecuted. Over the next 20 years or so, Japan managed to rid the country of all Christians. This was part of a larger plan to protect the country from European influence.

In 1639, leaders sealed Japan's borders except for one port city. It was open to only the Chinese and the Dutch. The Tokugawa shoguns controlled that port city, so they had tight control over all foreign contact. For the next 200 years, Japan remained closed to just about all European contact.

3. Why did the Japanese seal almost all of their borders?

____

____

As you read this section, take notes to answer the questions.

How did each of the following help to unify Japan?	
1. daimyo	2. Oda Nobunaga
3. Toyotomi Hideyoshi	4. Tokugawa Ieyasu

How did each of the following influence Japanese society and culture?	
5. Tokugawa Shogunate	6. Portuguese
7. Christian missionaries	8. "Closed country" policy

Spain Builds an American Empire

Terms and Names

Christopher Columbus Italian explorer who landed in the Americas

colony Land controlled by another nation

Hernando Cortés Conquistador who defeated the Aztec

conquistadors Spanish explorers in the Americas

Francisco Pizarro Conquistador who defeated the Inca

Atahualpa Last Incan emperor

mestizo Person with mixed Spanish and Native American blood

encomienda System of mining and farming using natives as slave labor

Before You Read

In the last chapter, you read about European exploration in the East.

In this section, you will study the Spanish and Portuguese exploration of the Americas.

As You Read

Use a diagram to trace the major events in the establishment of Spain's empire in the Americas.

THE VOYAGE OF COLUMBUS (Pages 119–120)

***How* did the voyage of Columbus change the Americas?**

In 1492, **Christopher Columbus,** an Italian sailor, led a voyage for Spain. He sailed west hoping to reach Asia. Instead, he landed in the Americas. Columbus thought that he had reached the East Indies in Asia. He misnamed the natives he met there, calling them Indians. He claimed the land for Spain. From then on, Spain began to create **colonies.** Colonies are lands controlled by another nation.

In 1500, a Portuguese explorer claimed Brazil. In 1501, Amerigo Vespucci explored the eastern coast of South America. He said that these lands were a new world. Soon after, a mapmaker showed the lands as a separate continent. He named them America after Vespucci.

Other voyages gave Europeans more knowledge about the world. Balboa reached the Pacific Ocean. Ferdinand Magellan sailed completely around the world.

1. Which voyages gave Europeans new knowledge of the world?

____

____

SPANISH CONQUESTS IN MEXICO
(**Pages** 120–122)

Why did Spain conquer the Aztecs?

Hernando Cortés was one of the Spanish **conquistadors,** or conquerors. In the 16th century, they began to explore the lands of the Americas. They were seeking great riches. In 1519, Cortés came to Mexico and defeated the powerful Aztec Empire led by Montezuma II.

2. What was the main goal of Cortéz in his conquests?

____

____

SPANISH CONQUESTS IN PERU
(**Pages** 122–123)

How did Spain build an empire?

About 15 years later, **Francisco Pizarro** led another Spanish force. It conquered the mighty Inca Empire of South America, led by **Atahualpa,** the last of the Incan emperors. Once again, the Spanish found gold and silver. By the mid-1500s, Spain had formed an American empire that stretched from modern-day Mexico to Peru. After 1540, the Spanish looked north of Mexico and explored the future United States.

The Spanish lived among the people they conquered. Spanish men married native women. Their children and descendants were called **mestizo**—people with mixed Spanish and Native American blood. The Spanish also formed large farms and mines that used natives as slave labor. This system was known as ***encomienda.***

One large area of the Americas—Brazil—was the possession of Portugal. In the 1830s, colonists began to settle there. Colonists built huge farms called plantations to grow sugar, which was in demand in Europe.

3. Give two examples of conquistadors and explain what they did.

____

____

SPAIN'S INFLUENCE EXPANDS
(**Page** 124)

Where did Spain hope to gain more power?

Soon Spain began to want even more power in the Americas. It started to look at land that is now part of the United States. Explorers like Coronado led expeditions to the area. Catholic priests went along.

4. What area did Coronado explore?

____

____

OPPOSITION TO SPANISH RULE
(**Page** 125)

Who opposed Spanish rule?

Spanish priests began to make some protests, however. One thing they criticized was the *encomienda* system. A monk named Bartolomé de Las Casas and others successfully called for the end of the system.

Native Americans also resisted new or continued Spanish rule. One of the most serious rebellions occurred in New Mexico. A Pueblo leader named Popé led a well-organized effort. It involved about 17,000 warriors and drove the Spanish back into New Spain for 12 years.

5. What challenges to their power did the Spanish face?

____

____

As you read about the empire Spain built in the Americas, take notes to answer questions about the time line below.

Year	Event	Question
1492	**Christopher Columbus sails westward from Spain, hoping to reach Asia.**	1. What was the significance of Columbus's voyages?
1519	**Ferdinand Magellan sets sail on a voyage that rounds the southern tip of South America.**	2. Magellan himself died in the Philippines. What was the importance of the voyage his crew completed?
1521	**Hernando Cortés conquers the Aztec.**	3. What factors helped the Spanish defeat the Aztec?
1533	**Francisco Pizarro conquers the Inca Empire.**	4. How did the Spanish treat the peoples they conquered?
1540	**Francisco Vásquez de Coronado explores the Southwest.**	5. What was unique about the Spanish colonization of the lands of New Mexico?
1542	**Spain abolishes the *encomienda* system.**	6. What was the long-term consequence of this action?

Name ______________ Class ______________ Date ______________

Section 2

European Nations Settle North America

Terms and Names

New France Area of the Americas explored and claimed by France

Jamestown First permanent settlement in America

Pilgrims Group of English people who founded a colony in Plymouth

Puritans People who did not agree with the practices of the Church of England

New Netherland Dutch colony begun in modern New York City

French and Indian War War between Britain and France over land in North America

Metacom Native American leader who led an attack on the villages of Massachusetts; also called King Philip

Before You Read

In the last chapter, you read about Spanish conquests.

In this section, you will see how other nations competed for power in North America.

As You Read

Use a chart to record information about early settlements.

COMPETING CLAIMS IN NORTH AMERICA (Pages 127–128)

***What* new colonies were formed in North America?**

In the early 1500s, the French began to explore North America. Jacques Cartier discovered and named the St. Lawrence River. He then followed it to the site of what is now Montreal. In 1608, Samuel de Champlain sailed as far as modern-day Quebec. In the next 100 years, the French explored and claimed the area around the Great Lakes and the Mississippi River all the way to its mouth at the Gulf of Mexico. The area became known as **New France**. The main activity in this colony was trade in beaver fur.

1. What was the main economic activity in New France?

____

____

THE ENGLISH ARRIVE IN NORTH AMERICA (Pages 128–129)

***Why* did the English settle in Massachusetts?**

The English also began to colonize North America. The first permanent settlement was at **Jamestown,** in modern Virginia, in 1607. The colony struggled at first. Many settlers died from disease, hunger, or war with the native peoples.

Soon, farmers began to grow tobacco to meet the high demand for it in Europe.

In 1620, a group known as **Pilgrims** founded a second English colony in Plymouth, in Massachusetts. These settlers and others who followed were deeply religious people who did not agree with the practices of the Church of England. They were called **Puritans.**

Meanwhile, the Dutch also started a new colony. They settled in the location of modern New York City and called it **New Netherland.** Like the French, they traded fur. The colony became known as a home to people of many different cultures. Europeans also took possession of many islands of the Caribbean. There they built tobacco and sugar plantations that used enslaved Africans as workers.

2. In which two places did English colonists first settle?

____

____

THE STRUGGLE FOR NORTH AMERICA (Pages 129–130)

Who fought for control of North America?

The European powers began to fight for control of North America. First, the English forced the Dutch to give up their colony. New Netherland was renamed New York. The English also started other colonies along the Atlantic coast, from New Hampshire to Georgia. These English colonists interfered with the French settlers in Canada.

The British and the French clashed over the Ohio Valley in 1754. The fight was called the **French and Indian War.** When it ended in 1763, France was forced to give up all its land in North America to England.

3. How did England gain land from the French?

____

____

____

NATIVE AMERICANS RESPOND (Pages 130–131)

How did native peoples respond to the colonists?

The native peoples responded to the colonists in many different ways. Many worked closely with the French and Dutch, joining in the fur trade and benefiting from it. Those who lived near the English, though, had stormier relations with colonists. More than just trade, the English were interested in settling the land and farming it. This was land that Native Americans would not be able to use for hunting or growing their own food.

Conflicts over land erupted into war several times. One of the bloodiest times was known as King Philip's War. The Native American ruler **Metacom** (also known as King Philip) led an attack on 52 colonial villages throughout Massachusetts. However, Metacom's forces were no match for the settlers' guns and cannons.

As in Spanish lands, the native peoples suffered even more from disease than from warfare. Thousands upon thousands of Native Americans died from European illnesses. This made it impossible for them to resist the growth of the colonies.

4. Why did Native Americans lose their way of life?

____

____

As you read this section, fill out the chart below by writing notes that describe aspects of each European settlement.

1. New France	
Explorers	Reasons for exploration

2. Jamestown	
Founders	Significance of colony

3. Plymouth and Massachusetts Bay colonies	
Settlers	Reasons for colonization

4. New Netherland	
Land claims	Reasons for colonization

Name ______________________ Class ______________ Date ______________

Section 3

The Atlantic Slave Trade

Terms and Names

Atlantic slave trade Buying and selling of Africans for work in the Americas

triangular trade European trade between the Americas, Africa, and Europe involving slaves and other goods

middle passage Voyage that brought captured Africans to the West Indies and the Americas

Before You Read

In the last section, you saw how different European nations settled in North America.

In this section, you will read about the slave trade that brought Africans to the Americas.

As You Read

Use an outline to list effects of the Atlantic slave trade.

THE CAUSES OF AFRICAN SLAVERY (Pages 132–133)

***What* was the Atlantic slave trade?**

Slavery has had a long history in Africa and in the world. For most of that history in Africa, though, large numbers of people had not been enslaved. That changed in the 600s, when Muslim traders started to take many slaves to Southwest Asia.

Most worked as servants, and they did have certain rights. Also, the sons and daughters of slaves were considered to be free. The European slave trade that began in the 1500s was larger. The enslaved Africans also were treated far more harshly.

In the Americas, Europeans first used Native Americans to work farms and mines. When the native peoples began dying from disease, the Europeans brought in Africans. The buying and selling of Africans for work in the Americas became known as the **Atlantic slave trade.** From 1500 to 1870, when the slave trade in the Americas finally ended, about 9.5 million Africans had been imported as slaves.

The Spanish first began the practice of bringing Africans to the Americas. However, the Portuguese increased the demand for slaves. They were looking for workers for their sugar plantations in Brazil.

1. Why were slaves brought to the Americas?

____

____

SLAVERY SPREADS THROUGHOUT THE AMERICAS (Pages 133–134)

***What* sorts of plantations existed in the Americas?**

Other European colonies also brought slaves to work on tobacco, sugar, and coffee plantations. About 400,000 slaves were brought to the English colonies in North America. Their population had increased to about 2 million in 1830.

Many African rulers joined in the slave trade. They captured people inland and brought them to the coast to sell to European traders.

2. How did some African rulers participate in the slave trade?

____

____

A FORCED JOURNEY (Pages 134–135)
***What* kinds of trade included human beings?**

Africans taken to the Americas were part of a **triangular trade** between Europe, Africa, and the Americas. European ships brought manufactured goods to Africa, trading them for people. They carried Africans across the Atlantic to the Americas, where they were sold into slavery. The traders then bought sugar, coffee, and tobacco to bring back to Europe.

Another triangle involved ships sailing from the northern English colonies in North America. They carried rum to Africa, people to the West Indies, and sugar and molasses back to the colonies to make more rum.

The part of the voyage that brought people to the Americas was called the **middle passage.** It was harsh and cruel. People were crammed into ships, beaten, and given little food. About 20 percent of the people on these ships died.

3. What was the triangular trade?

____

____

SLAVERY IN THE AMERICAS; CONSEQUENCES OF THE SLAVE TRADE (Pages 135–136)
***What* was life like for the slaves?**

Life on the plantations was harsh as well. People were sold to the highest bidder. They worked from dawn to dusk in the fields. They lived in small huts and had little food and clothing. Africans kept alive their traditional music and beliefs to try to maintain their spirits. Sometimes they rebelled. From North America to Brazil, from 1522 to the 1800s, there were small-scale slave revolts.

The Atlantic slave trade had a huge impact on both Africa and the Americas. In Africa many cultures lost generations of members. Africans began fighting Africans over the control of the slave trade.

The Africans' labor helped build the Americas. They brought skills and culture too. Many of the nations of the Americas have mixed race populations.

4. How did Africans change the Americas?

____

____

As you read this section, write notes to answer questions about the causes and consequences of the enslavement of Africans.

How did each of the following contribute to the development of the Atlantic slave trade?	
1. European colonization of the Americas	2. Portuguese settlement of Brazil
3. African rulers	4. African merchants

What were the consequences of the Atlantic slave trade for each of the following?	
5. African societies	6. Enslaved Africans
7. American colonies	8. Present-day American cultures

Section 4

The Columbian Exchange and Global Trade

Terms and Names

Columbian Exchange Global transfer of foods, plants, and animals during the colonization of the Americas

capitalism Economic system based on private ownership and the investment of wealth for profit

joint-stock company Company in which people pooled their wealth for a common purpose

mercantilism Economic policy of increasing wealth and power by obtaining large amounts of gold and silver and selling more goods than are bought

favorable balance of trade Condition resulting from selling more goods than are bought

Before You Read

In the last section, you read about the slave trade.

In this section, you will learn about other kinds of trade.

As You Read

Use a chart to take notes on the Columbian Exchange.

THE COLUMBIAN EXCHANGE (Pages 137–139)

What was the Columbian Exchange?

There was constant movement of people and products from Europe and Africa to the Americas. The large-scale transfer of foods, plants, and animals was called the **Columbian Exchange.** Important foods such as corn and potatoes were taken from the Americas to Europe, Africa, and Asia.

Some foods moved from the Old World to the New. Bananas, black-eyed peas, and yams were taken from Africa to the Americas. Cattle, pigs, and horses had never been seen in the Americas until the Europeans brought them. Deadly illnesses also moved to the Americas. They killed a large part of the Native American population.

1. What did the Columbian Exchange take from the Americas, and what did it bring?

____

____

GLOBAL TRADE (Pages 139–140)

How did business change?

The settling of the Americas and the growth of trade started an economic revolution. This revolution led to new business practices still followed today.

One was the rise of an economic system called **capitalism.** It is based on private ownership of property and the right of a business to earn a profit on money it has invested.

Another new business idea was the **joint-stock company.** In this type of company, many investors pool their money to start a business and share in the profits.

2. What is capitalism?

____

____

THE GROWTH OF MERCANTILISM

(**Pages** 140–141)

***Why* were colonies important in mercantilism?**

During the Commercial Revolution, European governments began to follow an idea called **mercantilism.** According to this theory, a country's power depended on its wealth. Getting more gold and silver increased a country's wealth. So did selling more goods than it bought. Selling more than it bought would result in a **favorable balance of trade.** Colonies played an important role because they provided goods that could be sold in trade.

The American colonies changed European society. Merchants grew wealthy and powerful. Towns and cities grew larger. Still, most people lived in the countryside, farmed for a living, and were poor.

3. Why were colonies important to European mercantilism?

____

____

As you read this section, note some cause-and-effect relationships relating to the European colonization of the Americas.

Causes	Event/Trend	Effects
	1. Columbian Exchange	
	2. Global trade	
	3. Inflation	
	4. Formation of joint-stock companies	
	5. Growth of mercantilism	

Section 1

Spain's Empire and European Absolutism

Terms and Names

Philip II Spanish king who took control of Portugal but failed in his invasion of England

absolute monarch King or queen with complete control

divine right Idea that a ruler receives the right to rule from God

Before You Read

In the last chapter, you read about Europe's new relationship to the Americas.

In this section, you will learn about changes occurring in Europe in the 1500s and 1600s.

As You Read

Use a chart to list the conditions that allowed European monarchs to gain power.

A POWERFUL SPANISH EMPIRE (Pages 155–157)

***How* did Spain's power increase and then decrease?**

Charles V of Spain ruled the Holy Roman Empire and other European countries. In 1556, he left the throne and split his holdings. His brother Ferdinand received Austria and the Holy Roman Empire. His son, **Philip II,** got Spain and its colonies.

Philip II then took control of Portugal when the king of Portugal, his uncle, died without an heir. Philip also got its global territories in Africa, India, and the East Indies. When he tried to invade England in 1588, though, he failed. The defeat made Spain weaker. However, Spain still seemed strong because of the wealth—gold and silver—that flowed in from its colonies in the Americas.

1. Who was Philip II?

____

____

GOLDEN AGE OF SPANISH ART AND LITERATURE (Pages 157–158)

***How* did works from the golden age of Spanish art and literature reflect the values and attitudes of the period?**

Spain's great wealth allowed monarchs and nobles to become patrons of artists. Two of the greatest artists of the 16th and 17th century were El Greco and Diego Velásquez. El Greco's work reflected the faith of Spain during this period. The paintings of Velásquez reflected the pride of the Spanish monarchy.

In literature, Miguel de Cervantes wrote *Don Quixote de la Mancha*, which ushered in the birth of the modern European novel.

The novel tells the story of a Spanish nobleman who reads too many books about heroic knights.

2. Who were some of the artists and writers of Spain's golden age?

____

____

THE SPANISH EMPIRE WEAKENS (Pages 158–159)

***What* weakened the Spanish Empire?**

Spain's new wealth led to some serious problems. The prices of goods constantly rose. Unfair taxes kept the poor from building up any wealth of their own. As prices rose, Spaniards bought more goods from other lands. To finance their wars, Spanish kings had to borrow money from banks in foreign countries. The silver from the colonies began to flow to Spain's enemies.

In the middle of these troubles, Spain lost land. Seven provinces of the Spanish Netherlands rose in protest against high taxes and attempts to crush Protestantism in the Netherlands. These seven provinces were Protestant, whereas Spain was strongly Catholic. In 1579, they declared their independence from Spain and became the United Provinces of the Netherlands. The ten southern provinces (present-day Belgium) were Catholic and remained under Spanish control.

3. Why did Spain lose its power?

____

____

THE INDEPENDENT DUTCH PROSPER (Pages 159–160)

***Why* did the Dutch prosper?**

The United Provinces of the Netherlands was different from other European states of the time. It was a republic, not a kingdom. Each province had a leader elected by the people.

The Dutch also practiced religious tolerance, letting people worship as they wished. Dutch merchants established a trading empire. They had the largest fleet of merchant ships in the world. They were also the most important bankers in Europe.

4. Give two reasons for the success of the Dutch in trading.

____

____

ABSOLUTISM IN EUROPE (Pages 160–161)

***What* is absolutism?**

Though he lost his Dutch possessions, Philip continued to hold tight control over Spain. He wanted to control the lives of his people. Philip and others who ruled in the same way were called **absolute monarchs.** They believed in holding all power. They also believed in **divine right.** This is the idea that a ruler receives the right to rule from God.

Widespread unrest in Europe in the 17th century led to an increase in absolute rule, or **absolutism,** and its restrictions. Absolute rulers used their increased power to impose order. They wanted to free themselves from the limitations imposed by the nobility and government bodies.

5. What did absolute monarchs believe?

____

____

As you read about the Spanish Empire, briefly note the causes or effects (depending on which is missing) of each event or situation.

Causes	Effects
1. The gold and silver coming from its vast empire made Spain incredibly wealthy.	
2.	Spain suffered from severe inflation.
3.	The Spanish economy declined and at times Spain was bankrupt.
4. Philip raised taxes in the Netherlands and tried to crush Protestantism.	
5.	The Dutch became wealthy from trade and banking.
6.	European monarchs became increasingly more powerful.

Name ______________________ Class ______________ Date ______________

The Reign of Louis XIV

Terms and Names

Edict of Nantes Order that gave Huguenots the right to live in peace in Catholic France

Cardinal Richelieu Chief minister of France who reduced the power of the nobles

skepticism Belief that nothing could be known for certain

Louis XIV French king who was an absolute ruler

intendant Official of the French government

Jean Baptiste Colbert Chief Minister of Finance under Louis XIV

War of the Spanish Succession War fought by other European nations against France and Spain when those two states tried to unite their thrones

Before You Read

In the last section, you were introduced to the idea of absolutism.

In this section, you will read about absolute power in France.

As You Read

Use a time line to list the major events of Louis XIV's reign.

RELIGIOUS WARS AND POWER STRUGGLES; WRITERS TURN TOWARD SKEPTICISM

(Pages 162–164)

***What* changes were occurring in France?**

France was torn by eight religious wars between Catholics and Protestants from 1562 to 1598.

In 1589, a Protestant prince, Henry of Navarre, became King Henry IV. In 1593, he changed religions. He became a Catholic to please the majority of his people. In 1598, he issued an order called the **Edict of Nantes.** It gave Huguenots—French Protestants—the right to live in peace and have their own churches in some cities.

Henry rebuilt the French economy and brought peace to the land. He was followed by his son, Louis XIII, a weak king. However, Louis had a very capable chief minister, **Cardinal Richelieu.** Richelieu ruled the land for Louis and increased the power of the crown.

The cardinal ordered the Huguenots not to build walls around their cities. He also said nobles had to destroy their castles. As a result, Protestants and nobles could not hide within walls to defy the king's power. Richelieu used people from the middle class—not nobles—to work in his government. That also reduced the power of the nobles.

French thinkers had reacted to the religious wars with horror. They developed a new philosophy called **skepticism.** Nothing could be known for certain, they argued. Doubting old ideas was the first step to learning the truth, they said.

1. How did the monarchy get stronger in France?

____

____

LOUIS XIV COMES TO POWER

(**Pages** 164–165)

How did Louis XIV rule?

In 1643, **Louis XIV** became king at the age of about five. Cardinal Mazarin, who succeeded Richelieu as minister, ruled for Louis until he was 22. Louis became a powerful ruler, who had total control of France. He was determined to never let nobles challenge him.

He kept the nobles out of his government. He gave more power to government officials called **intendants** and made sure that they answered only to him. He also worked hard to increase the wealth of France. His chief minister of finance, **Jean Baptiste Colbert,** tried to build French industry. Colbert wanted to persuade French people to buy French-made goods and not those from other countries. He urged people to settle in the new French colony of Canada in North America. The fur trade there brought wealth to France.

2. How did Louis make sure he kept his power?

____

____

THE SUN KING'S GRAND STYLE; LOUIS FIGHTS DISASTROUS WARS

(**Pages** 165–168)

What changes did Louis make?

Louis enjoyed a life of luxury at his court. He built a huge and beautiful palace at Versailles near Paris. He also made sure that nobles had to depend on his favor to advance in society.

Louis made France the most powerful nation in Europe. France had a larger population and a bigger army than any other country. However, Louis made some mistakes that later proved costly. After winning some wars against neighboring countries, he became bolder and tried to seize more land. Other nations allied to stop France in the late 1680s. The high cost of these wars combined with poor harvests to produce problems at home in France.

The final war fought in Louis's time was fought over succession to the throne of Spain and lasted from 1700 to 1713. In this **War of the Spanish Succession,** France and Spain attempted to set up united thrones. The rest of Europe felt threatened and joined in war against them. Both France and Spain were forced to give up some of their American and European colonies to England. England was the new rising power.

3. How did Louis XIV bring disaster to France?

____

____

As you read about the French monarchy, write notes to answer the questions.

Wars between the Huguenots and Catholics create chaos in France.	
1. How did Henry of Navarre end the crisis and restore order?	
2. How did Cardinal Richelieu strengthen the French monarchy?	
3. What effect did the religious wars have on French intellectuals?	

Louis XIV became the most powerful monarch of his time.	
4. What steps did Jean Baptiste Colbert take to turn France into an economic power?	
5. In what ways did Louis XIV support the arts?	
6. Why did Louis fail in his attempts to expand the French Empire?	
7. What was the legacy of Louis XIV?	

Name ______________________ Class ______________ Date ______________

Central European Monarchs Clash

Terms and Names

Thirty Years' War Conflict over religion, territory, and power among European ruling families

Maria Theresa Empress of Austria whose main enemy was Prussia

Frederick the Great Leader of Prussia who sought to increase his territory

Seven Years' War Conflict from 1756 to 1763 in which the forces of Britain and Prussia battled those of Austria, France, Russia, and other countries

Before You Read

In the last section, you read how absolute power grew in France.

In this section, you will learn about absolutism in Austria and Prussia.

As You Read

Use a chart to compare Maria Theresa with Frederick the Great.

THE THIRTY YEARS' WAR

(**Pages** 169–170)

***What* caused the Thirty Years' War?**

Germany had suffered from religious wars that ended in 1555. Rulers of each German state agreed that they would decide whether their lands would be Catholic or Protestant. Relations between sides became tense over the next decades. Then in 1618, a new war broke out and lasted for 30 terrible years. It was called the **Thirty Years' War.**

During the first half of the war, Catholic forces led by Ferdinand, the Holy Roman Emperor, won. However, Germany suffered because he allowed his large army to loot towns. Then the Protestant king of Sweden, Gustavus Adolphus, won several battles against him.

In the last years of the war, France helped the Protestants. Although France was a Catholic nation, Richelieu feared the growing power of the Hapsburg family, which was headed by Frederick.

The Thirty Years' War ended in 1648 with the Peace of Westphalia. It had been a disaster for Germany. About 4 million people had died, and the economy was in ruins. It took Germany two centuries to recover.

The peace treaty weakened the power of Austria and Spain. But it made France stronger. The French gained German territory. The treaty also made German princes independent of the Holy Roman Emperor. It ended religious wars in Europe. Lastly, the treaty introduced a new way of negotiating peace—a method still used today. All states involved in the fighting meet to settle the problems of a war and decide the terms of peace.

1. What were three results of the Thirty Years' War?

____

____

____

____

STATES FORM IN CENTRAL EUROPE (Page 171)

Who ruled Austria?

The formation of strong states took place slowly in central Europe. The economies there were less developed than in western Europe. Most people were still peasants. This region had not built an economy based on cities and commercialism. Nobles enjoyed great influence. This helped them keep the serfs on the land and prevent the rise of strong rulers. Still, two important states arose.

The Hapsburg family ruled Austria, Hungary, and Bohemia. Their empire linked many different peoples—Czechs, Hungarians, Italians, Croatians, and Germans. **Maria Theresa,** the daughter of Charles VI, was empress of Austria in the mid–1700s. She managed to increase her power and reduce that of the nobles. She was opposed by the kings of Prussia, a new powerful state in northern Germany.

2. Who were the Hapsburgs?

____

____

____

____

PRUSSIA CHALLENGES AUSTRIA (Pages 172–173)

What was Prussia?

Like Austria, Prussia rose to power in the late 1600s. Like the Hapsburgs of Austria, Prussia's ruling family, the Hohenzollerns, also had ambitions.

Prussia was a strong state that gave much power to its large, well-trained army. In 1740, **Frederick the Great** of Prussia invaded one of Maria Theresa's lands. Austria fought hard to keep the territory, but lost. Still, in fighting the War of the Austrian Succession, Maria Theresa managed to keep the rest of her empire intact.

The two sides fought again, beginning in 1756. In the **Seven Years' War,** Austria abandoned Britain, its old ally, for France and Russia. Prussia joined with Britain. The Prussians and British won. In that victory, Britain gained economic domination of India.

3. What effect did fighting between Austria and Prussia have on Britain?

____

____

____

____

Name ______________________ Class ______________ Date ______________

Section 3, *continued*

As you read about the absolute monarchs that ruled in Central Europe, fill out the chart by writing notes in the appropriate spaces.

The Thirty Years' War	
1. Note two causes of the war.	
2. Note four consequences of the war and the Peace of Westphalia.	

Central Europe	
3. Note two differences between the economies of western and central Europe.	
4. Note two reasons why central European empires were weak.	

Prussia and Austria	
5. Note three steps the Hapsburgs took to become more powerful.	
6. Note three steps the Hohenzollerns took to build up their state.	

Name ______________________ Class ______________ Date ______________

Section 4

Absolute Rulers of Russia

Terms and Names

Ivan the Terrible Ruler who added lands to Russia, gave it a code of laws, and also used his secret police to execute "traitors"

boyar Russian noble who owned land

Peter the Great Important leader of Russia who started westernization

westernization Use of western Europe as a model of change

Before You Read

In the last section, you read how Austria and Prussia became strong states.

In this section, you will learn how Russia developed into a powerful state.

As You Read

Use a cluster diagram to list the important events of Peter the Great's reign.

THE FIRST CZAR (Pages 174–175)

***Who* was Ivan the Terrible?**

Ivan III had begun centralizing the Russian government. His son, Vasily, continued the work of adding territory to the growing Russian state. Ivan's grandson, Ivan IV, was called **Ivan the Terrible.** He came to the throne in 1533, when he was three years old.

At first, landowning nobles, known as **boyars,** tried to control Ivan. Eventually, he ruled successfully on his own. He added lands to Russia and gave the country a code of laws. After his wife, Anastasia, died, however, his rule turned harsh. He used secret police to hunt down enemies and kill them. Ivan even murdered his oldest son.

A few years after he died, Russian nobles met to name a new ruler. They chose Michael Romanov, the grandnephew of Ivan the Terrible's wife. He began the Romanov dynasty, which ruled Russia for about 300 years.

1. What good and bad did Ivan the Terrible do?

____

____

____

PETER THE GREAT COMES TO POWER (Page 175)

***Who* was Peter the Great?**

The Romanovs restored order to Russia. In the late 1600s, Peter I came to power. He was called **Peter the Great** because he was one of Russia's greatest reformers. He began an intense program of trying to modernize Russia. He also continued the trend of increasing the czar's power.

When Peter came to power, Russia was still a land of boyars and serfs. Serfdom lasted much longer in Russia than it did in western Europe. It continued into the mid–1800s.

When a Russian landowner sold a piece of land, he sold the serfs with it. Landowners could give away serfs as presents or to pay debts. It was also against the law for serfs to run away from their owners.

Most boyars knew little of western Europe. But Peter admired the nations of western Europe. He traveled in Europe to learn about new technology and ways of working. It was the first time a czar traveled in the West.

2. Why did Peter the Great visit Europe?

____

____

____

____

PETER RULES ABSOLUTELY
(**Pages** 176–177)

***What* changes did Peter the Great make?**

Peter the Great wanted Russia to be the equal of the countries of western Europe. He wanted Russia to be strong both in its military and in its trade.

To meet these goals, Peter changed Russia. His first steps were to increase his powers, so he could force people to make the changes he wanted. He put the Russian Orthodox Church under his control. He reduced the power of nobles. He built up the army and made it better trained.

Peter also changed Russia through **westernization.** He took several steps to make Russia more western. He brought in potatoes as a new food, began Russia's first newspaper, gave more social status to women, and told the nobles to adopt Western clothes. He promoted education.

Peter also knew Russia needed a seaport that would make it easier to travel to the west. He fought a long war with Sweden to gain land along the shores of the Baltic Sea. There he built a grand new capital city, St. Petersburg. By the time of Peter's death in 1725, Russia was an important power in Europe.

3. How did Peter the Great increase his power?

____

____

____

____

As you read this section, complete the chart by explaining how Peter the Great solved each problem he encountered in his efforts to westernize Russia.

Problems	Solutions
1. Russian people did not believe that change was necessary.	
2. The Russian Orthodox Church was too strong.	
3. The great landowners had too much power.	
4. The Russian army was untrained and its tactics and weapons were outdated.	
5. Russian society had to change to compete with the modern states of Europe.	
6. To promote education and growth, Russia needed a seaport for travel to the West.	
7. The port needed to be built.	
8. The new city needed to be settled.	

Name ______________________ Class ______________ Date ______________

Parliament Limits the English Monarchy

Terms and Names

Charles I King of England who was executed

English Civil War War fought from 1642 to 1649 between the Royalists, or Cavaliers, and the Puritan supporters of Parliament

Oliver Cromwell Leader of the Puritans

Restoration Period after the monarchy was restored in England

habeas corpus Law giving prisoners the right to obtain a document saying that the prisoner cannot go to jail without being brought before a judge

Glorious Revolution Bloodless overthrow of King James II

constitutional monarchy Government in which laws limit the monarch's power

cabinet A group of government ministers that was a link between the monarch and Parliament

Before You Read

In the last section, you saw how power was becoming more absolute in Russia.

In this section, you will see how the power of the monarch was challenged and weakened in England.

As You Read

Use a chart to list the causes of the English monarchs' conflicts with Parliament.

MONARCHS DEFY PARLIAMENT

(**Page** 180)

***Why* was there tension between the monarchy and Parliament?**

When Queen Elizabeth I died, her cousin James, king of Scotland, became king of England. The reign of James I began a long series of struggles between king and Parliament. They fought over money. James's religious policies also angered the Puritans in Parliament.

During the reign of his son, **Charles I,** there was continued conflict between king and Parliament. Parliament forced Charles to sign the Petition of Right in 1628. By signing, Charles agreed that the king had to answer to Parliament. But he then dissolved Parliament and tried to raise money without it.

1. How did Charles I make Parliament angry?

____

ENGLISH CIVIL WAR (**Pages** 181–182)
***Who* fought the English Civil War?**

When Charles tried to force Presbyterian Scots to follow the Anglican Church, Scotland threatened to invade England. Charles needed money to fight. When Charles called a new Parliament to get money, it quickly passed laws to limit his power.

Soon England was fighting a civil war. Charles and his Royalists were opposed by the supporters of Parliament. Many of Parliament's supporters were Puritans.

The **English Civil War** lasted from 1642 to 1649. Under the leadership of **Oliver Cromwell,** the forces of the Puritans won. They tried and executed Charles for treason against Parliament. This was the first time a king had faced a public trial and execution. Cromwell became a military dictator, ruling until 1658. He crushed a rebellion in Ireland and tried to reform society at home.

2. What happened as a result of the English Civil War?

____

RESTORATION AND REVOLUTION
(**Page** 182)
***What* was the Restoration?**

Soon after Cromwell's death, the government collapsed. Parliament asked Charles's older son to restore the monarchy. Charles II's rule beginning in 1660 is called the **Restoration.**

Charles II's reign was calm. Parliament passed an important guarantee of freedom called **habeas corpus.** It gave every prisoner the right to get an order to be brought before a judge. The judge would then decide whether the prisoner should be tried or set free. This kept monarchs from putting people in jail just for opposing them. It also meant that people would not stay in jail forever without a trial.

After Charles II's death in 1685, his brother became King James II. His pro-Catholic policies angered the English. They feared that he would restore Catholicism. In 1688, seven members of Parliament contacted James's older daughter, Mary, and her husband, William of Orange, prince of the Netherlands. Both were Protestants. The members of Parliament wanted William and Mary to replace James II on the throne. James was forced to flee to France. When that took place, the bloodless revolution was called the **Glorious Revolution.**

3. Why did the Glorious Revolution take place?

____

LIMITS ON MONARCH'S POWER
(**Page** 183)
***How* was the power of the monarchy decreased in England?**

William and Mary agreed to rule according to the laws made by Parliament. That is, Parliament became their partner in governing. England was now a **constitutional monarchy,** where laws limited the ruler's power.

William and Mary also agreed to accept the Bill of Rights. It guaranteed the people and Parliament certain rights.

By the 1700s, it was clear that the government of England would come to a standstill if the monarch disagreed with Parliament or vice versa. This led to the development of the **cabinet.** This group of government ministers became the first link between the monarch and Parliament.

4. What three changes gave Parliament more power in England?

____

As you read this section, take notes to fill in the diagram describing relations between Parliament and each English ruler listed.

1. King James I
(1603–1625)

↓

2. Charles I
(1625–1649)

↓

3. Oliver Cromwell
(1649–1658)

↓

4. Charles II
(1660–1685)

↓

5. James II
(1685–1688)

↓

6. William and Mary
(1689–1702)

Name ______________________ Class ______________ Date ______________

Enlightenment and Revolution

Section 1

The Scientific Revolution

Terms and Names

Scientific Revolution New way of thinking about the natural world based on careful observation and a willingness to question

heliocentric theory Theory that the sun is at the center of the universe

geocentric theory View which held that the earth was the center of the universe

Galileo Galilei Scientist who was forced by the Catholic Church to take back scientific ideas that disagreed with the church's view

scientific method Logical procedure for gathering and testing ideas

Isaac Newton Scientist who discovered laws of motion and gravity

Before You Read

In the last chapter, you learned about wars and political changes in Europe.

In this section, you will read how the Enlightenment transformed Europe and helped lead to the American Revolution.

As You Read

Use a web diagram to record the events and circumstances that led to the Scientific Revolution.

THE ROOTS OF MODERN SCIENCE (Pages 189–190)

***How* did modern science begin?**

During the Middle Ages, few scholars questioned beliefs that had been long held. Europeans based their ideas on what ancient Greeks and Romans believed or on the Bible. People still thought that the earth was the center of the universe. They believed that the sun, moon, other planets, and stars moved around it.

In the mid-1500s, attitudes began to change. Scholars started what is called the **Scientific Revolution.** It was a new way of thinking about the natural world. It was based on careful observation and the willingness to question old beliefs. European voyages of exploration helped to bring about the Scientific Revolution. When Europeans explored new lands, they saw plants and animals that ancient writers had never seen. These discoveries led to new courses of study in the universities of Europe.

1. What was the Scientific Revolution?

____

A REVOLUTIONARY MODEL OF THE UNIVERSE (Pages 190–191)

***How* did new ideas change accepted thinking in astronomy?**

The first challenge to accepted thinking in science came in astronomy. In the early 1500s, Nicolaus Copernicus, a Polish astronomer, studied the stars and planets.

He developed a **heliocentric theory.** Heliocentric meant sun-centered. It said that Earth, like all the other planets, revolved around the sun. Copernicus did not publish his findings until just before his death. He had been afraid that his ideas would be attacked because they went against the **geocentric theory.** This theory held that the earth was at the center of the universe. In the early 1600s, Johannes Kepler used mathematics to prove that Copernicus's basic idea was correct.

An Italian scientist—**Galileo Galilei**—made several discoveries that also undercut ancient ideas. He made one of the first telescopes and used it to study the planets. He found that Jupiter had moons, the sun had spots, and Earth's moon was rough. Some of his ideas about the earth, the sun, and the planets went against the teaching of the Catholic Church. Church authorities forced Galileo to take back his statements. Still, his ideas spread.

2. What old belief about the universe did the new discoveries destroy?

____

THE SCIENTIFIC METHOD

(**Pages** 191–192)

***Why* was the scientific method an important development?**

Interest in science led to a new approach, the **scientific method.** With this method, scientists ask a question based on something they have seen in the physical world. They form a hypothesis, or an attempt to answer the question. Then they test the hypothesis by making experiments or checking other facts. Finally, they change the hypothesis if needed.

The English writer Francis Bacon helped create this new approach to knowledge. He said scientists should base their thinking on what they can observe and test. The French mathematician René Descartes also influenced the use of the scientific method. His thinking was based on logic and mathematics.

3. What thinkers helped advance the use of the scientific method?

____

NEWTON EXPLAINS THE LAW OF GRAVITY; THE SCIENTIFIC REVOLUTION SPREADS

(**Pages** 192–194)

***What* scientific discoveries were made?**

In the mid-1600s, the English scientist **Isaac Newton** described the law of gravity. Using mathematics, Newton showed that the same force ruled both the motion of planets and the action of bodies on the earth.

Other scientists made new tools to study the world around them. One invented a microscope. Others invented tools for understanding weather.

Doctors also made advances. One made drawings that showed the different parts of the human body. Another learned how the heart pumped blood through the body. In the late 1700s, Edward Jenner first used the process called vaccination to prevent disease. By giving a person the germs from a cattle disease called cowpox, he helped that person avoid getting the more serious human disease of smallpox.

Scientists made progress in chemistry as well. One questioned the old idea that things were made of only four elements—earth, air, fire, and water. He and other scientists separated oxygen from air.

4. How did the science of medicine change?

____

As you read about the revolution in scientific thinking, take notes to answer the questions.

How did the following help pave the way for the Scientific Revolution?		
1. The Renaissance		
2. Age of European exploration		

What did each scientist discover about the universe?		
3. Nicolaus Copernicus		
4. Johannes Kepler		
5. Galileo Galilei		
6. Isaac Newton		

What important developments took place in the following areas?		
7. Scientific instruments		
8. Medicine		
9. Chemistry		

The Enlightenment in Europe

Terms and Names

Enlightenment Age of Reason

social contract According to Thomas Hobbes, an agreement people make with government

John Locke Philosopher who wrote about government

philosophes Social critics in France

Voltaire Writer who fought for tolerance, reason, freedom of religious belief, and freedom of speech

Montesquieu French writer concerned with government and political liberty

Rousseau Enlightenment thinker who championed freedom

Mary Wollstonecraft Author who wrote about women's rights

Before You Read

In the last section, you read how the Scientific Revolution began in Europe.

In this section, you will learn how the Enlightenment began in Europe.

As You Read

Use an outline to organize the summaries' main ideas and details.

TWO VIEWS ON GOVERNMENT

(**Pages** 195–196)

***What* were the views of Hobbes and Locke?**

The **Enlightenment** was an intellectual movement. Enlightenment thinkers tried to apply reason and the scientific method to laws that shaped human actions. They hoped to build a society founded on ideas of the Scientific Revolution. Two English writers—Thomas Hobbes and John Locke—were important to this movement. They came to very different conclusions about government and human nature.

Hobbes wrote that there would be a war of "every man against every man" if there were no government. To avoid this war, Hobbes said, people formed a **social contract.** It was an agreement between people and their government. People gave up their rights to the government so they could live in a safe and orderly way. The best government, he said, is that of a strong king who can force all people to obey.

John Locke believed that people have three natural rights. They are life, liberty, and property. The purpose of government is to protect these rights. When it fails to do so, he said, people have a right to overthrow the government.

1. How were Hobbes's and Locke's views different?

____

THE PHILOSOPHES ADVOCATE REASON (Pages 196–198)

Who were the philosophes?

French thinkers called **philosophes** had five main beliefs: (1) thinkers can find the truth by using reason; (2) what is natural is good and reasonable, and human actions are shaped by natural laws; (3) acting according to nature can bring happiness; (4) by taking a scientific view, people and society can make progress and advance to a better life; and (5) by using reason, people can gain freedom.

The most brilliant of the philosophes was the writer **Voltaire.** He fought for tolerance, reason, freedom of religious belief, and freedom of speech. Baron de **Montesquieu** wrote about separation of powers—dividing power among the separate branches of government. The third great philosophe was Jean Jacques **Rousseau.** He wrote in favor of human freedom. He wanted a society in which all people were equal. Cesare Beccaria was an Italian philosphe. He spoke out against abuses of justice.

2. Name the types of freedoms that Enlightenment thinkers championed.

____

____

____

WOMEN AND THE ENLIGHTENMENT; LEGACY OF THE ENLIGHTENMENT (Pages 199–200)

What were Enlightenment views about individuals?

Many Enlightenment thinkers held traditional views about women's place in society. They wanted equal rights for all men but paid no attention to the fact that women did not have such rights. Some women protested this unfair situation. "If all men are born free," stated British writer **Mary Wollstonecraft,** "how is it that all women are born slaves?"

Enlightenment ideas strongly influenced the American and French revolutions. Enlightenment thinkers also helped spread the idea of progress. By using reason, they said, it is possible to make society better. Enlightenment thinkers helped make the world less religious and more worldly. They also stressed the importance of the individual.

3. Explain the influence of Enlightenment ideas.

____

____

____

Name ______________________ Class ______________ Date ______________

As you read this section, fill in the diagram by describing the beliefs of Enlightenment thinkers and writers.

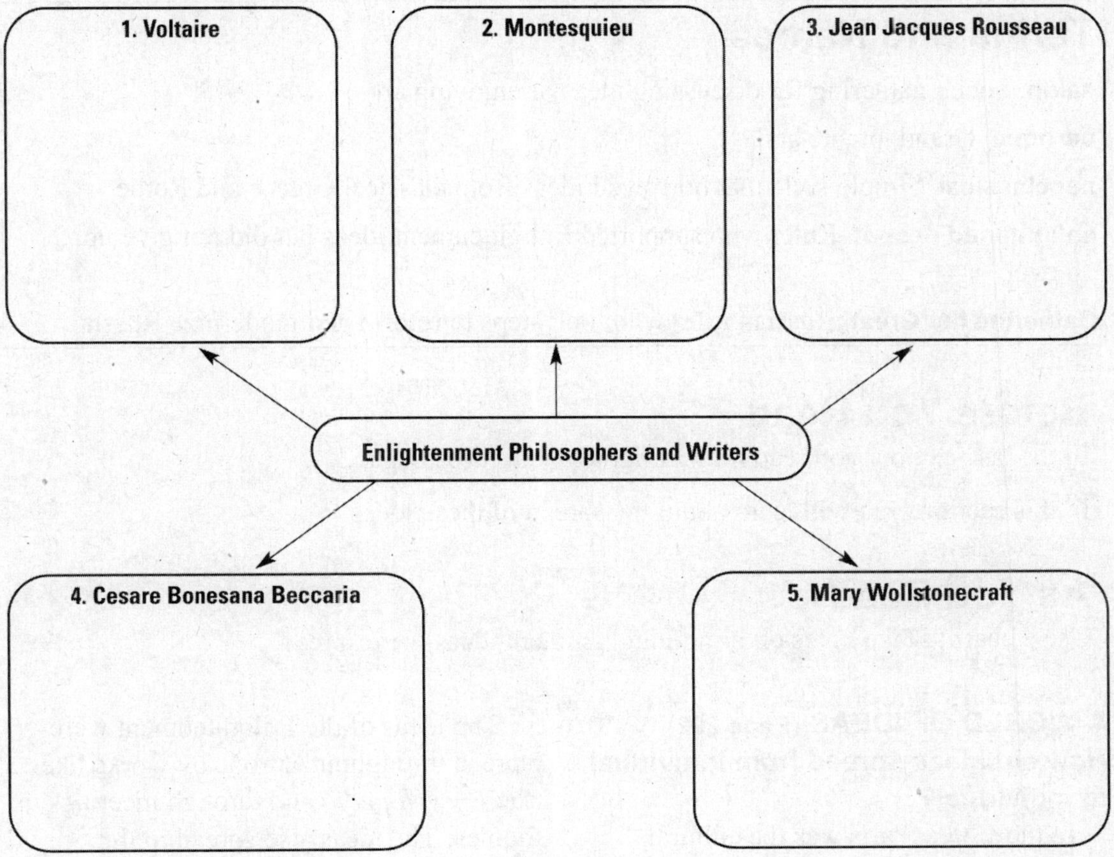

Section 3

The Enlightenment Spreads

Terms and Names

salon Social gathering for discussing ideas or enjoying art

baroque Grand, ornate style

neoclassical Simple style that borrowed ideas from classical Greece and Rome

enlightened despot Ruler who supported Enlightenment ideas but did not give up power

Catherine the Great Russian ruler who took steps to reform and modernize Russia

Before You Read

In the last section, you read how Enlightenment ideas began.

In this section, you will learn about the spread of these ideas.

As You Read

Use a chart to take notes on how Enlightenment ideas were spread.

A WORLD OF IDEAS (Page 202)

***How* did ideas spread from individual to individual?**

In the 1700s, Paris was the cultural center of Europe. People came there from other countries to hear the new ideas of the Enlightenment. Writers and artists held social gatherings called **salons.** A woman named Marie-Thérèse Geoffrin became famous for hosting these discussions.

Geoffrin also supplied the money for one of the major projects of the Enlightenment. With her funds, Denis Diderot and other thinkers wrote and published a huge set of books called the *Encyclopedia*. Their aim was to gather all that was known about the world. The French government and officials in the Catholic Church did not like many of the ideas that were published in the *Encyclopedia*. They banned the books at first. Later, however, they changed their minds.

The ideas of the Enlightenment were spread throughout Europe by works like the *Encyclopedia* and through meetings in homes. The ideas also spread to the growing middle class. This group was becoming wealthy but had less social status than nobles. They also had very little political power. Ideas about equality sounded good to them.

1. Why were salons important?

____

____

____

NEW ARTISTIC STYLES (Page 203)

***How* did art and literature change?**

The arts—painting, architecture, music, and literature—moved in new directions in the late 1700s. They used Enlightenment ideas of order and reason.

Earlier European painting had been very grand and highly decorated. It was a style known as **baroque.** Now styles began to change. A new simpler, yet elegant, style of painting and architecture developed. This style borrowed ideas and themes from Classical Greece and Rome. That is the reason it was called **neoclassical.**

In music, the style of the period is called classical. Three important composers of the time were Franz Joseph Haydn, Wolfgang Amadeus Mozart, and Ludwig von Beethoven. They composed music that was elegant and original. New musical forms were developed, including the sonata and the symphony.

In literature, the novel became popular. This new form presented long stories with twisting plots. It explored the thoughts and feelings of characters. A number of European authors, including women, began writing novels. These books were popular with the middle class. They liked entertaining stories in everyday language.

2. What new styles and forms appeared in art, music, and literature?

____

____

____

ENLIGHTENMENT AND MONARCHY (Pages 204–205)

Who were the enlightened despots?

Some Enlightenment thinkers believed that the best form of government was a monarchy. In it, a ruler respected people's rights. These thinkers tried to influence rulers to rule fairly. Rulers who followed Enlightenment ideas in part but were unwilling to give up much power were called **enlightened despots.**

Frederick the Great of Prussia was an enlightened despot. He gave his people religious freedom and improved schooling. He also reformed the justice system. However, he did nothing to end serfdom, which made peasants slaves to the wealthy landowners. Joseph II of Austria did end serfdom. Once he died, though, the nobles who owned the lands were able to undo this reform.

Catherine the Great of Russia was another of the rulers influenced by Enlightenment ideas. She tried to reform Russia's laws but met resistance. She had hoped to end serfdom. But a bloody peasants' revolt persuaded her to change her mind. Instead, she gave the nobles even more power over serfs. Catherine did manage to gain new land for Russia. Russia, Prussia, and Austria agreed to divide Poland among themselves. As a result, Poland disappeared as a separate nation for almost 150 years.

3. In what way was Frederick the Great typical of an enlightened despot?

____

____

____

As you read about art, literature, and politics in the Age of Reason, explain how each of the following people reflected Enlightenment ideas.

The Arts	
1. Denis Diderot	
2. Franz Joseph Haydn	
3. Wolfgang Amadeus Mozart	
4. Ludwig van Beethoven	
5. Samuel Richardson	

Government	
6. Frederick the Great	
7. Joseph II	
8. Catherine the Great	

Section 4

The American Revolution

Terms and Names

Declaration of Independence Document declaring American independence from Britain

Thomas Jefferson Author of the Declaration of Independence

checks and balances System in which each branch of government checks, or limits, the power of the other two branches

federal system System of government in which power is divided between the national and state governments

Bill of Rights First ten amendments to the U.S. Constitution; protections of basic rights for individuals

Before You Read

In the last section, you read about the spread of Enlightenment ideas in Europe.

In this section, you will learn how Enlightenment ideas influenced the American Revolution.

As You Read

Use a chart to list the problems American colonists faced in shaping their republic and solutions they found.

BRITAIN AND ITS AMERICAN COLONIES (Page 206)

How were the colonies governed?

The British colonies in North America grew in population and wealth during the 1700s. Population went from about 250,000 in 1700 to 2,150,000 in 1770. Economically, they prospered on trade with the nations of Europe. The 13 colonies also had a kind of self-government. People in the colonies began to see themselves less and less as British subjects. Still, Parliament passed laws that governed the colonies. One set of laws banned trade with any nation other than Britain.

1. How did the colonists' image of themselves clash with their status as colonists?

____

____

AMERICANS WIN INDEPENDENCE (Pages 207–209)

What caused Britain and America to grow apart?

The high cost of the French and Indian War led Parliament to tax the colonists. The colonists became very angry. They had never before paid taxes directly to the British government. They said that the taxes violated their rights.

Since Parliament had no members from the colonies, they said, Parliament had no right to tax them.

The colonists met the first tax, passed in 1765, with a boycott of British goods. Their refusal to buy British products was very effective. It forced Parliament to repeal the law.

Over the next decade, the colonists and Britain grew further apart. Some colonists wanted to push the colonies to independence. They took actions that caused Britain to act harshly. Eventually, the conflict led to war. Representatives of the colonies met in a congress and formed an army. In July 1776, they announced that they were independent of Britain. They issued the **Declaration of Independence.** It was based on Enlightenment ideas. **Thomas Jefferson** wrote it.

From 1775 to 1781, the colonies and the British fought a war in North America. The colonists had a poorly equipped army, and Britain was one of the most powerful nations in the world. However, in the end, the colonies won their independence.

The British people grew tired of the cost of the war and pushed Parliament to agree to a peace. The Americans were also helped greatly by aid from France. In 1783, the two sides signed a treaty. In it, Britain recognized the independent United States of America.

2. Name some of the steps that led to the American Revolution.

____

____

____

____

AMERICANS CREATE A REPUBLIC

(Pages 210–211)

***What* are some fundamental ideas in the U.S. Constitution?**

The 13 states formed a new government under the Article of Confederation. This government was very weak. States held all the power and the central government had little. This proved unworkable. In 1787, American leaders met again. They wrote a new framework of government.

The Constitution of the United States drew on many Enlightenment ideas. It used Montesquieu's idea of separation of powers into three branches of government. Through a system of **checks and balances,** each branch was able to prevent other branches from abusing their power. The Constitution also set up a **federal system.** Under this system, power was divided between national and state governments.

The Constitution also used Locke's idea of putting power in the hands of the people. It used Voltaire's ideas to protect the right to free speech and freedom of religion. It used Beccaria's ideas about a fair system of justice.

Many of these rights were ensured in a set of additions to the Constitution called the **Bill of Rights.** The inclusion of a bill of rights helped win approval for the Constitution.

3. Explain how the Constitution divides power.

____

____

____

____

As you read this section, note some causes and effects relating to the American Revolution and the establishment of the United States as a republic.

Causes	Events	Effects
	1. British Parliament passes Stamp Act.	
	2. British close Boston harbor and station troops in city.	
	3. Second Continental Congress votes to form an army under command of George Washington.	
	4. France enters the war in 1778.	
	5. By approving the Articles of Confederation, states create a weak national government.	

Name ______________________ Class ______________ Date ______________

Section 1

The French Revolution Begins

Terms and Names

Old Regime System of feudalism

estate Social class of people

Louis XVI Weak king who came to French throne in 1774

Marie Antoinette Unpopular queen; wife of Louis XVI

Estates-General Assembly of representatives from all three estates

National Assembly French congress established by representatives of the Third Estate

Tennis Court Oath Promise made by Third Estate representatives to draw up a new constitution

Great Fear Wave of panic

Before You Read

In the last chapter, you read about the Enlightenment and the American Revolution.

In this section, you will learn about the beginning of the French Revolution.

As You Read

Use a chart to take notes on the causes and effects of the early stages of the French Revolution.

THE OLD ORDER (Pages 217–218)

***How* was French society unequal?**

In the 1700s, France was the leading country of Europe. It was the center of the new ideas of the Enlightenment. However, beneath the surface there were major problems. Soon the nation would be torn by a violent revolution.

One problem was that people were not treated equally in French society. A political and social system called the **Old Regime** remained in place. The French were divided into three classes, or **estates.** The First Estate consisted of the Roman Catholic clergy. The Second Estate was made up of nobles. Only about 2 percent of the people belonged to these two estates. Yet they owned 20 percent of the land. They had easy lives.

Everybody else belonged to the Third Estate. This huge group included the bourgeoisie—merchants and skilled workers—city workers, and peasants.

Members of the Third Estate were angry. They had few rights. They paid up to half of their income in taxes, while the rich paid almost none.

1. What were the three classes of French society?

____

____

THE FORCES OF CHANGE
(**Pages** 218–219)
***Why* were the French ready for the revolution?**

Three factors led to revolution. First, the Enlightenment spread the idea that everyone should be equal. The powerless people in the Third Estate liked that. Second, the French economy was failing. High taxes kept profits low, and food supplies were short. The government owed money. Third, King **Louis XVI** was a weak leader. His wife, **Marie Antoinette,** was unpopular. She was from Austria, France's long-time enemy, and was noted for her extravagant spending.

In the 1780s, France was deep in debt. Louis tried to tax the nobles. Instead, they forced the king to call a meeting of the **Estates-General,** an assembly of delegates of the three estates.

2. What three factors led to revolution?

____

____

DAWN OF THE REVOLUTION
(**Pages** 220–221)
***How* did the Revolution begin?**

The meeting of the Estates-General began in May 1789 with arguments over how to count votes. In the past, each estate had cast one vote. The Third Estate now wanted each delegate to have a vote. The king and the other estates did not agree to the plan because the Third Estate was larger and would have more votes.

The Third Estate then broke with the others and met separately. In June 1789, its delegates voted to rename themselves the **National Assembly.** They claimed to represent all the people. This was the beginning of representative government for France.

At one point, the members of the Third Estate found themselves locked out of their meeting. They broke down a door leading to a tennis court. Then they promised to stay there until they made a new constitution. This promise was called the **Tennis Court Oath.**

Louis tried to make peace. He ordered the clergy and nobles to join the National Assembly. However, trouble erupted. Rumors flew that foreign soldiers were going to attack French citizens. On July 14, an angry crowd captured the Bastille, a Paris prison. The mob wanted to get gunpowder for their weapons in order to defend the city.

3. Why did the National Assembly form?

____

____

A GREAT FEAR SWEEPS FRANCE
(**Page** 221)
***What* was the Great Fear?**

A wave of violence called the **Great Fear** swept the country. Peasants broke into and burned nobles' houses. They tore up documents that had forced them to pay fees to the nobles. Late in 1789, a mob of women marched from Paris to the king's palace at Versailles. They were angry about high bread prices and demanded that the king come to Paris. They hoped he would end hunger in the city. The king and queen left Versailles, never to return.

4. What happened during the Great Fear?

____

As you read about the dawn of revolution in France, write notes to answer questions about the causes of the French Revolution.

How did each of the following contribute to the revolutionary mood in France?	
1. The three estates	2. Enlightenment ideas
3. Economic crisis	4. Weak leadership

How did each of the following events lead to the French Revolution?	
5. Meeting of the Estates-General	6. Establishment of the National Assembly
7. Tennis Court Oath	8. Storming of the Bastille

Revolution Brings Reform and Terror

Terms and Names

Legislative Assembly Assembly that replaced the National Assembly in 1791

émigrés Nobles and others who left France during the peasant uprisings and who hoped to come back to restore the old system

sans-culottes Radical group of Parisian wage-earners

Jacobin Member of the Jacobin Club, a radical political organization

guillotine Machine for beheading people

Maximilien Robespierre Revolutionary leader who tried to wipe out every trace of France's past monarchy and nobility

Reign of Terror Period of Robespierre's rule

Before You Read

In the last section, you read how the French Revolution began.

In this section, you will learn what course it took and where it led.

As You Read

Use a flow chart to identify the major events that followed the creation of the Constitution of 1791.

THE ASSEMBLY REFORMS FRANCE (Pages 222–223)

***What* reforms resulted from the revolution?**

In August 1789, the National Assembly took steps to change France. It made a revolutionary statement called the Declaration of the Rights of Man. One new law ended all the special rights that members of the First and Second Estates had enjoyed. Another law gave all French men equal rights. Though women did not get these rights, it was a bold step. Other laws gave the state power over the Catholic Church.

The new laws about the church divided people who had supported the Revolution. Catholic peasants remained loyal to the church. They were angry that the church would be part of the state. Thereafter, many of them opposed the Revolution's reforms.

For months, the assembly worked on plans for a new government. During this time, Louis was fearful for his safety. One night, he and his family tried to escape the country. They were caught, brought back to Paris, and placed under guard. This escape attempt made the king and queen more unpopular. It also increased the power of his enemies.

1. What new laws came into being?

____

DIVISIONS DEVELOP (Pages 223–224)
***What* groups called for different kinds of changes?**

In the fall of 1791, the assembly drew up a new constitution. It took away most of the king's power. The assembly then turned over its power to a new assembly, the **Legislative Assembly.**

This new assembly soon divided into groups. Radicals wanted sweeping changes in the way government was run. Moderates wanted some changes in government, but not as many as the radicals. Conservatives upheld the idea of a limited monarchy and wanted few changes in government.

There were groups outside the Legislative Assembly who wanted to influence the government, too. One group wanted an end to revolutionary changes. This group included the **émigrés,** nobles and others who had fled France during the uprisings. Another group wanted even greater changes. This group included the **sans-culottes.** These wage-earners and small shopkeepers wanted a greater voice in government.

2. In what ways did the émigrés and sans-culottes have opposite goals?

____

____

WAR AND EXECUTION
(Pages 224–226)
***What* caused the French people to take extreme measures?**

At the same time, France faced serious trouble on its borders. Kings in other countries feared that revolution would spread to their lands. They wanted to use force to restore control of France to Louis XVI. Soon foreign soldiers were marching toward Paris. Many people thought that the king and queen were ready to help the enemy. Angry French citizens imprisoned them. Many nobles were killed in other mob actions.

The government took strong steps to meet the danger from foreign troops. It took away all the king's powers. In 1792, the National Convention—another new government—was formed. **Jacobins,** members of a radical political club, soon took control of this new government. They declared Louis a common citizen. He was then tried for treason and convicted. Like many others, the king was beheaded by a machine called the **guillotine.** The National Convention also ordered thousands of French people into the army.

3. What happened to the king?

____

____

THE TERROR GRIPS FRANCE; END OF THE TERROR (Pages 226–227)
***What* was the Reign of Terror?**

Maximilien Robespierre became leader of France. He headed the Committee of Public Safety. It tried and put to death "enemies of the Revolution." Thousands were killed. Robespierre's rule, which began in 1793, was called the **Reign of Terror.** It ended in July 1794, when Robespierre himself was put to death.

The French people were tired of the killing and the unrest. They wanted a return to order. Moderate leaders drafted a new, less revolutionary plan of government.

4. Where did the Reign of Terror lead?

____

____

As you read about the events of the French Revolution, answer the questions about the time line.

Date	Event	Question
1789 Aug.	National Assembly adopts Declaration of the Rights of Man.	1. What are some rights this document guarantees French citizens?
1790	National Assembly reforms status of church.	2. What caused the peasants to oppose many of these reforms?
1791 Sept.	National Assembly hands power to Legislative Assembly.	3. What political factions made up the Legislative Assembly?
1792 April	Legislative Assembly declares war on Austria.	4. What did European monarchs fear from France?
Aug.	Parisians invade Tuileries and imprison royal family.	
Sept.	Parisian mobs massacre more than 1,000 prisoners.	5. What effects did the September Massacres have on the government?
1793 Jan.	Ex-king Louis XVI is executed.	
July	Robespierre leads Committee of Public Safety; Reign of Terror begins.	6. What was the stated aim of Robespierre and his supporters?
1794 July	Robespierre is executed; Reign of Terror ends.	7. What were some consequences of the Reign of Terror?
1795	National Convention adopts new constitution.	

Section 3

Napoleon Forges an Empire

Terms and Names

Napoleon Bonaparte Military leader who seized power in France

coup d'état A sudden takeover of a government

plebiscite Vote by the people

lycée Government-run public school

concordat Agreement

Napoleonic Code Complete set of laws set up by Napoleon that eliminated many injustices

Battle of Trafalgar British defeat of Napoleon's forces at sea

Before You Read

In the last section, you read about the Revolution's extremes, including the Reign of Terror.

In this section, you will learn how Napoleon grabbed power and brought order to France.

As You Read

Use a time line to take notes on the events that led to Napoleon's crowning as emperor of France.

NAPOLEON SEIZES POWER
(**Pages** 229–230)

***How* did Napoleon rise to power?**

Napoleon Bonaparte was born in 1769 on the Mediterranean island of Corsica. When he was nine years old, his parents sent him to military school. In 1785, he finished school and became an artillery officer. When the revolution broke out, Napoleon joined the army of the new government.

In 1795, Napoleon led soldiers against French royalists who were attacking the National Convention. For this, he was thought of as the savior of the French republic.

By 1799, the unsettled French government had lost the people's support. In a bold move, Napoleon used troops to seize control of the government. This was a **coup d'état,** or a sudden takeover of power. Napoleon then assumed dictatorial powers.

1. How did Napoleon get control of the government?

____

____

NAPOLEON RULES FRANCE
(**Pages** 230–231)

***How* did Napoleon use the Revolution's ideas in his government?**

At first, Napoleon pretended to be the rightfully elected leader of France.

In 1800, a **plebiscite,** or vote of the people, was held to approve a new constitution. The people voted for it overwhelmingly, and Napoleon took power as first consul.

Napoleon made several changes that were meant to build on the Revolution's good ideas:

1. He made tax collection more fair and orderly. As a result, the government could count on a steady supply of money.
2. He removed dishonest government workers.
3. He started **lycées**—new public schools for ordinary citizens.
4. He gave the church back some of its power. He signed a **concordat,** or agreement, with the pope. This gave him the support of the organized church.
5. He wrote a new set of laws, called the **Napoleonic Code,** which gave all French citizens the same rights. However, the new laws took away many individual rights won during the Revolution. For example, they limited free speech and restored slavery in French colonies.

2. What changes did Napoleon make?

____

____

____

____

____

NAPOLEON CREATES AN EMPIRE

(Pages 231–233)

***What* goals did Napoleon have beyond France's borders?**

Napoleon had hoped to make his empire larger in both Europe and the New World. In 1801, he had sent soldiers to retake the island of present-day Haiti. Slaves in that colony had seized power during a civil war. But his troops failed. Napoleon then gave up on his New World plans. In 1803, he sold the largest part of France's North American land—the huge Louisiana Territory—to the United States.

Napoleon had been stopped in the Americas. So he then moved to add to his power in Europe. In 1804, he made himself emperor of France. He took control of the Austrian Netherlands, parts of Italy, and Switzerland. Napoleon's only loss during this time was to the British navy in the **Battle of Trafalgar.** This loss kept him from conquering Britain.

3. Where did Napoleon succeed in adding lands, and where did he fail?

____

____

____

____

____

As you read about Napoleon, note the goals and results of some of his actions.

Actions	Goal(s)	Result(s)
1. Establishment of national bank and efficient tax-collection system		
2. Enacting Napoleonic Code of law		
3. Sending troops to Saint Domingue		
4. Selling Louisiana Territory to the United States		
5. Waging Battle of Trafalgar		

Napoleon's Empire Collapses

Terms and Names

blockade Forced closing of ports

Continental System Napoleon's policy of preventing trade and communication between Great Britain and other European nations

guerrilla Spanish peasant fighter

Peninsular War War that Napoleon fought in Spain

scorched-earth policy Policy of burning fields and slaughtering livestock so that enemy troops would find nothing to eat

Waterloo Battle in Belgium that was Napoleon's final defeat

Hundred Days Napoleon's last bid for power, which ended at Waterloo

Before You Read

In the last section, you read how Napoleon built his power.

In this section, you learn why he lost it.

As You Read

Use a chart to take notes on mistakes Napoleon made and the impact they had on the French Empire.

NAPOLEON'S COSTLY MISTAKES (Pages 234–236)

***What* mistakes did Napoleon make abroad?**

Napoleon's own personality posed a threat to his empire. His love of power pushed him to expand his empire. His efforts to extend French rule led to his empire's collapse.

Napoleon made three costly mistakes. His first mistake was caused by his desire to crush Britain. He wanted to hurt the British economy. So in 1806 he ordered a **blockade.** This was an effort to stop all trade between Britain and the other European nations. Napoleon called this policy the **Continental System.** It was supposed to make continental Europe more self-sufficient.

The effort failed because some Europeans secretly brought in British goods. At the same time, the British put their own blockade around Europe. Because the British navy was so strong, it worked well. Soon the French economy, along with others on the European continent, weakened.

Napoleon's second mistake was to make his brother king of Spain in 1808. The Spanish people were loyal to their own king. With help from Britain, bands of peasant fighters called **guerrillas** fought Napoleon for five years. Napoleon lost 300,000 troops during this **Peninsular War.** (The war gets its name from the Iberian Peninsula on which Spain is located.)

Napoleon's third mistake was perhaps his worst. In 1812, he tried to conquer Russia, far to the east. He entered Russia with more than 400,000 soldiers. As the Russians retreated, however, they followed a **scorched-earth policy.** They burned their fields and killed their livestock so Napoleon's armies could not eat what they left behind.

Although the French got as far as Moscow, winter was coming. Napoleon was forced to order his soldiers to head back. On the way home, bitter cold, hunger, and Russian attacks killed thousands. Thousands more deserted. By the time Napoleon's army left Russian territory, only 10,000 of his soldiers were able to fight.

1. What happened to Napoleon in Russia?

____

____

____

____

____

NAPOLEON'S DOWNFALL

(Pages 236–237)

***What* other defeats did Napoleon suffer?**

Other leaders saw that Napoleon was now weaker. Britain, Russia, Prussia, Sweden, and Austria joined forces and attacked France. Napoleon was defeated at the Battle of Leipzig, in Germany, in 1813. In 1814, Napoleon gave up his throne and was exiled, or sent away, to the tiny island of Elba off the Italian coast.

Louis XVIII took the throne in Paris. But he quickly became unpopular. The peasants feared the new king would undo the land reforms of the Revolution.

News of Louis XVIII's trouble was all Napoleon needed to try to regain his empire. In March 1815, he escaped from Elba and boldly returned to France. He took power and raised another army.

The rest of the European powers raised armies to fight against Napoleon. Led by the Duke of Wellington, they defeated Napoleon in his final battle near a Belgian town called **Waterloo.** This defeat ended Napoleon's last attempt at power, which was called the **Hundred Days.** He was then sent to the far-off island of St. Helena in the southern Atlantic Ocean. He died there in 1821.

2. What was Napoleon's last attempt at power, and where did it end?

____

____

____

____

____

Name ______________________ Class ______________ Date ______________

Section 4, *continued*

As you read about Napoleon's downfall, write notes in the chart to explain how each action contributed to his final defeat.

Action		Notes
1. Ordered a blockade to prevent trade and communication between Great Britain and other European nations	→	
2. Sent an army to invade Portugal and began the Peninsular War	→	
3. In June 1812, invaded Russia with his Grand Army	→	
4. Entered Moscow on September 14, 1812, and stayed in the ruined city for five weeks	→	
5. Raised another army and fought the Battle of Leipzig	→	
6. Escaped Elba, reclaimed title of emperor, and fought Battle of Waterloo	→	

Section 5

The Congress of Vienna

Terms and Names

Congress of Vienna Meetings in Vienna for the purpose of restoring order to Europe

Klemens von Metternich Key leader at the Congress of Vienna

balance of power Condition in which no one country becomes a threat to the other

legitimacy Bringing back to power the kings that Napoleon had driven out

Holy Alliance League formed by Russia, Austria, and Prussia

Concert of Europe Series of alliances to help prevent revolution

Before You Read

In the last section, you saw how Napoleon's empire collapsed.

In this section, you will learn how the rest of Europe reacted to both the French Revolution and Napoleon's rise and fall.

As You Read

Use a chart to take notes on how the three goals of Metternich's plan at the Congress of Vienna solved a political problem.

METTERNICH'S PLANS FOR EUROPE (Pages 238–239)

***What* was the Congress of Vienna?**

In 1814, leaders of many nations met to draw up a peace plan for Europe. This series of meetings was called the **Congress of Vienna.** The most important person at the Congress of Vienna was the foreign minister of Austria, **Klemens von Metternich.** He shaped the peace conditions that were finally accepted.

Metternich had three goals at the congress. First, he wanted to make sure that the French would not attack another country again. Second, he wanted a **balance of power** in which no one nation was strong enough to threaten other nations. Third, he wanted **legitimacy.** This meant restoring monarchs to the thrones they had before Napoleon's conquests. The other leaders agreed with Metternich's ideas.

Metternich achieved his first goal when the congress strengthened the small nations that surrounded France. Meanwhile, France was not punished too severely. It remained independent and kept some overseas possessions. This helped achieve Metternich's second goal to create a balance of power.

The congress also worked to fulfill Metternich's third goal. Many rulers were returned to power in states throughout Europe, including France.

The Congress of Vienna created very successful peace agreements. None of the great powers fought against one another for 40 years. Some did not fight in a war for the rest of the century.

1. What three goals did Metternich have?

____

____

____

____

____

POLITICAL CHANGES BEYOND VIENNA (Pages 239–241)

How did European leaders respond to the effects of the French Revolution?

Many European rulers were nervous about the effects of the French Revolution. In 1815, Czar Alexander of Russia, Emperor Francis I of Austria, and King Frederick William III of Prussia formed the **Holy Alliance.** Other alliances created by Metternich were called the **Concert of Europe.** The idea of these alliances was for nations to help one another if revolution came.

Across Europe, conservatives held control of European governments. Conservatives were people who opposed the ideals of the French Revolution. They also usually supported the rights and powers of royalty. They did not encourage individual liberties. They did not want any calls for equal rights.

But many other people still believed in the ideals of the French Revolution. They thought that all people should be equal and share in power. Later they would again fight for these rights.

People in the Americas also felt the desire for freedom. Spanish colonies in the Americas revolted against the restored Spanish king. Many colonies won independence from Spain. National feeling grew in Europe, too. Soon people in areas such as Italy, Germany, and Greece would rebel and form new nations. The French Revolution had changed the politics of Europe and beyond.

2. What happened to ideas about freedom and independence?

____

____

____

____

____

As you read about the meeting of the Congress of Vienna, fill in the diagram below.

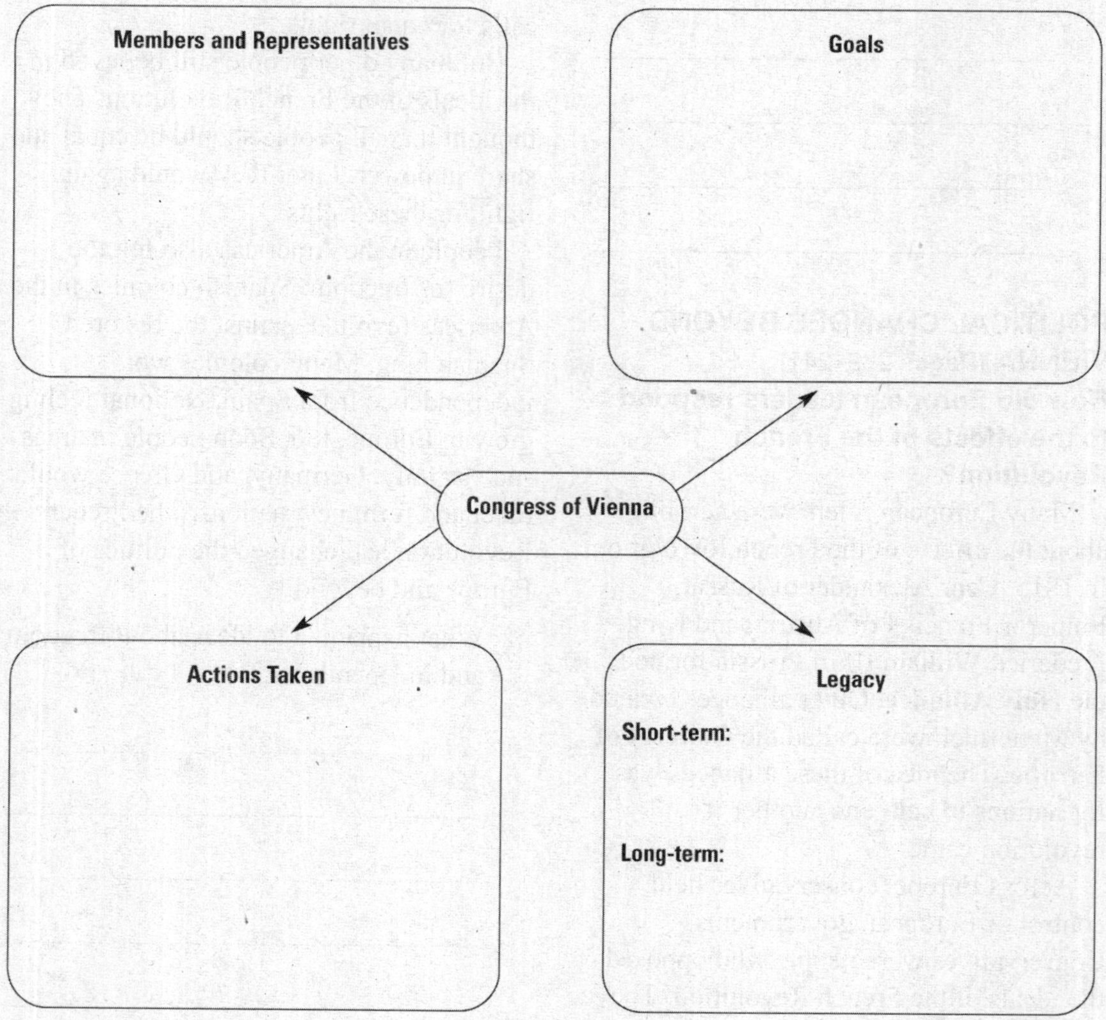

Latin American Peoples Win Independence

Terms and Names

peninsulares Latin Americans born in Spain

creoles Spaniards born in Latin America

mulattos Africans or people of mixed European and African ancestry

Simón Bolívar Leader of Venezuelan independence movement

José de San Martín Leader who helped win independence for Chile and Argentina

Miguel Hidalgo Priest who began the revolt against Spanish rule in Mexico

José Morelos Leader of the Mexican revolt after Hidalgo was defeated

Before You Read

In the last section, you read about revolution and the Congress of Vienna.

In this section, you will learn how Latin American countries got their independence.

As You Read

Use a chart to identify details about Latin American independence movements.

COLONIAL SOCIETY DIVIDED

(**Pages** 247–248)

***What* classes existed in Latin American society?**

In Latin America, society was divided into six classes of people. ***Peninsulares***—those born in Spain—were at the top. Next were **creoles,** or Spaniards who had been born in Latin America. Below them were mestizos. Mestizos had mixed European and Indian ancestry. Next were **mulattos,** with mixed European and African ancestry, and then Africans. At the bottom were Indians.

1. Which groups of society were of European ancestry?

____

____

REVOLUTIONS IN THE AMERICAS

(**Page** 248)

***Where* in Latin America was independence first declared?**

In the early 1800s, colonial peoples in Latin America fought for independence. The French colony of Saint Domingue was the first Latin American colony to fight for independence.

Almost all of the people who lived in the French colony were slaves of African origin. In 1791, about 100,000 of them rose in revolt. Toussaint L'Ouverture, a former slave, became their leader. In 1802 Napoleon sent troops to the island to end the rebellion. They failed. In 1804, the colony declared its independence as Haiti.

2. How did Haiti become independent?

____

____

CREOLES LEAD INDEPENDENCE

(**Pages** 248–250)

***Why* did Creoles want independence?**

Creoles felt that they were not treated fairly. This bad feeling boiled over when Napoleon overthrew the king of Spain and named his own brother as king. Creoles in Latin America had no loyalty to the new king. They revolted. Even after the old king was restored, they did not give up their fight for freedom.

Two leaders pushed much of South America to independence. **Simón Bolívar** was a writer, fighter, and political thinker. He survived defeats and exile to help win independence for Venezuela in 1821. **José de San Martín** helped win independence for Argentina in 1816 and Chile in 1818. Bolívar led their combined armies to a great victory in 1824. This victory gained independence for all the Spanish colonies.

3. Which two great leaders led the fights for independence in Venezuela, Chile, and Argentina?

____

____

MEXICO ENDS SPANISH RULE; BRAZIL'S ROYAL LIBERATOR

(**Pages** 251–252)

***How* did Mexico and Brazil achieve independence?**

In Mexico, mestizos and Indians led the fight for independence. In 1810, **Miguel Hidalgo,** a village priest, called for a revolt against Spanish rule. Creoles united with the Spanish government to put down this revolt by the lower classes.

Hidalgo lost, but Padre **José María Morelos** took over leadership of the rebels. Fighting continued until 1815, when the creoles won.

After a revolution in Spain put a new government in power, the creoles joined with the other groups fighting for independence. In 1821, Mexico won its independence. In 1823, the region of Central America separated itself from Mexico.

In Brazil, 8,000 creoles signed a paper asking the son of Portugal's king to rule an independent Brazil. He agreed. Brazil became free that year through a bloodless revolt.

4. How were the drives for independence in Mexico and Brazil different?

____

____

As you read this section, fill out the chart below to help you better understand why and how Latin Americans fought colonial rule.

Independence for Haiti

Reasons	Strategy
1. Why did slaves in the French colony of Saint-Domingue revolt?	2. What events led up to General Dessalines's declaration of independence for Haiti?

South American Wars of Independence

Reasons	Strategy
3. How did events in Europe lead to revolution in the Spanish colonies?	4. What tactics did José de San Martín and Simón Bolívar use to defeat Spanish forces in South America?

End of Spanish Rule in Mexico

Reasons	Strategy
5. What is the significance of the *grito de Dolores*?	6. What role did Indians, mestizos, and Creoles play in Mexico's independence from Spain?

Section 2

Europe Faces Revolutions

Terms and Names

conservative People who supported the monarchy

liberal People who wanted to give more power to elected legislatures

radical People who wanted to end the rule by kings and give full voting rights to all people

nationalism Belief that a person's loyalty belongs to the nation itself instead of to the nation's ruler

nation-state Country with its own independent government

the Balkans Region including all or part of present-day Greece, Albania, Bulgaria, Romania, Turkey, and former Yugoslavia

Louis-Napoleon Winner of the presidential election in France in 1848; later emperor

Alexander II Ruler of Russia who freed the serfs

Before You Read

In the last section, you read about Latin American independence movements.

In this section, you will learn about revolutions in Europe.

As You Read

Use a web diagram to identify major revolutions in Europe.

CLASH OF PHILOSOPHIES; NATIONALISM DEVELOPS

(**Pages** 253–255)

***What* forces and peoples struggled for power?**

There was a power struggle in Europe in the first half of the 1800s. Three forces were involved. **Conservatives** wanted to continue to support the kings who had ruled these lands for many centuries. These were nobles and other people who owned large amounts of property. **Liberals** wanted to give more power to elected legislatures. They were typically middle-class merchants and business people. **Radicals** wanted the end of rule by kings and full voting rights for all.

At the same time, another movement arose in Europe—**nationalism.** This was the belief that a person's loyalty should go not to the country's ruler but to the nation itself. When the nation also had its own independent government, it became a **nation-state.** Nationalists thought that people with a common language and culture were a nation. And they had the right to their own government. These ideas grew out of the French Revolution.

1. What different goals did conservatives, liberals, and radicals have?

____

NATIONALISTS CHALLENGE CONSERVATIVE POWER

(**Pages** 255–256)

***What* changes were occurring in Western Europe?**

The first people to win self-rule during this period were the Greeks. Greece had been part of the Ottoman Empire for centuries. The Ottomans controlled most of **the Balkans.** That region includes most of modern Greece, Albania, Bulgaria, Romania, Turkey, and the former Yugoslavia. In 1821, the Greeks revolted against Turkish rule. The Greeks won their independence by 1830.

Other revolts broke out in other parts of Europe. In 1830, the Belgians declared their independence from rule by the Dutch. Nationalists began a long struggle to unify all of Italy. The Poles revolted against Russian rule. Conservatives managed to put down these rebellions. However, new ones broke out again in 1848 among Hungarians and Czechs. Once again, they were put down forcibly.

2. What groups challenged conservative rule?

____

RADICALS CHANGE FRANCE

(**Page** 256)

***Why* did French radicals lose?**

Events differed in France. Riots in 1830 forced the king to flee, and a new king was put in his place. Another revolt broke out in 1848. The king was overthrown and a republic established. However, the radicals who had won began arguing. They differed over how much France should be changed. Some wanted only political changes. Others wanted social and economic changes that would help the poor.

When these forces began to fight in the streets, the French gave up on the radical program. They introduced a new government. It had a legislature and a strong president. The new president was **Louis-Napoleon,** Napoleon Bonaparte's nephew. He later named himself emperor of France. He built railroads and helped industry. The economy got better and more people had jobs.

3. What did Louis-Napoleon accomplish for France?

____

REFORM IN RUSSIA (**Pages** 256–257)

***How* did Alexander II change Russia?**

In the early 1800s, Russia still did not have an industrial economy. The biggest problem was that serfdom still existed there. Peasants were bound to the nobles whose land they worked. Russia's rulers were reluctant to free the serfs, though. They feared they would lose the support of the nobles.

A new ruler of Russia, **Alexander II,** decided to free the serfs. Though it seemed bold, Alexander's move went only part way. Nobles kept half their land and were paid for the other half that went to the peasants. The former serfs were not given the land. They had to pay for it. This debt kept them still tied to the land. The czar's efforts to make changes ended when he was assassinated in 1881. Alexander III, the new czar, brought back tight control over the country. He also moved to make the economy more industrial.

4. What major reform was made in Russia at this time?

____

As you read about uprisings in Europe, make notes in the chart to explain the outcomes of each action listed.

Action		Outcome
1. French citizens' armies win their revolution for liberty and equality.	→	
2. Greeks revolt against the Ottoman Turks.	→	
3. Nationalist groups in Budapest, Prague, and Vienna demand independence and self-government.	→	
4. Charles X tries to set up an absolute monarchy in France.	→	
5. Paris mobs overthrow monarchy of Louis-Philippe.	→	
6. Louis-Napoleon Bonaparte is elected president of France and later assumes the title of Emperor Napoleon III.	→	
7. In the Crimean War, Czar Nicholas I threatens to take over part of the Ottoman Empire.	→	
8. Alexander II issues the Edict of Emancipation.	→	

Nationalism

Case Study: Italy and Germany

Terms and Names

Russification A policy of forcing Russian culture on ethnic groups in the Russian Empire

Camillo di Cavour Prime minister who unified northern Italy

Giuseppe Garibaldi Leader of the Red Shirts who won control over parts of southern Italy

Otto von Bismarck Leader who worked to expand Prussia

Junker Wealthy German landholders

realpolitik Tough, practical politics

kaiser Emperor

Before You Read

In the last section, you read about revolutions and reform in western Europe.

In this section, you will learn about nationalism.

As You Read

Use a time line to list major events in the unification of Italy and of Germany.

NATIONALISM: A FORCE FOR UNITY OR DISUNITY (Pages 258–259)
***What* is nationalism?**

Nationalists thought that many factors linked people to one another. First was nationality, or a common ethnic ancestry. Shared language, culture, history, and religion were also seen as ties that connected people. People sharing these traits were thought to have the right to a land they could call their own. Groups with their own government were called nation-states.

Leaders began to see that this feeling could be a powerful force for uniting a people. The French Revolution was a prime example of this. However, nationalism could also be a force to rip apart empires. This happened in three empires in Europe.

1. What shared characteristics can unite people and create a strong national feeling?

____

____

NATIONALISM SHAKES AGING EMPIRES (Pages 259–260)
***Why* did nationalism divide empires?**

Feelings of nationalism threatened to break apart three aging empires. The Austrian Empire was forced to split in two.

One part was Austria, the other was Hungary. In Russia, harsh rule and a policy called **Russification** that forced other peoples to adopt Russian ways helped produce a revolution in 1917. This revolution overthrew the czar. Like the other two, the Ottoman Empire broke apart around the time of World War I.

2. What three empires were torn apart by nationalism?

____

____

CAVOUR UNITES ITALY

(**Pages** 260–261)

***How* did nationalism unite Italy?**

Italians used national feeling to build a nation, not destroy an empire. Large parts of Italy were ruled by the kings of Austria and Spain. Nationalists tried to unite the nation in 1848. But the revolt was beaten down. Hopes rested with the Italian king of the state of Piedmont-Sardinia. His chief minister was Count **Camillo di Cavour.** Cavour worked to expand the king's control over other areas of the north.

Meanwhile, **Giuseppe Garibaldi** led an army of patriots that won control of southern areas. Garibaldi put the areas he conquered under control of the Italian king. In 1866, the area around Venice was added to the king's control. By 1870, the king completed the uniting of Italy.

3. Who helped unify Italy?

____

____

BISMARCK UNITES GERMANY; A SHIFT IN POWER (Pages 261–263)

***How* was Germany united?**

Germany had also been divided into many different states for many centuries. Since 1815, 39 states had joined in a league called the German Confederation. Prussia and Austria-Hungary controlled this group. Over time, Prussia rose to become more powerful. Leading this move was prime minister **Otto von Bismarck.** He was supported by wealthy landowners called **Junkers.** Bismarck was a master of **realpolitik**—tough power politics.

Bismarck worked to create a new **confederation** of German states. Prussia controlled it. To win the loyalty of German areas in the south, he purposefully angered a weak France so that it would declare war on Prussia. Prussia won the Franco-Prussian War in 1871. The war with France gave the southern German states a nationalistic feeling. They joined the other states in naming the king of Prussia as emperor, or **kaiser,** of a strong united Germany.

These events changed the balance of power in Europe. Germany and Britain were the strongest powers, followed by France. Austria, Russia, and Italy were all even weaker.

4. What was the result of the defeat of France and the uniting of Germany?

____

____

As you read this section, take notes to answer questions about nationalism as a force for disunity and unity.

How did nationalism lead to the breakup of these empires?		
1. Austro-Hungarian	2. Russian	3. Ottoman

How did each of the following help unify Italy?		
4. Camillo di Cavour	5. Giuseppe Garibaldi	6. King Victor Emmanuel

How did each of the following lead to German unification?		
7. Policy of realpolitik	8. Seven Weeks' War	9. Franco-Prussian War

Section 4

Revolutions in the Arts

Terms and Names

romanticism Movement in art and ideas that focused on nature and the thoughts and feelings of individuals

realism Movement in art that tried to show life as it really was

impressionism Style of art using light and light-filled colors to produce an "impression"

Before You Read

In the last section, you read how political borders changed in Europe.

In this section, you will learn about changes in the arts in Europe.

As You Read

Use a chart to note details about movements in the arts.

THE ROMANTIC MOVEMENT
(**Pages** 264–265)

***What* is romanticism?**

In the early 1800s, the Enlightenment gradually gave way to another movement, called **romanticism.** This movement in art and ideas focused on nature and on the thoughts and feelings of individuals. Gone was the idea that reason and order were good things. Romantic thinkers valued feeling, not reason, and nature, not society. Romantic thinkers held idealized views of the past as simpler, better times. They valued the common people. As a result, they enjoyed folk stories, songs, and traditions. They also supported calls for democracy. However, not all romantic artists and thinkers supported all of these ideas.

Romantic writers had different themes. During the first half of the 19th century, the Grimm brothers collected German folk tales. They also created a German dictionary and worked on German grammar. These works celebrated being German long before there was a united German nation. Other writers wrote about strong individuals. Some wrote about beauty and nature.

Germany produced one of the greatest early Romantic writers. Johann Wolfgang von Goethe wrote *The Sorrows of Young Werther*. It was a story about a young man who kills himself after he falls in love with a married woman.

British Romantic poets William Wordsworth and Samuel Taylor Coleridge honored nature as the source of truth and beauty. A type of horror story called a Gothic novel became popular. Novels such as Mary Shelley's *Frankenstein* were tales about good and evil.

Romanticism was important in music as well. Composers wrote music to appeal to the hearts and souls of listeners. Ludwig van Beethoven, a German, was the foremost of these composers. Romanticism made music a popular art form.

1. What did Romantic thinkers and artists value?

____

2. For what purposes did writers use realism?

____

THE SHIFT TO REALISM IN THE ARTS (Pages 266–267)

What is realism?

In the middle 1800s, the grim realities of industrial life made the dreams of romanticism seem silly. A new movement arose—**realism.** Artists and writers tried to show life as it really was. They used their art to protest unfair social conditions. French writer Emile Zola's books revealed harsh working conditions for the poor. They led to new laws aimed at helping those people. In England, Charles Dickens wrote many novels that showed how poor people suffered in the new industrial economy.

A new device, the camera, was developed in this period. Photographers used cameras to capture realistic images on film.

IMPRESSIONISTS REACT AGAINST REALISM (Page 267)

What is impressionism?

In the 1860s, Parisian painters reacted against the realistic style. This new art style—**impressionism**—used light and light-filled colors to produce an impression of a subject or moment in time. Impressionist artists like Claude Monet and Pierre-Auguste Renoir glorified the delights of the life of the rising middle class in their paintings. Composers created music that set a mood by using different music structures, instruments, or patterns.

3. What was the focus of impressionist art and music?

____

As you read this section, take notes to answer questions about the artistic and intellectual movements of the 1800s.

Nationalism ushers in a romantic movement in arts and ideas.

1. How did the ideas of romanticism contrast with Enlightenment ideas?	2. How were the ideas of romanticism reflected in literature?
3. How was romanticism reflected in art?	4. How did romanticism affect the music of the time?

Realism in art and literature replaces romantic idealism.

5. What trends or events led to a shift from romanticism to realism?	6. How did photography exemplify the art of the new industrial age?
7. What were some themes common to realist novels?	8. What did realist novelists hope to accomplish with their exposés?

Section 1

The Beginnings of Industrialization

Terms and Names

Industrial Revolution Great increase in machine production that began in England in the 18th century

enclosure Large closed-in field for farming

crop rotation Planting a different crop in a different field each year

industrialization Process of developing machine production of goods

factors of production Conditions needed to produce goods and services

factory Building where goods are made

entrepreneur Person who organizes, manages, and takes on the financial risk of a business enterprise

Before You Read

In the last section, you read about romanticism and realism in the arts.

In this section, you will read about the beginning of the Industrial Revolution.

As You Read

Use a time line to note important events in Britain's industrialization.

INDUSTRIAL REVOLUTION BEGINS IN BRITAIN (Pages 283–284)

***How* did the Industrial Revolution begin?**

The **Industrial Revolution** was the great increase in production that began in England during the 18th century. Before the Industrial Revolution, people made most goods by hand. By the middle of the 1700s, more and more goods were made by machines.

The Industrial Revolution began with an agricultural revolution. In the early 1700s, large landowners in Britain bought much of the land that had been owned by poorer farmers. The landowners collected these lands into large fields closed-in by fences or hedges. These fields were called **enclosures.** Many of the poor farmers who lost their lands became tenant farmers. Others gave up farming and moved to the cities.

New farm methods made farmers more productive. For example, Jethro Tull invented a seed drill that made planting more efficient. Farmers also practiced **crop rotation.** Crop rotation is the practice of planting a different crop in a different field each year.

The increase in farm output made more food available. People enjoyed better diets. The population of Britain grew. Fewer farmers were needed to grow food.

More people began to make goods other than food. The growth in the number of people in cities to work in factories helped create the Industrial Revolution.

For several reasons, Britain was the first country to industrialize. **Industrialization** is the process of developing machine production of goods.

Great Britain had all the resources needed for industrialization. These resources included coal, water, iron ore, rivers, harbors, and banks. Britain also had all the **factors of production** that the Industrial Revolution required. These factors of production included land, labor (workers), and capital (wealth).

1. Why was Britain the first country to industrialize?

____

____

INVENTIONS SPUR INDUSTRIALIZATION (Pages 284–286)

What inventions helped change business?

The Industrial Revolution began in the textile industry. Several new inventions helped businesses make cloth and clothing more quickly. Richard Arkwright invented the water frame in 1769. It used water power to run spinning machines that made yarn. In 1779, Samuel Compton invented the spinning mule that made better thread. In 1787, Edmund Cartwright developed the power loom. The power loom was a machine that sped up the cloth-making process.

These new inventions were large and expensive machines. Business owners built large **factories** to house and run these machines. These factories were built near rivers because these machines needed water power to run them.

2. How was the textile industry changed by the new inventions?

____

____

IMPROVEMENTS IN TRANSPORTATION; THE RAILWAY AGE BEGINS (Pages 287–288)

The invention of the steam engine in 1705 brought in a new source of power. The steam engine used fire to heat water and produce steam. The power of the steam drove the engine. Eventually steam-driven engines were used to run factories.

At the same time, improvements were being made in transportation. Robert Fulton, an American, invented the first steam-driven boat. This invention allowed people to send goods more quickly over rivers and canals.

Starting in the 1820s, steam brought a new burst of industrial growth. George Stephenson, a British engineer, set up the world's first railroad line. It used a steam-driven locomotive. Soon, railroads were being built all over Britain.

The railroad boom helped business owners move their goods to market more quickly. It created thousands of new jobs in several different industries. The railroad had a deep effect on British society. For instance, people could now travel throughout the country more quickly.

3. What effects did the invention of the steam engine have?

____

____

As you read this section, make notes in the chart to explain how each factor listed contributed to an Industrial Revolution in Great Britain.

1. Agricultural revolution	
2. Abundant natural resources	
3. Political stability	
4. Factors of production	
5. Technological advances in the textile industry	
6. Entrepreneurs	
7. Building of factories	
8. Railroad boom	

Section 2

Industrialization

Case Study: Manchester

Terms and Names

urbanization City building and the movement of people to cities

middle class A social class of skilled workers, professionals, business people, and wealthy farmers

Before You Read

In the last section, you saw how the Industrial Revolution began.

In this section, you will read about some of its effects.

As You Read

Use an outline to organize the summaries' main ideas and details.

INDUSTRIALIZATION CHANGES LIFE (**Pages** 289–291)

***How* did industrialization change people's ways of life?**

Industrialization brought many changes to the British people. More people could use coal to heat their homes, eat better food, and wear better clothing.

Another change was **urbanization**—city building and the movement of people to cities. For centuries, most people in Europe had lived in the country. By the 1800s, more and more people lived in cities, where they had come to find jobs.

Living conditions were bad in crowded cities. Many people could not find good housing, schools, or police protection. Filth, garbage, and sickness were part of life in the slums. A person in a city could expect to live 17 years. In the countryside, a person could expect to live 38 years.

Working conditions were also bad. The average worker spent 14 hours a day on the job, 6 days a week. Many workers were killed or seriously injured in accidents.

1. What were major changes in living conditions and working conditions?

____

____

CLASS TENSIONS GROW; POSITIVE EFFECTS OF THE INDUSTRIAL REVOLUTION
(**Pages** 291–292)

***Who* were the members of the middle class?**

Some people's lives were improved in the new economy. The Industrial Revolution created new wealth for the **middle class,** which included skilled workers, professionals, business people, and wealthy farmers. People in the middle class enjoyed comfortable lives in pleasant homes. This class began to grow in size. Some people grew wealthier than the nobles who had been in control for many centuries.

The Industrial Revolution had many good effects. It created wealth. It created jobs for workers and over time helped many of them live better lives. It produced better diets, better housing, and better clothing at lower prices.

2. What were three positive effects of industrialization?

____

____

THE MILLS OF MANCHESTER

(**Pages** 292–294)

What **changes occurred in Manchester?**

The English city of Manchester is a good example of how industrialization changed society. Rapid growth made the city crowded and filthy. The factory owners risked their money and worked long hours to make their businesses grow. In return, they enjoyed huge profits and built huge houses. The workers also worked long hours, but had few benefits. Many of these workers were children, some only six years old. The British government did not limit the use of children as workers until 1819.

The large amount of industry in Manchester caused environmental problems. Coal smoke and cloth dyes from the factories polluted the air and water. Yet, Manchester also created many jobs, a variety of consumer goods, and great wealth.

3. Why is Manchester a good example of how industrialization changed cities?

____

____

As you read this case study, take notes to answer questions about how industrialization changed the way people lived and worked.

What changes did industrialization bring about for the following groups of people?	
1. Poor city dwellers	
2. Factory workers	
3. Wealthy merchants, factory owners, shippers	
4. Children	
5. Lower middle class of factory overseers and skilled workers	
6. Large landowners and aristocrats	

What were the long-term consequences of the Industrial Revolution for each of the following?	
7. The environment	8. Education

Industrialization Spreads

Terms and Names

stock Right of ownership in a company called a corporation

corporation Business owned by stockholders who share in its profits but are not responsible for its debts

Before You Read

In the last section, you read about some of the effects of industrialization.

In this section, you will see how industrialization spread to other nations.

As You Read

Use a Venn diagram to compare industrialization in the United States and in Europe.

INDUSTRIAL DEVELOPMENT IN THE UNITED STATES

(**Pages** 295–297)

***How* did industrialization begin in the United States?**

Other countries began to industrialize after Great Britain. The United States was one of the first. Like Britain, the United States had a great deal of coal and water to create power. There was also plenty of iron. In addition, the immigrants that came to the United States created a large supply of workers.

The United States also benefited from conflict with Britain. During the War of 1812, Britain stopped shipping goods to the United States. As a result, American industries began to make many of the goods that Americans wanted.

In the United States, industrialization began in the textile industry. In 1789, Samuel Slater, a British worker, brought the secret of Britain's textile machines to North America. Slater built a machine to spin thread.

In 1813, a group of Massachusetts investors built textile factories in Waltham, Massachusetts. Just a few years later they built even more factories in the Massachusetts town of Lowell. Thousands of workers, mostly young girls, came to these towns to work in the factories.

American industry first grew in the Northeast. In the last decades of the 1800s, industrial growth spread to other areas of the nation. This boom was fueled by large supplies of coal, oil, and iron. New inventions, including the electric light, also helped. As in Britain, railroad building was also a big part of American industrial growth.

Businesses needed huge sums of money to do big projects. To raise money, companies sold **stock.** Stocks are shares of ownership in a company. All those who held stock were part owners of the company. This form of business organization is called a corporation.

1. How did industrialization begin in the United States?

____

____

____

CONTINENTAL EUROPE INDUSTRIALIZES (Pages 297–298)

***Where* did industrialization begin in continental Europe?**

Industrial growth also spread from England to the European continent. Belgium was the first to industrialize. It was rich in iron and coal and had good waterways.

Germany was divided politically until the late 1800s. As a result, it did not develop much industry at first. However, the Ruhr Valley in western Germany was rich in coal. The Ruhr Valley eventually became a leading industrial region.

Across Europe, small areas began to change to the new industries. Industrial growth did not occur in France until after 1830. It was helped by the government's construction of a large network of railroads. Some countries, such as Austria-Hungary and Spain, faced transportation problems that held them back from industrializing.

2. Which nations industrialized first, and why?

____

____

____

THE IMPACT OF INDUSTRIALIZATION (Page 299)

***How* did industrialization change the world?**

The Industrial Revolution changed the world. Countries that industrialized gained more wealth and power than those that did not. The countries of Europe soon began to take advantage of lands in Africa and Asia.

The Europeans wanted to use these lands as sources of raw materials for their factories. European merchants saw the people on other continents as little more than markets for European goods. The European nations took control of the lands in many areas of the world outside of Europe. This practice is called imperialism.

The Industrial Revolution that took place in the1700s and 1800s changed life forever in the countries that industrialized. Problems caused by industrialization led to movements for social reform.

3. How did industrialization lead to imperialism?

____

____

____

As you read this section, take notes to answer the questions about industrialization in different parts of the world.

Industrial development in the United States paralleled industrialization in Britain.	
1. What were some favorable conditions that sparked industrialization in both Britain and the United States?	
2. What factors led to the great expansion of U.S. industry in the late 1800s?	

Industrialization eventually reached continental Europe.	
3. How did the Napoleonic wars affect the development of industry in Europe?	
4. How would you characterize the expansion of industry throughout Europe during the early 1800s?	

Industrialization revolutionized every aspect of society worldwide.	
5. How did industrialization shift the world balance of power?	
6. In what ways did industrialization benefit society?	

Section 4

Reforming the Industrial World

Terms and Names

laissez faire Economic theory that argues that governments should not interfere with business affairs

Adam Smith Philosopher who defended laissez-faire economics

capitalism Economic system in which people invest money to make a profit

utilitarianism Belief that an idea is only as good as it is useful

socialism Belief that businesses should be owned by society as a whole

Karl Marx Economic thinker who wrote about a radical form of socialism

communism Form of socialism in which all production is owned by the people

union Organized groups of workers that bargain with business owners to get better pay and working conditions

strike Organized refusal to work

Before You Read

In the last section, you saw how industrialization spread to different nations.

In this section, you will learn about new ideas and reforms.

As You Read

Use a chart to summarize the characteristics of capitalism and socialism.

THE PHILOSOPHERS OF INDUSTRIALIZATION

(**Pages** 300–301)

***What* is capitalism?**

Industrialization led to new ways of thinking about society. Some economists thought that the government should leave business owners alone. Their view is called **laissez faire.**

Adam Smith argued that governments should not put limits on business. He and others, including British economists Thomas Malthus and David Ricardo, supported a system called **capitalism.** In a capitalist economy, people invest their money in businesses to make a profit.

Smith and the others believed that society would benefit over time from this system. Supporters of laissez faire opposed laws to protect workers.

1. How does capitalism work?

____

RISE OF SOCIALISM; MARXISM; RADICAL SOCIALISM

(**Pages** 301–304)

***What* is socialism?**

Other thinkers challenged capitalism. One group was called the **utilitarians.** According to utilitarianism, an idea or practice is good only if it is useful.

The utilitarians thought it was unfair that workers should work so hard for such little pay and live in such poor conditions. They thought the government should work to end great differences in wealth among people.

Some thinkers wanted society as a whole to own businesses. This way a few people would not grow wealthy at the expense of everyone else. Instead, all people would enjoy the benefits of increased production. This view—called **socialism**—grew out of a belief in progress and a concern for justice.

A German thinker named **Karl Marx** proposed a form of socialism that became known as Marxism. He said that factory owners and workers would struggle for power. Over time, he said, the capitalist system would destroy itself. The workers would rebel against the wealthy few.

Marx wrote *The Communist Manifesto*. It described **communism,** a form of socialism in which production is controlled by the people. In the early 1900s, these ideas would bring revolution.

2. How are capitalism and socialism different?

____

LABOR UNIONS AND REFORM LAWS (Pages 304–305)

How did workers take action to improve their lives?

While thinkers discussed these different ideas, workers fought to improve their lives. Many workers joined **unions.** A union is a group of workers that tries to bargain with employers for better pay and better working conditions.

When employers resisted these efforts, the workers went on **strike,** or refused to work. British and American workers struggled for a long time to win the right to form unions. By the late 1800s, workers in both countries had made some progress.

The British Parliament and reformers in the United States also tried to fix other social problems. Britain passed laws to limit how much work women and children could do. Groups in the United States pushed for similar laws.

3. How did both the government and workers themselves try to improve workers' lives?

____

THE REFORM MOVEMENT SPREADS (Pages 305–306)

What other reforms were taking place at this time?

Another major reform movement of the 1800s was the effort to abolish slavery. The British Parliament ended the slave trade in 1807. It then abolished slavery throughout British territories in 1833.

Slavery was finally abolished in the United States in 1865, after the Civil War. Spain ended slavery in Puerto Rico in 1873 and in Cuba in 1886. In 1888 Brazil became the last country to ban slavery.

Women were active in many reform movements. As they fought for the end of slavery, many women began to fight for equal rights for women. The movement began in the United States in 1848. In 1888, women from around the world formed a group dedicated to this cause.

Reformers took on other projects as well. Some pushed for—and won—improved education. Others tried to improve conditions in prisons.

4. Name two major reform movements of the 1800s.

____

As you read about the age of reforms, take notes to answer the questions about the ideas of the philosophers and reformers of the Industrial Revolution.

The Economic Philosophers	What were the basic ideas of each philosopher?
1. Adam Smith	
2. Thomas Malthus	
3. David Ricardo	

The Social Reformers	How did each reformer try to correct the ills of industrialization?
4. John Stuart Mill	
5. Robert Owen	
6. Charles Fourier and Henri de Saint-Simon	
7. Karl Marx and Friedrich Engels	
8. William Wilberforce	
9. Jane Addams	
10. Horace Mann	

Democratic Reform and Activism

Terms and Names

suffrage Right to vote

Chartist movement Movement in England to give the right to vote to more people and to obtain other rights

Queen Victoria Leader of Britain when democratic changes were occurring

Third Republic Government formed in France after Napoleon III was exiled

Dreyfus affair Events surrounding the framing of a Jewish officer in the French army

anti-Semitism Prejudice against Jews

Zionism Movement to establish a separate homeland in Palestine for the Jews

Before You Read

In the last section, you read about the Industrial Revolution.

In this section, you will read about democratic reforms in Great Britain and France.

As You Read

Use a chart to list and evaluate events in this section according to whether they expanded or impeded democracy.

BRITAIN ENACTS REFORMS

(**Pages** 313–314)

***How* did Britain become more democratic?**

Since the 1600s, Britain's government had been a constitutional monarchy. A king or queen ruled the country, but the elected legislature—Parliament—held the real power.

Still, very few people could vote for members of Parliament. Only men who owned property—about five percent of the population—had the right to vote. That situation changed in the 1800s. The Reform Bill of 1832 was the first step. Middle-class people across England protested the fact that they could not vote. Worried by revolutions sweeping Europe, Parliament passed the Reform Bill. This law gave **suffrage,** the right to vote, to many in the middle class.

Those who still could not vote began the **Chartist Movement.** They wanted the vote and other rights. They presented their demands to Parliament in The People's Charter of 1838. Although they did not get what they wanted at first, over time their demands became law.

The leader of England during all these changes was **Queen Victoria.** She was queen for 64 years. She performed her duties wisely and capably, but during her reign Parliament gained more power.

The era that she was queen is known as the Victorian Age.

1. How did power shift in Britain in the 1800s?

____

____

____

____

WOMEN GET THE VOTE

(Page 315)

***How* did women campaign for the right to vote?**

By 1890, a few countries had given the right to vote to all men. But none gave the right to vote to all women. In the 1800s, women in the United States and Britain campaigned peacefully for the vote.

In 1903, a group called the Women's Social and Political Union began a stronger campaign for women's suffrage in Britain. This campaign included rallies, parades, and demonstrations during speeches of government officials. But women in Britain and the United States did not win the right to vote until after World War I.

2. When did women get the right to vote in Britain and the United States?

____

____

____

____

FRANCE AND DEMOCRACY

(Pages 315–316)

***What* was the Dreyfus affair?**

The road to democracy in France was rocky. France lost a war with Prussia. The National Assembly met to decide on a new government. Finally, in 1875, a new government—the **Third Republic**—was formed. It lasted over 60 years. They were years marked by fighting between many political parties.

In the 1860s, French society was divided over the case of an army officer named Alfred Dreyfus. Dreyfus was accused of being a traitor. The charge was made mainly because Dreyfus was a Jew. Many people believed the charge was true. Dreyfus was found guilty. The issue became known as the **Dreyfus affair.** A few years later, evidence showed that Dreyfus had been framed. He was later declared innocent.

The Dreyfus affair revealed **anti-Semitism,** or prejudice against Jews, in Europe. In Eastern Europe, anti-Semitism was bad. The Russian government even allowed organized attacks on Jewish villages. From the 1880s on, many Jews fled to the United States. In the 1890s, a movement called Zionism began. Its goal was a separate homeland for the Jews in Palestine.

3. Where in Europe was anti-Semitism found?

____

____

____

____

As you read about democratic reforms in Great Britain, answer the questions about the time line.

Year	Event
1830	**Revolution breaks out in France.**
1832	**Parliament passes the Reform Bill.**
1837	**Queen Victoria comes to throne.**
1838	**Chartists submit The People's Charter to Parliament.**
1867	**Parliament extends suffrage to working-class men.**
1884	**Parliament extends suffrage to male rural workers.**
1903	**Emmeline Pankhurst forms the Women's Social and Political Union.**

1. How did this revolution affect parliamentary leaders in Britain?

2. How did this bill advance democracy in Great Britain?

3. Why did the British monarchy become so powerless in the 1800s?

4. What demands did the Chartists make in their petition?

5. Why did ordinary people want a greater voice in government?

6. What were the objectives of this group?

Self-Rule for British Colonies

Terms and Names

dominion Nation in the British Empire allowed to govern its own domestic affairs

Maori Polynesian people who settled in New Zealand

Aborigine Native people of Australia

penal colony Place where convicts are sent to serve their sentences as an alternative to prison

home rule Local control over domestic affairs

Irish Republican Army Unofficial military force seeking independence

Before You Read

In the last section, you read about democracy and prejudice in Britain, France, and other parts of Europe.

In this section, you will read about the fight for self-rule in British colonies.

As You Read

Use a chart to compare progress toward self-rule by recording significant events in Canada, Australia, New Zealand, and Ireland.

CANADA STRUGGLES FOR SELF-RULE (Pages 317–318)

***How* was the dominion of Canada formed?**

Britain had colonies all over the world. Three of them—Canada, Australia, and New Zealand—were settled by colonists from Europe. Over time, the people in these colonies wanted to control their own governments.

The white settlers of Canada were split into two groups. One group included French-speaking Catholics that lived in the colony. Britain had won Canada from France in 1763. The other group was English-speaking and mostly Protestant. The two groups did not get along. In 1791, Britain split the colony into two provinces. Each colony had its own government.

But the French-speaking people were not happy with British rule. After several rebellions, the British Parliament put the two provinces back together under one government. Other smaller colonies were added to create the Dominion of Canada. As a **dominion,** Canada had the right to make all laws concerning its own affairs. But Parliament kept the right to control Canadian relations with other countries. By 1871, Canada stretched all the way from the Atlantic Ocean to the Pacific Ocean.

1. Why does Canada today contain both French-speaking and English-speaking people?

____

____

AUSTRALIA AND NEW ZEALAND

(Pages 318–319)

***How* were Australia and New Zealand settled?**

New Zealand became part of the British Empire in 1769. Britain claimed Australia in 1770. Australia was a **penal colony.** The first settlers there were convicted criminals. The **Aborigines,** as Europeans later called the native people of Australia, were nomadic. They fished and hunted.

The settlement of New Zealand went slowly because the British government recognized that the native people—the **Maori**—had rights to the land. By the 1840s, though, the number of British settlers in New Zealand was growing.

During the 1850s, Australia and New Zealand became self-governing. But they stayed in the British Empire. In the early 1900s they became dominions. Australia was the first country to use the secret ballot in elections. New Zealand—in 1893—was the first country to give women the right to vote.

2. How were the native people of Australia and New Zealand treated differently?

____

THE IRISH WIN HOME RULE

(Pages 320–321)

***Why* did the British hesitate to give Ireland independence?**

Irish self-rule took a long time to achieve. The Irish opposed English rule from its start in the 1100s. Religious conflict also divided the Catholic Irish and the small group of English Protestants who lived in the north.

In the 1840s, the Irish suffered a terrible famine. Many died of starvation and disease. Others lost their land. Millions of Irish people emigrated, or left Ireland. Most went to the United States or Britain.

In the late 1800s, some Irish pushed for complete independence. Most argued for **home rule**—the right to govern internal affairs. The British government opposed this move. They were afraid that the Catholic majority would treat harshly the Protestants in the north. In 1914, Parliament enacted a home rule bill for the southern part of Ireland. When World War I delayed its enactment, Irish nationalists rebelled. **The Irish Republican Army,** a military force seeking independence, attacked British officials in Ireland.

Finally, Britain split Ireland in two. Northern Ireland remained part of Britain. The southern part became independent. Violence continued in Ireland off and on for decades. In 1998, the people of Ireland and Britain signed an agreement to solve their problems peacefully.

3. Why was Ireland split into two parts?

____

____

As you read this section, note some of the causes and effects of conflicts between Britain and its colonies.

Causes	Actions/Events	Effects
	1. Parliament creates Upper Canada and Lower Canada in 1791.	
	2. Nova Scotia and New Brunswick join with the Province of Canada to form the Dominion of Canada in 1867.	
	3. British annex New Zealand in 1838.	
	4. British government formally joins Ireland to Britain in 1801.	
	5. During the Great Famine, British government forces Irish peasants to continue paying rent.	
	6. Irish nationalists rebel in Dublin in 1916.	

Name ____________________ Class ____________ Date ____________

War and Expansion in the United States

Terms and Names

manifest destiny Belief that the United States would rule the land from the Atlantic Ocean to the Pacific Ocean

Abraham Lincoln 16th president of the United States

secede To leave the nation

U.S. Civil War War fought between the North and South from 1861–1865

Emancipation Proclamation 1863 proclamation to free the slaves in the Confederate states

segregation Separation by race

Before You Read

In the last section, you read about the struggle for self-rule in British colonies.

In this section, you will read about changes in the United States during the same time period.

As You Read

Use a time line to take notes on major events of the United States in the 19th century.

AMERICANS MOVE WEST

(**Pages** 324–325)

***What* was manifest destiny?**

The United States expanded across North America and fought a bloody civil war. In the early 1800s the nation grew in size. It bought a huge piece of land from France in the Louisiana Purchase. It won a war with Mexico in the 1840s, and gained even more land.

Many believed in **manifest destiny**—the belief that the United States would control land from the Atlantic Ocean to the Pacific. As white settlers moved farther west, Native Americans suffered. In the 1830s, thousands of Native Americans were forced to move from their homes in the East to the present state of Oklahoma.

The growth of the nation raised serious questions. The Southern states used slave labor to grow crops such as cotton. People in the South hoped to extend slavery to the western lands. But many Northerners believed that slavery was wrong and should be ended.

1. What problems did the movement westward bring?

____

____

CIVIL WAR TESTS DEMOCRACY

(**Pages** 325–327)

Why was the Civil War fought?

The struggle over slavery led to the **U.S. Civil War.** The Southern states **seceded,** or pulled out of, the Union. The Southerners formed their own nation known as the Confederate States of America. War broke out after Confederate forces fired on a Union fort in 1861. The fighting lasted four years.

The North won the war. During the war, President **Abraham Lincoln** issued the **Emancipation Proclamation.** This proclamation declared that the people enslaved in the Confederate states were free. After the war, the Constitution was amended, or changed, to outlaw slavery. Another change to the Constitution made African Americans citizens.

In the first few years after the war, newly freed African Americans enjoyed equal rights. But whites soon regained control of the governments of the Southern states. They passed laws that took away the rights of blacks. The white governments also set up **segregation,** or separation, of blacks and whites. African Americans have continued to fight for equality since then.

2. What changes came about as a result of the Civil War?

____

____

____

THE POSTWAR ECONOMY

(**Page** 327)

What happened after the war?

After the Civil War, the nation experienced quick industrial growth. A sharp rise in immigration from Europe and Asia helped cause this growth. By 1914, more than 20 million people had come to the United States.

Many of these new citizens moved to the West. The government offered free land to people who moved there.

In addition, Congress set aside money to build a railroad across the continent. The railroad linked the different regions of the nation. By 1900, nearly 200,000 miles of track crossed the country. The growth of the railroads helped American industry grow.

3. What helped cause the rise in industrial growth?

____

____

____

As you read this section, take notes to answer the questions about the United States in the nineteenth century.

From 1783 to 1853, the United States added new territory.	
1. What was the significance of the Louisiana Purchase?	
2. How did the United States extend its northern and southern boundaries?	
3. What lands did the United States acquire as a result of the Mexican-American War?	
4. How did the idea of manifest destiny affect Native Americans?	

Civil War breaks out between the North and South.	
5. What issues caused conflict between the North and South?	
6. What were the immediate causes of the U.S. Civil War?	
7. Why did Abraham Lincoln issue the Emancipation Proclamation?	
8. What were the long-term economic effects of the Civil War?	

Name ______________________ Class ______________ Date ______________

Nineteenth-Century Progress

Terms and Names

assembly line Arrangement by which a product in a factory is moved from worker to worker, with each worker completing a single step in the task

Charles Darwin Scientist who developed the theory of evolution

theory of evolution Theory that all life on earth developed from simpler forms of life

radioactivity Form of energy released as atoms decay

psychology Study of the mind

mass culture Art and entertainment appealing to a large audience

Before You Read

In the last section, you read about political change in the United States.

In this section, you will learn about progress in science and other fields.

As You Read

Use a web diagram to connect people with their ideas and inventions.

INVENTIONS MAKE LIFE EASIER

(**Pages** 328–330)

***How* did inventions change ways of life?**

In the late 1800s, new inventions changed how people lived. Inventors around the world worked to make new machines. Thomas Edison received patents on more than 1,000 inventions. Among them were the electric light bulb and phonograph. Alexander Graham Bell invented the telephone. Guglielmo Marconi created the first radio.

There were changes in transportation, too. Henry Ford made the car affordable to ordinary people. He had a factory with an **assembly line.** It allowed him to build cheap cars. These cars were affordable for ordinary people. In 1903, the Wright brothers flew the first motor-powered airplane flight. Soon there was an aircraft industry.

1. What were three important inventions during this period?

____

NEW IDEAS IN MEDICINE

(**Page** 330)

***What* new ideas appeared in medicine?**

Until the mid-1800s, no one knew about germs. French scientist Louis Pasteur discovered that microscopic animals could live in food. Pasteur called these tiny creatures bacteria. Scientists such as Joseph Lister soon realized that bacteria could cause disease.

2. What relevance did Pasteur's ideas have to the treatment of disease?

____

____

NEW IDEAS IN SCIENCE

(**Pages** 331–332)

***What* new ideas appeared in science?**

English scientist **Charles Darwin** developed the **theory of evolution.** This theory said that all life on earth had developed from simpler life forms over millions of years. This theory was hotly debated. Many people did not accept this idea. They said it went against the Bible.

In the mid-1880s, an Austrian monk named Gregor Mendel showed that parents passed on their personal traits to their offspring. The science of genetics began.

Other scientists made new discoveries in chemistry and physics. They found that all matter is made of tiny particles called atoms. Marie and Pierre Curie discovered **radioactivity.** Radioactivity is the energy that is released when atoms decay.

3. Tell what each of the following discovered or developed: Charles Darwin, Gregor Mendel, Marie and Pierre Curie.

____

____

____

____

SOCIAL SCIENCES EXPLORE BEHAVIOR (Page 332)

***What* is psychology?**

In the late 1800s, some thinkers began to study the human mind. This new social science was called **psychology**. The Russian scientist Ivan Pavlov conducted a series of experiments. These experiments convinced him that people responded to certain situations because of how they were trained.

Sigmund Freud, an Austrian doctor, argued that a person's actions are shaped by forces in the subconscious mind. These views shocked many. They seemed to overturn the idea that people could use their reason to build better lives.

4. What did Freud reveal about the mind?

____

____

____

____

THE RISE OF MASS CULTURE

(**Pages** 332–333)

***What* is mass culture?**

In earlier times, most art, music, and the theater had been of interest to only the wealthy. With the rise of the middle class, a new mass culture developed.

This new **mass culture** appealed to a wide audience. People went to music halls to enjoy singing and dancing. In the early 1900s, they watched the first silent movies. People also enjoyed sporting events, both as participants and as spectators.

5. What new forms of entertainment became popular?

____

____

____

____

As you read this section, take notes to answer the questions about the technological and scientific advances of the late 1800s.

The Inventors	What were their most significant inventions or innovations?
1. Thomas Edison	
2. Alexander Graham Bell	
3. Guglielmo Marconi	
4. Henry Ford	
5. Wilbur and Orville Wright	

The Scientists	What were their most significant discoveries or theories?
6. Louis Pasteur	
7. Charles Darwin	
8. Gregor Mendel	
9. Marie and Pierre Curie	
10. Ivan Pavlov	

The Scramble for Africa

Terms and Names

imperialism Control by a strong nation over a weaker nation

racism Belief that one race is superior to others

Social Darwinism Use of Charles Darwin's ideas about evolution to explain human societies

Berlin Conference Meeting at which Europeans agreed on rules for colonizing Africa

Shaka Zulu chief who created a large centralized state

Boer Dutch colonist in South Africa

Boer War War between the British and the Boers

Before You Read

In the last section, you read about movements for democracy and self-rule.

In this section, you will learn about imperialism in Africa.

As You Read

Use an outline to list the forces and events surrounding imperialism in Africa.

AFRICA BEFORE EUROPEAN DOMINATION; FORCES DRIVING IMPERIALISM (Pages 339–341)

***Why* did imperialism begin in the 1800s?**

In the early 1800s, Europeans controlled a few areas along the coast of Africa. By the mid-1800s, Europeans were expanding their control to new lands. This policy is called **imperialism.**

There were four basic reasons for imperialism. The first reason for imperialism had to do with money. Europeans wanted colonies to provide raw materials for their factories. The Europeans also wanted to sell their goods in their new colonies.

National pride was a second reason for imperialism. Some nations wanted to gain colonies to show their national strength.

Racism was a third reason for imperialism. Racism is the belief that one race is better than others. Many Europeans believed that whites were better than other races.

Racism is related to Social Darwinism. **Social Darwinism** is the use of Charles Darwin's ideas about evolution to explain human societies. One of Darwin's ideas was "survival of the fittest." This idea was that the fittest, or strongest, species would survive. Weak species would not survive.

People who believed in Social Darwinism argued that fit people and nations survived. They also believed that weak people and nations would not survive.

Christian missionaries also supported imperialism. They thought that European rule would end the slave trade. The missionaries also wanted to convert the people of other continents to Christianity.

Europeans began to take lands in Africa for these reasons. Technology helped the Europeans succeed. The African peoples were divided. It was hard for them to resist European advances.

1. What are four reasons for imperialism?

____

____

____

THE DIVISION OF AFRICA (Pages 341–342)

How did European nations claim African lands?

The "scramble for Africa" began in the 1880s. Diamonds were discovered in South Africa in 1867. Gold was discovered there in 1886. Europeans became more interested in the continent.

The European nations did not want to fight over the land. They met at the **Berlin Conference** in 1884–85. They agreed that any nation could claim any part of Africa by telling the others and by showing that it had control of the area. Europeans quickly grabbed land. By 1914, only Liberia and Ethiopia were free from European control.

2. What was the purpose of the Berlin Conference?

____

____

____

THREE GROUPS CLASH OVER SOUTH AFRICA (Pages 342–344)

What groups fought over South Africa?

In South Africa, three groups struggled over the land. In the early 1800s, the Zulu chief **Shaka** fought to win more land. Shaka's successors were not able to keep his kingdom intact. The Zulu land was taken over by the British in 1887.

Meanwhile, the British took control of the Dutch colony on the southern coast. Thousands of Dutch settlers, called **Boers,** moved north to escape the British. This movement is known as the Great Trek. The Boers fought the Zulus whose land they were entering.

At the end of the century, Boers fought a vicious war against the British called the **Boer War.** The Boers lost this war. The Boers then joined the British-run Union of South Africa.

3. Who were the Boers, and whom did they fight?

____

____

____

As you read about the European colonization of Africa, fill out the chart by writing notes in the appropriate spaces.

The Forces of Imperialism	
1. Note three motives behind the European race for colonies.	
2. Note two technological advantages Europeans had over the Africans.	
3. Note two factors within Africa that made it vulnerable to European conquest.	

The Division of Africa	
4. Note two outcomes of the Berlin Conference in 1884 and 1885.	
5. Note three groups that clashed over territory and resources in South Africa.	
6. Note one outcome of the Boer War.	

Imperialism

Case Study: Nigeria

Terms and Names

paternalism Governing in a "parental" way by providing for needs but not giving rights

assimilation Absorbing colonized people into the culture of the imperialist nation

Menelik II Leader of Ethiopian resistance

Before You Read

In the last section, you learned about the reasons for imperialism.

In this section, you will read about how the colonies were controlled.

As You Read

Use a web to record the forms and methods of European imperialism in Africa, the resistance it met with, and its impact.

A NEW PERIOD OF IMPERIALISM; A BRITISH COLONY (Pages 345–348)

***What* forms and methods did imperialist nations use to control their colonies?**

Each imperial power had goals for its colonies. Imperialist nations had four forms of control: colony, protectorate, sphere of influence, and economic imperialism.

A colony is an area ruled by a foreign government. A protectorate runs its own daily affairs, but is controlled by an imperialist nation. A sphere of influence is an area where an imperialist nation has exclusive economic rights. Economic imperialism refers to a situation where an independent nation is controlled by foreign businesses rather than foreign governments.

Imperialist nations also developed two basic methods to manage their colonies. France and other European nations used direct control. They felt native peoples could not handle the tough job of running a country. Instead, the imperialist power governed. This policy was called **paternalism.** The French also had a policy of **assimilation.** All colonial institutions were patterned after French institutions. The French hoped that the native peoples would learn French ways.

Britain used indirect control. In this system, local rulers had power over daily matters. There were also councils of native people and government officials. These councils were supposed to help native people learn to govern themselves in the British method. When the United States began to colonize, it also used the indirect method of control.

Britain tried to rule Nigeria through indirect control. The British let local chiefs manage their areas. The system did not always work. The local chiefs in some regions of Nigeria resented having their power limited by the British.

1. What forms and methods did imperialists use to control and manage colonies?

____

____

AFRICAN RESISTANCE

(**Pages** 348–349)

***How* did Africans resist imperialism?**

Some Africans resisted imperialism. People in Algeria fought against the French for almost 50 years. In German East Africa, thousands of Africans died when they tried to use magic to fight German machine guns.

Only Ethiopia resisted the Europeans successfully. There, Emperor **Menelik II** played one European country against another. In 1896, he used European weapons to defeat an Italian army.

2. Who resisted imperialism in Africa, and what were the results?

____

____

THE LEGACY OF COLONIAL RULE

(**Page** 350)

***How* did colonial rule affect Africa?**

Africans enjoyed some benefits from colonial rule. European governments reduced local conflicts. The Europeans also brought Africa deeper into the world economy. Railroads, dams, and telephone and telegraph lines were built.

But imperialism mostly caused damage. Africans lost control over much of their land. Many African traditions were destroyed. People were forced out of their homes. Many were made to work in bad conditions. The boundaries that Europeans drew had no relation to ethnic divisions in Africa. These boundaries caused problems when the colonies became independent nations.

3. What were three benefits and three problems of colonial rule?

____

____

As you read this section, take notes to answer the questions.

European nations used various forms of colonial control.	
1. How did the British control Nigeria and other British colonies?	
2. What method of management did the French use with their colonies?	

African societies tried to resist European attempts at colonization.	
3. How did Algeria's resistance to French rule differ from the East Africans' resistance to German rule?	
4. Why was Ethiopia able to successfully resist European rule?	

European colonial rule greatly transformed African society.	
5. How did Africans benefit from colonial rule?	
6. What were the negative consequences of colonial rule for the African continent?	

Europeans Claim Muslim Lands

Terms and Names

geopolitics Interest in or taking of land for its location or products

Crimean War Conflict in which the Ottoman Empire halted Russian expansion near the Black Sea

Suez Canal Human-made waterway connecting the Red and Mediterranean Seas

Before You Read

In the last section, you read about imperialism in Africa.

In this section, you will learn about imperialism in Muslim lands.

As You Read

Use a diagram to note three details that support the main idea that Muslim states failed to keep European imperialists out of their lands.

OTTOMAN EMPIRE LOSES POWER (Page 352)

***When* did the Ottoman Empire become weak?**

The Ottoman Empire was based in modern Turkey. But it controlled lands in Eastern Europe, North Africa, and Southwest Asia.

This empire lasted for hundreds of years, but by the 1800s, it was weak. The ruling party broke up into quarreling factions. Corruption and theft caused financial chaos. The Ottomans had once embraced modern technologies but now were falling behind the Europeans.

Nationalism began to stir among people in the empire. In 1830, Greece won its independence and Serbia won the right to govern itself. European nations eyed what remained of the empire hungrily.

1. What happened when the Ottoman Empire weakened?

____

____

____

____

____

EUROPEANS GRAB TERRITORY (Pages 352–354)

***Where* did Europeans grab territory?**

Geopolitics is the interest in or taking of land for its location or products. It played an important role in the fall of the Ottoman Empire. Russia hoped to win control of the Black Sea so it could ship grain into the Mediterranean Sea. Russia fought a war with the Ottomans in the 1850s called the **Crimean War.**

Russia lost the war when Britain and France joined on the side of the Ottomans. Still, the Ottomans later lost almost all of their land in Europe and parts of Africa. Muslim leaders, seeing this decline, decided to modernize their countries.

Russia also fought Great Britain in a war known as the "Great Game." Russia sought to extend its empire and gain access to India, one of Britain's most valuable colonies. The British defended India and also attempted to spread its empire beyond India's borders. Much of the war was fought in the independent Muslim kingdom of Afghanistan. After decades of fighting, both countries withdrew and agreed to respect Afghanistan's independence.

2. Why did Russia engage in the Crimean War and the Great Game?

____

____

____

____

EGYPT INITIATES REFORMS; PERSIA PRESSURED TO CHANGE

(Pages 354–356)

What measures did Muslim countries take to avoid imperialist domination?

Some Muslim leaders tried to adopt reforms to block European control of their lands. In Egypt, Muhammad Ali broke away from Ottoman control. He reformed the army and the economy. Ali's grandson continued to modernize the empire. He joined with the French in building the **Suez Canal.** It connected the Mediterranean to the Red Sea.

The canal was extremely expensive to build. Egypt quickly found that it could not afford to repay the money it owed. The British took control of the canal. Later the British took over the rest of the country as well.

In Persia, the Russians and the British competed for control. Russia wanted to use Persia to gain access to the Persian Gulf and Indian Ocean. Twice Russia forced Persia to give up territories through military victories.

Britain wanted to use Afghanistan as a buffer between India and Russia. In 1857, Britain forced Persia to give up all claims to Afghanistan.

In the early 1900s, oil was discovered in Persia. A British company signed an agreement with Persia's ruler to develop these oil fields. Persians rebelled against their ruler, who was corrupt, and the growing influence of Europeans. Then Russia and Britain stepped in and took control of the land.

In Muslim lands, the Europeans gained control by using economic imperialism and creating spheres of influence. Some Muslim countries tried to modernize. But these efforts came too late to prevent Europeans from taking over.

3. What happened in Egypt and in Persia?

____

____

____

____

Name ______________________ Class ______________ Date ______________

Section 3, *continued*

As you read this section, explain how each of the factors listed contributed to the decline of Muslim states.

Factor		Effect
1. Death of Suleyman I	→	
2. Rise of nationalism	→	
3. Geopolitics	→	
4. Construction of the Suez Canal	→	
5. Discovery of oil in Persia	→	

Section 4

British Imperialism in India

Terms and Names

sepoy Indian soldier under British command

"jewel in the crown" Term referring to India as the most valuable of all British colonies

Sepoy Mutiny Uprising of Indian soldiers against the British

Raj British rule over India from 1757 to 1947

Before You Read

In the last section, you saw how Europeans grabbed Muslim lands.

In this section, you will read about British control of India.

As You Read

Use a diagram to identify the effects in India of the decline of the Mughal Empire, colonial policies, and the Sepoy Mutiny.

BRITISH EXPAND CONTROL OVER INDIA (Pages 357–358)

***How* did British rule affect India?**

The Mughal Empire of India fell into decline in the early 1700s. By the mid-1700s, the British East India Company was the most important power in India. The company held huge amounts of land. The company even had its own army. This army was led by British officers. It was staffed by **sepoys,** Indian soldiers.

India was the main supplier of raw materials for Britain. The British called India the **"jewel in the crown"** because it was Britain's most valuable colony.

India enjoyed some benefits from British rule. India's rail system was the third largest in the world. The railroad helped make India's economy more modern. The British made other improvements, too. They built telephone and telegraph lines, dams, bridges, and canals. They also improved sanitation and public health and built schools.

But British rule also caused problems. A great deal of wealth flowed from India to Britain. Indian industry died out because of British trade laws. Many farmers and villages could no longer feed themselves because they were forced to grow cash crops. India suffered famines in the late 1800s. In addition, most British officials had racist attitudes that threatened Indian culture.

1. What problems did British rule bring?

____

____

____

____

____

THE SEPOY MUTINY (Pages 359–360)

Why did Indians rebel?

By the mid-1800s, many Indians resented British rule. In 1857, some Indian soldiers heard rumors about British weapons. The rumors offended the Indians' religious feelings. The British handled the situation badly. The Indian soldiers rebelled. This rebellion has been called the **Sepoy Mutiny.** It took the East India Company and British troops a year to put it down.

The Sepoy Mutiny failed because the Indians were divided. Muslims and Hindus did not trust each other. After the revolt, the British government took direct control of British India. The term **Raj** refers to British rule over India from 1757 to 1947.

2. What was the Sepoy Mutiny?

____
____
____
____

NATIONALISM SURFACES IN INDIA (Page 361)

What were the goals of the Indian nationalist movement?

Indians also resisted British control in other ways. Leaders such as Ram Mohun Roy urged changes in traditional Indian practices. He wanted to make Indian society more modern and to free India of foreign control.

Nationalist feelings also started to grow in India. Indians resented the British discrimination against them. Indians were barred from the best jobs in the Indian Civil Service. British workers were paid more than Indian workers doing the same job.

Indians formed two groups—the Indian National Congress and the Muslim League. Both groups pushed the British to make changes. In the early 1900s, they called for self-government.

3. What groups called for change?

____
____
____
____
____

As you read about imperialism in India, briefly note the cause or effect (depending on which is missing) of each situation.

Causes		Effects
1.	→	East India Company gains control of India.
2. British establish a railroad network in India.	→	
3.	→	Villagers are no longer self-sufficient; food production declines and famine sets in.
4. The Sepoy Mutiny occurs and uprisings spread over much of northern India.	→	
5.	→	Indians form Indian National Congress and then the Muslim League, which eventually call for self-government.
6. British partition Bengal into Hindu and Muslim sections.	→	

Imperialism in Southeast Asia

Terms and Names

Pacific Rim Southeast Asian mainland and islands along the rim of the Pacific Ocean

King Mongkut King who helped Siam modernize

Emilio Aguinaldo Leader of Filipino nationalists

annexation Adding of territory

Queen Liliuokalani Last Hawaiian ruler of Hawaii

Before You Read

In the last section, you saw how the Indians reacted to imperialism.

In this section, you will read about imperialism in Southeast Asia.

As You Read

Use a web diagram to identify a Western power and the areas it controlled.

EUROPEAN POWERS INVADE THE PACIFIC RIM (Pages 362–363)

Which Western powers grabbed land in Southeast Asia?

European nations also grabbed land in the **Pacific Rim,** Southeast Asia and the islands on the edge of the Pacific Ocean. The lands of Southeast Asia were perfect for plantation agriculture. Sugar, coffee, cocoa, rubber, coconuts, bananas, and pineapples were important products.

The Dutch controlled Indonesia. Many of the Dutch who moved to Indonesia thought of Indonesia as their home. They set up a class system that kept the Dutch at the top. Wealthy and educated Indonesians came next. Plantation workers were at the bottom. The Dutch forced farmers to use one-fifth of their land for export crops.

The British took the port of Singapore plus Malaysia and Burma (modern Myanmar). They used Singapore as a base for trade. It became one of the world's busiest ports. The British encouraged the Chinese to move to Malaysia. The Malaysians have become a minority in their own country. Tension between the Malays and the Chinese remains to this day.

France grabbed Indochina (modern Laos, Cambodia, and Vietnam). The French ruled Indochina directly and tried to push French culture on the Indochinese. The French did not encourage industry. Rice became a major crop. Although the Vietnamese grew more rice than before, they ate less of it because so much rice was sent out of the region. This problem set the stage for Vietnamese resistance to French rule.

Colonialism brought some features of modern life to these regions. But economic change benefited Europeans more than the local people. Even so, schooling, health, and sanitation were improved. Millions of people migrated to new regions of Southeast Asia. But the mix of cultures did not always go smoothly. Even today, some conflict between groups results from this period.

1. What major problems did colonialism bring?

____

____

____

____

SIAM REMAINS INDEPENDENT (Pages 363–364)

How did imperialism affect Siam?

One land—Siam (modern Thailand)—stayed independent. Siam was surrounded by lands taken by the French and British. The French and British did not want the other to control Siam. The Siamese kings played the French and British against one another to remain free of both nations.

King Mongkut and his son modernized Siam. They started schools and reformed the government. They also built railroads and telegraph lines and ended slavery. These changes happened with little social turmoil.

2. How did Siam confront imperialism?

____

____

____

____

U.S. IMPERIALISM IN THE PACIFIC ISLANDS (Pages 364–365)

What lands did the United States acquire?

In the late 1800s, the United States also began to seek colonies. After the Spanish-American War in 1898, the United States took control of Puerto Rico, Guam, and the Philippine Islands.

Filipino nationalists led by **Emilio Aguinaldo** fought against the Americans for their freedom. The United States defeated the rebels but promised to give the Philippines self-rule later. In the meantime, American businesses took advantage of Filipino workers.

American businessmen grew wealthy from sugar plantations in Hawaii. But they wanted to make more money. They also asked for the **annexation,** or addition, of Hawaii to the United States. That way they would get more money when they sold sugar in the United States. The American businessmen had a great deal of power in Hawaii.

In the 1890s, **Queen Liliuokalani** tried to regain control of her country for the Hawaiian people. The American businessmen overthrew her. They declared a republic. In 1898, it became a territory of the United States.

3. What happened in the Philippines?

____

____

____

____

As you read about the cclonization of Southeast Asia, write notes about each group.

1. Dutch East India Company		
Lands claimed	Major products	Impact of colonization

2. British		
Lands claimed	Immigration policy	Impact of colonization

3. French		
Lands claimed	Method of management	Impact of colonization

4. Americans		
Lands claimed	Method of management	Impact of colonization

Section 1

China Resists Outside Influence

Terms and Names

Opium War War between Britain and China over the opium trade

extraterritorial rights Rights of foreign residents to follow the laws of their own government rather than those of the host country

Taiping Rebellion Rebellion against the Qing Dynasty

sphere of influence Area in which a foreign nation controls trade and investment

Open Door Policy Policy proposed by the United States giving all nations equal opportunities to trade in China

Boxer Rebellion Rebellion aimed at ending foreign influence in China

Before You Read

In the last section, you read about imperialism in Asia.

In this section, you will see how China dealt with foreign influence.

As You Read

Use a chart to identify the internal and external problems faced by China in the 1800s and early 1900s.

CHINA AND THE WEST

(Pages 371–372)

Was **China able to resist foreign influence?**

In the late 1700s, China had a strong farming economy based on growing rice. Other crops, such as peanuts, helped to feed its large population. The Chinese made silk, cotton, and ceramics. Mines produced salt, tin, silver, and iron. China needed nothing from the outside world.

China limited its trade with European powers. All goods shipped to China had to come through one port. Britain bought so much Chinese tea that it was eager to find something that the Chinese would want in large quantities. In the early 1800s, the British began shipping opium, a dangerous drug, to China. The opium came mostly from India. The Chinese tried to make the British stop.

As a result of the **Opium War** that followed, the British took possession of Hong Kong. Later, the United States and European nations won **extraterritorial rights** and the right to trade in five ports. The Chinese resented these treaties but could not stop them.

1. What happened as a result of the Opium War?

____

GROWING INTERNAL PROBLEMS

(Pages 372–373)

What **problems did China face?**

China had internal problems as well. The population had grown quickly. When rains were too light or too heavy, millions starved. The Chinese government was weak and too corrupt to solve its problems.

A leader arose who hoped to save China. His name was Hong Xiuquan, and he led the **Taiping Rebellion.** More than one million peasants joined his army. The rebels won control of large parts of the south. The government needed 14 years to put down this rebellion. The fighting destroyed much farmland. At least 20 million people died.

2. What was the Taiping Rebellion?

____

____

____

FOREIGN INFLUENCE GROWS

(**Pages** 373–374)

***What* was the official attitude toward reform?**

In the late 1800s, one person ruled China—the Dowager Empress Cixi. She supported a few reforms in education, civil service, and the military. Despite her efforts to bring change, China continued to face problems.

Other countries were well aware of China's weakness, and they took advantage of the situation. Throughout the late 1800s, many foreign nations won a **sphere of influence** in China. A sphere of influence is a region in which a foreign nation controls trade and investment.

The United States opposed these spheres of influence. Americans urged an **Open Door Policy,** in which all powers had equal access to Chinese markets. The Europeans agreed. This policy did not help China, however. Although it was not a colony or group of colonies, China was dominated by foreign powers.

3. How did foreigners begin to gain control over China?

____

____

____

AN UPSURGE IN CHINESE NATIONALISM

(**Pages** 374–375)

***What* actions resulted from growing nationalism?**

Humiliated by their loss of power, many Chinese wanted strong reforms. In 1898, the young Emperor Guangxu, Cixi's nephew, tried to put in place broader reforms.

Conservatives didn't like this. The retired Empress Cixi had him arrested and she took back control of the government. China had lost a chance for reform.

Some Chinese peasants and workers formed the Society of Harmonious Fists, known as the Boxers. They wanted to get rid of all Western influence. That included any Chinese who had accepted Western culture or the Christian religion. At the start of the **Boxer Rebellion** in early 1900, Boxers surrounded Beijing's European section. After many weeks, they were driven out by a multinational army.

Cixi finally began to allow major reforms. But change came slowly. In 1908, Chinese officials said that China would become a constitutional monarchy by 1917. However, unrest soon returned.

4. What was the Boxer Rebellion?

____

____

As you read this section, note some of the causes and effects of events and policies that affected China.

Causes	Events/Policies	Effects
	1. Opium War	
	2. Taiping Rebellion	
	3. Self-strengthening movement	
	4. Open Door policy	
	5. Boxer Rebellion	

Modernization in Japan

Terms and Names

Treaty of Kanagawa Treaty between the United States and Japan opening trade between the two nations

Meiji era Period of rule by Emperor Mutsuhito from 1867 to 1912

Russo–Japanese War War between Russia and Japan fought in 1904

annexation Adding of territory

Before You Read

In the last section, you read about foreign influence in China.

In this section, you will learn about the steps taken by Japan to modernize.

As You Read

Use a chart to list the steps that Japan took toward modernization and the events that contributed to its growth as an imperialistic power.

JAPAN ENDS ITS ISOLATION

(**Pages** 376–377)

***How* did isolation end in Japan?**

From the early 1600s to the mid-1800s, Japan traded with China and the Dutch and had diplomatic contact with Korea. But beyond that, Japan was largely isolated. British, French, Russian, and American officials tried to convince the Japanese to open up. But the Japanese repeatedly refused.

That situation changed in 1853 when American steamships with cannons entered Japanese waters. The next year, Japan and the United States signed the **Treaty of Kanagawa.** It agreed to open Japan to trade with America. Soon afterwards, Japan made similar deals with European nations.

Many Japanese were upset with the shogun, the military dictator, who had agreed to these new treaties. The Emperor Mutsuhito got their support and managed to overthrow the shogun. For the first time in centuries, the emperor ruled Japan directly. He reigned for 45 years, from 1867 to 1912. This period is called the **Meiji era.** The name Meiji means "enlightened rule."

The emperor wanted to modernize Japan. He sent government officials to Europe and the United States. From what they saw, they shaped a new Japan. They modeled the government after the strong central government of Germany. They patterned the army after Germany's and the navy after Britain's. They adapted the American system of schooling for all children.

The emperor also supported changes to Japan's economy. The country mined coal and built railroads and factories. In just a few years, Japan's economy was as modern as any in the world.

1. What steps did Emperor Mutsuhito take to modernize Japan?

____

____

____

____

____

IMPERIAL JAPAN (Pages 377–379)

How did Japan increase its influence in Asia?

By 1890, Japan had the strongest military in Asia. It asked foreigners to give up their special rights in Japan. The European nations agreed. Japan felt equal to the Western nations.

Japan became more imperialistic as its power grew. When China broke an agreement not to send armies into Korea, Japan went to war. It drove China out of Korea and gained Taiwan and some other islands as new colonies. In 1904, Japan and Russia fought the **Russo–Japanese War** over China's Manchurian territory. Japan surprised the world by defeating a larger power that was supposed to be stronger.

The next year, Japan attacked Korea. Japan made Korea a protectorate. Japanese officials took more and more power away from the Korean government. The Korean king was unable to get help for his government from other countries. By 1910, Japan achieved **annexation** of Korea.

The Japanese were harsh rulers. They shut down Korean newspapers. They allowed only Japanese history and language to be taught. They took land from Korean farmers and gave it to Japanese settlers. They built factories run by Japanese only. Koreans were not allowed to start new businesses. Koreans resented these actions. They began a nationalist movement and protested against Japanese rule.

2. How did Japan expand its empire to Korea?

____

____

____

____

____

Name ______________________ Class ______________ Date ______________

As you read about the modernization of Japan, answer the questions about the time line.

Year	Event
1853	**Matthew Perry arrives in Tokyo harbor.**
1854	**Japan signs the Treaty of Kanagawa.**
1867	**Mutsuhito establishes a new government.**
1885	**Japan and China pledge not to send armies into Korea.**
1894	**Sino-Japanese war begins.**
1904	**Russia and Japan go to war over Manchuria.**
1910	**Japan annexes Korea.**

1. What was the American motive in sending the fleet?
2. How did the United States benefit from the terms of the treaty?
3. What steps did the Meiji take to modernize Japan?
4. Why were both countries interested in Korea?
5. How did the war begin?
6. What consequences did the war have?
7. What was the cause of this war?
8. What were some consequences?
9. How did the Japanese rule Korea?

U.S. Economic Imperialism

Terms and Names

caudillo Military dictator

Monroe Doctrine U.S. statement of opposition to European influence in the Americas

José Martí Cuban writer who fought for Cuban independence

Spanish–American War War fought between the United States and Spain in 1898, in which the Americans supported the Cuban fight for independence

Panama Canal Man-made waterway connecting the Atlantic and Pacific Oceans

Roosevelt Corollary Statement that the United States had the right to exercise "police power" in the Western Hemisphere

Before You Read

In the last section, you saw how Japan increased its power and became an imperialist nation.

In this section, you will read about U.S. economic imperialism in Latin America.

As You Read

Use a time line to list the major events in U.S. involvement in Latin America.

LATIN AMERICA AFTER INDEPENDENCE (Pages 382–383)

***What* conditions existed among the new nations of Latin America?**

In the early 1800s, the new nations of Latin America had serious problems. Most people were poor laborers. They worked on farms for large landowners who took advantage of them.

Another problem was political unrest. Local military leaders who wanted power ruled Latin American nations as **caudillos,** or military dictators. Landowners kept the caudillos in power. The landowners refused to give power to the poor people. Only people with property could vote.

Sometimes reformers did take office. But they never lasted long. When their reforms threatened the power of the wealthy too much, a dictator would rise and remove them from office.

1. What problems did the people in the new nations of Latin America face?

____

____

ECONOMIES GROW UNDER FOREIGN INFLUENCE (Pages 383–384)

***What* nations controlled Latin American economies?**

Spain's trade laws in Latin America ended when Spain lost control of those lands. The new countries could now trade with any nation. Britain and the United States became the chief trading partners.

Businesses in these nations soon dominated Latin American economies.

The Latin American economies depended on exports. Other countries benefited from trade with Latin America more than the Latin Americans did.

Latin America did not develop its own manufacturing industries. It had to import manufactured goods. These goods cost more than what was earned from exports.

In addition, Latin American countries often borrowed money from foreign banks. When they could not repay the loans, lenders took control of the businesses. In this way, much of Latin America fell into foreign hands.

2. Why was Latin America's need to import goods a problem?

____

____

____

A LATIN AMERICAN EMPIRE

(**Pages** 384–387)

How did the United States gain Latin American territories?

In 1823, President James Monroe issued the **Monroe Doctrine.** It warned European nations against interfering in the American continents. The United States did not really enforce this policy until the end of the century.

In the 1890s, the people of Cuba were fighting for their independence from Spain. The writer **José Martí** was one of them. American businesses had economic interests on the island. Also, Spain had placed Cuban civilians in concentration camps. This upset many Americans. For these reasons, the United States fought against Spain in the **Spanish–American War.**

The United States won the war and gained several new territories. The United States put a military government in place in Cuba. This step made many Cubans angry at the United States.

Into the early part of the 20th century, ships traveling from the east to the west coast had to go around the southern tip of South America. This took many weeks. Americans wanted to find a quicker route. They hoped to build a canal across Panama.

President Roosevelt offered $10 million to Colombia—to which Panama belonged—for the right to build this canal. When Colombia asked for more money, the United States helped the people of Panama revolt for independence. In return, the United States won a ten-mile-wide zone in Panama in which to build the **Panama Canal.** The canal opened in 1914.

In 1904, Roosevelt extended the Monroe Doctrine. He said that the United States had the right to act as "an international police power" in the western hemisphere. This statement is known as the **Roosevelt Corollary.** Over the next few decades, the United States acted on the Roosevelt Corollary many times. When trouble arose in various countries, the United States sent its troops. Sometimes they stayed for many years.

3. How did the United States win a zone in Panama for a canal?

____

____

____

As you read this section, answer the questions about three factors that set the stage for economic imperialism in Latin America.

Factor 1: Legacy of Colonial Rule	
1. In what ways did landowners "enslave" peasant workers?	
2. How was land distributed during colonial times?	
3. What political problems did independent nations face as a result of European colonial rule?	

Factor 2: Foreign Trade	
4. How did advances in technology affect Latin American trade?	
5. How did foreign countries gain control of Latin American industries?	
6. Why did Latin American nations remain poor and unindustrialized after they gained independence?	

Factor 3: "The Colossus of the North"	
1. Why did President Monroe issue the Monroe Doctrine?	
2. How did the Spanish-American War make the United States the dominant imperial power in Latin America?	
3. How did the United States expand its influence in Latin America in the early 1900s?	

Name ______________________ Class ______________ Date ______________

Section 4

Turmoil and Change in Mexico

Terms and Names

Antonio López de Santa Anna Leader in Mexico's fight for independence

Benito Juárez Leader of *La Reforma*

La Reforma Movement in Mexico aimed at achieving land reform, better education, and other goals

Porfirio Díaz Dictator who came to power after Juárez

Francisco Madero Enemy of Díaz who believed in democracy

"Pancho" Villa Popular leader of the Mexican revolution

Emiliano Zapata Leader of a powerful revolutionary army

Before You Read

In the last section, you read about U.S. economic imperialism in Latin America.

In this section, you will read about revolution and reform in Mexico.

As You Read

Use a chart to compare the major accomplishments of the Mexican leaders discussed in this section.

SANTA ANNA AND THE MEXICAN WAR (Pages 388–389)

***Who* was Santa Anna?**

Antonio López de Santa Anna was a leading figure in the early history of independent Mexico. He fought for Mexican independence from Spain in 1821. He fought against Spain again in 1829 when Spain tried to recapture Mexico. He served as Mexico's president four times.

But in the 1830s, Santa Anna was unable to stop Texas from winning independence from Mexico. In the 1840s, the United States annexed Texas. This angered many Mexicans.

When a border dispute between Mexico and Texas turned into armed conflict, the United States invaded Mexico. Santa Anna led his nation's army and was defeated. Mexico surrendered huge amounts of land to the United States.

1. What losses did Mexicans suffer under Santa Anna?

____

____

____

JUÁREZ AND *LA REFORMA* (Pages 389–391)

***What* was *La Reforma*?**

Another important leader of the middle 1800s was **Benito Juárez.** Juárez wanted to improve conditions for the poor.

He led a movement called ***La Reforma***—"the reform." *La Reforma* aimed to break the power of the large landowners and give more schooling to the poor. Juárez and his supporters won control of the government in 1858.

But conservatives who opposed *La Reforma* did not give up. They plotted with France to retake Mexico. In 1862, Napoleon III of France sent an army that captured the country in 18 months. Napoleon III named a European noble as emperor. But Juárez and his followers kept fighting. Five years later, they drove the French from Mexican soil and executed the emperor.

2. How did conservatives oppose *La Reforma*?

____

____

PORFIRIO DÍAZ AND "ORDER AND PROGRESS" (Pages 391–392)

Who was Porfirio Díaz?

Juárez again pressed for his reforms. He made some progress but died in office in 1872. Soon after he died, a new leader emerged. **Porfirio Díaz** was a leader in Mexican politics for more than 30 years. Díaz brought order to the country. He ended raids by bandits and brought some economic growth, but he limited political freedom. A leader named **Francisco Madero** called for the overthrow of Díaz.

3. What were the benefits and drawbacks of Díaz's rule?

____

____

REVOLUTION AND CIVIL WAR (Pages 392–393)

Who were Villa and Zapata?

In the early 1900s, calls for reform got louder. Francisco **"Pancho" Villa** and **Emiliano Zapata** called for better lives for the poor. They raised armies and forced Díaz to step down. But political unrest continued. For many years, leaders struggled for power. In 1917, Mexico adopted a new constitution that survived all of the turmoil.

Conflict continued until a new political party gained control of Mexico in 1929. The Institutional Revolutionary Party (PRI) brought peace and political stability to a troubled land.

4. What was the main goal of Villa and Zapata?

____

____

As you read this section, take notes to answer questions about revolution and reform in Mexico.

What were the major accomplishments of each leader? What was the political legacy of each?	
1. Antonio López de Santa Anna	
2. Benito Juárez	
3. Porfirio Díaz	

What role did each of the following play in the Mexican Revolution?	
4. Francisco Madero	
5. Francisco "Pancho" Villa	
6. Emiliano Zapata	
7. Venustiano Carranza	

Section 1

Marching Toward War

Terms and Names

militarism Glorifying war and preparing for it

Triple Alliance Military agreement between Germany, Austria-Hungary, and Italy

Kaiser Wilhelm II Emperor of Germany

Triple Entente Military agreement among Britain, France, and Russia

Before You Read

In the last chapter, you read about political changes around the globe.

In this section, you will learn about the First World War.

As You Read

Use a time line to list major events that led to the start of World War I.

RISING TENSIONS IN EUROPE

(**Pages** 407–408)

***Why* didn't peace last in Europe?**

Many people in Europe had joined groups to work for peace. However, developments would soon lead Europe into war.

One of those developments was nationalism—a deep feeling of attachment to one's own nation. This force helped unify the people of a country. It also created competition between countries.

By 1900, six nations were rivals for power in Europe. These nations, called the Great Powers, were Germany, Austria-Hungary, Great Britain, Russia, Italy, and France. They competed economically, and they competed for neighboring land.

Imperialism was another force that helped lead to war. France and Germany were each seeking to control parts of Africa. They almost came to war twice in the early 1900s. Mistrust was a huge problem.

The third factor leading to war was a growing arms race. Each country in Europe—except Great Britain—built a large army. Glorifying war and preparing for it is called **militarism.**

1. What were three factors leading to war?

____

____

____

TANGLED ALLIANCES

(**Pages** 408–409)

***What* caused countries to fear one another?**

Growing rivalries led the nations to make military alliances. Prussia's chancellor, Otto von Bismarck, feared that France would want revenge for its defeat in the Franco-Prussian War. He set out to isolate France. In 1879, he formed a **Triple Alliance** with Austria-Hungary and Italy. He also signed a treaty with Russia.

Kaiser Wilhelm II of Germany did not want to share power with Bismarck. He forced Bismarck to resign and followed his own foreign policy. He let the agreement with Russia end. Russia soon allied itself with France. This alliance meant that Germany would have to fight enemies on its eastern and western borders if there were a war with either country. Wilhelm II then moved to make the German navy larger.

Britain grew alarmed. It began to build more ships. It also entered into the **Triple Entente** alliance with France and Russia. The six Great Powers had now formed two camps—Germany, Austria-Hungary, and Italy against Britain, France, and Russia.

2. What two groups of nations developed?

____

____

____

____

____

CRISIS IN THE BALKANS

(**Pages** 409–410)

What part did the Balkans play in the increasing tensions?

Meanwhile, trouble was brewing in the Balkans, in southeastern Europe. The Ottoman Empire controlled this area. But it was breaking apart. Both Austria-Hungary and Russia wanted some of this land.

The kingdom of Serbia was also in this region. It wanted to bring other Slavic peoples who lived in the Balkans under its control. In 1908, Austria-Hungary seized Bosnia and Herzegovina. These lands had Slavic peoples. This action angered the Serbs. However, their Russian allies were unwilling to support them, and they backed down.

By 1914, the situation was different. Serbia had gained land in other parts of the region and felt strong. Austria worried that Serbia might interfere with its control of Bosnia and Herzegovina.

In June 1914, a Serbian killed Archduke Franz Ferdinand, the heir to the throne of Austria-Hungary. Austria-Hungary declared war on Serbia. Russia came to Serbia's defense. Soon most of Europe was at war.

3. How were the Serbians involved in the start of World War I?

____

____

____

____

____

As you read this section, answer the questions below about the situations and events that led to war in Europe.

a. What is it?

b. How did it increase tensions among European nations?

1. Nationalism	a. b.
2. Imperialism	a. b.
3. Militarism	a. b.
4. Triple Alliance (1882)	a. b.
5. Triple Entente (1907)	a. b.
6. Assassination in Sarajevo	a. b.

Europe Plunges into War

Terms and Names

Schlieffen Plan Germany's plan for winning the war on two fronts

Allies Great Britain, France, Russia, and other nations who fought on their side

Central Powers Germany, Austria-Hungary, and other nations who fought on their side

trench warfare Fighting from trenches dug in the battlefield

Western Front Region of northern France where much fighting took place

Eastern Front Region along German-Russian border where much fighting took place

Before You Read

In the last section, you read how World War I began.

In this section, you will learn the details of this costly and tragic war.

As You Read

Use an outline to organize the main ideas and details in this section.

THE GREAT WAR BEGINS (Page 411)
How did so many nations become involved?

The system of alliances turned the war between Austria-Hungary and Serbia into a wider war. Russia moved against Austria-Hungary. It figured that Germany would support Austria-Hungary. So it moved troops against Germany as well. Germany declared war on Russia. Soon after, it also declared war on Russia's ally, France.

Germany had a plan for winning the war on two fronts. This was the **Schlieffen Plan.** It called for a rapid push through France, a quick defeat of that nation, and a turn to face Russia in the east. To capture France quickly, Germany moved through Belgium. Belgium was a neutral country. Britain was outraged by Germany's action. It declared war on Germany. France, Britain, and Russia were called the **Allies.** They were later joined by Italy, which broke with Germany and Austria-Hungary. Bulgaria and the Ottoman Empire joined Germany and Austria-Hungary. They were called the **Central Powers.**

1. Who were the Allies and Central Powers?

____

____

____

____

____

____

A BLOODY STALEMATE

(**Pages** 412–414)

***What* kind of warfare was used?**

After the German army moved almost to Paris, French defenses strengthened and stopped them in September 1914. Both sides became bogged down in a bloody conflict. Soldiers dug deep trenches into the ground. **Trench warfare** began.

When soldiers left the trenches to storm enemy lines, they faced powerful weapons. Machine guns, tanks, poison gas, and larger pieces of artillery killed hundreds of thousands of soldiers. This was how the war was fought in France, which was called the **Western Front.**

2. What was the war like on the Western Front?

____

____

____

____

____

THE BATTLE ON THE EASTERN FRONT (Pages 414–415)

***What* happened on the Eastern Front?**

The war on the **Eastern Front** showed more movement at first—but it was equally destructive. Russian armies attacked both Germany and Austria-Hungary. They had some early success but were driven back in both places. One reason was that Russia did not have a fully industrial economy. It could not keep troops supplied.

Still, Russia had a huge population and could send millions to war. The large Russian army provided a constant threat to Germany. This threat prevented Germany from putting its full resources against the Allies in the west.

3. What weaknesses and strengths did Russia have?

____

____

____

____

____

As you read this section, note the effects of each of the actions or situations (causes) listed below.

Causes	Effects
1. Russia mobilizes along the German border.	
2. Germany declares war on France.	
3. The Allies defeat the Germans in the Battle of the Marne.	
4. Machine guns, tanks, poison gas, and airplanes are used in battles along the Western Front.	
5. Russian forces attack both Austria and Germany.	
6. The Allies are unable to ship war supplies to Russia's ports.	

Section 3

A Global Conflict

Terms and Names

unrestricted submarine warfare Using submarines to sink any ship without warning

total war War in which countries use all their resources for the war

rationing Control of the amounts and kinds of goods people can have

propaganda One-sided information designed to persuade

armistice Agreement to stop fighting

Before You Read

In the last section, you read how the war was fought in Europe.

In this section, you will learn how the war affected the world.

As You Read

Use a web diagram to show the effects of World War I.

WAR AFFECTS THE WORLD
(**Pages** 417–419)

***What* other areas of the world were involved?**

The Allies hoped to take a part of the Ottoman Empire called the Dardanelles. The attack failed with great loss of life. A more successful operation was headed by a British officer named T. E. Lawrence. He helped lead an Arab revolt against Ottoman rule. As a result, the Allies were able to capture several important cities in Southwest Asia.

Japan took German colonies in China and the Pacific Ocean. The Allies also captured three of the four German colonies in Africa.

The British had used their strong navy to block all supplies from reaching Germany. The Germans responded by increasing their submarine attacks on ships bringing food and supplies to the Allies. They used **unrestricted submarine warfare**. This meant sinking any ship without warning in the waters around Great Britain.

When American ships were sunk and lives were lost, the American people grew angry. Then the British intercepted a secret message from Germany to Mexico. This message asked Mexico to ally itself with Germany. In return, Germany offered to help Mexico regain land lost to the United States in the 1840s. In April 1917, Congress declared war on Germany.

1. What areas outside of Europe were affected by the war?

____

WAR AFFECTS THE HOME FRONT
(**Pages** 419–420)

***What* happened on the home fronts?**

By 1917, the war had already killed millions. It had drastically changed the lives of millions more—people at home as well as soldiers fighting on the fronts.

This "Great War," as it was called, was a **total war.** It demanded all the resources of the countries that fought it.

Governments took control of factories. It told them what to produce and how much of it to make. Governments also used **rationing.** This limited how much food and other goods people could buy and hold. That way armies in the field would have the supplies they needed. Governments used **propaganda** to get support for the war. They also took steps to stop dissent, or opposition to the war.

With so many men in the military, women played a growing role in the economies of the countries at war. They worked in factories, offices, and shops. They built planes and tanks, grew food, and made clothing. These changes had an impact on people's attitudes toward what kind of work women could do.

2. What were three ways that the war affected people's day-to-day lives?

____

THE ALLIES WIN THE WAR

(Pages 420–421)

***Why* did the Allies win?**

In 1917, the United States entered the war. And Russia left it. Suffering during the war chipped away at the Russian people's support for the czar. In March, he stepped down. The new government hoped to continue fighting the war, but the Russian armies refused. Just months later, a new revolution broke out. Communists seized Russia's government. They quickly made a treaty with Germany and gave up huge amounts of land in return for peace.

In March 1918, Germany tried one final attack. Once again, the German army nearly reached Paris. But the soldiers were tired, and supplies were short. The Allies—now with fresh American troops—drove the Germans back.

Bulgaria and the Ottoman Empire surrendered. In October, a revolution overthrew the emperor of Austria-Hungary. In November, Kaiser Wilhelm II was forced to step down in Germany. The new government signed an **armistice,** an agreement to stop fighting. On November 11, 1918, Europe was finally at peace.

3. What were the final problems that Germany and Austria-Hungary faced?

____

THE LEGACY OF THE WAR

(Pages 421–423)

***What* was the cost of the war?**

World War I had a devastating effect on the world. About 8.5 million soldiers had died. Another 21 million had been wounded. Countless civilians had suffered as well. The economies of the warring nations had suffered serious damage, too. Farms were destroyed, and factories ruined. One estimate said the war had caused $338 billion in damage.

The war also had an emotional cost. People felt all the suffering did not seem to have a purpose. The art and literature of the years after the war reflected a new sense of hopelessness.

4. Name one political, economic, and emotional cost of the war.

____

____

____

____

____

Name ______________________ Class ______________ Date ______________

As you read about the effects of the war on countries throughout the world, make notes to answer questions related to the time line.

Date	Event	Question
Feb. 1915	**Gallipoli campaign begins.**	1. What was the purpose of the Gallipoli campaign?
Jan. 1917	**Germany announces a policy of unrestricted submarine warfare.**	
Feb. 1917	**British intercept the Zimmermann note.**	2. Why did the United States enter the war?
April 1917	**United States enters the war.**	
		3. Why did the czar's government collapse?
Nov. 1917	**Lenin seizes power in Russia.**	4. What did this treaty accomplish?
March 1918	**Germany and Russia sign Treaty of Brest-Litovsk.**	5. What was the significance of this battle?
July 1918	**Allies and Germans fight Second Battle of the Marne.**	6. What events signaled the final defeat of the Central Powers?
Nov. 1918	**World War I ends.**	

Section 4

A Flawed Peace

Terms and Names

Woodrow Wilson President who proposed the Fourteen Points and represented the United States at Versailles

Georges Clemenceau France's premier and delegate at Versailles

Fourteen Points Plan for a just and lasting peace

self-determination Allowing people to decide for themselves about what kind of government they want

Treaty of Versailles Agreement at the end of World War I between Germany and the Allied Powers

League of Nations International group with the goal of keeping peace among nations

Before You Read

In the last section, you read how World War I spread and finally ended.

In this section, you will learn about the harsh peace that followed.

As You Read

Use a chart to record the reaction by Germany, Africans, Asians, Italy, and Japan to the Treaty of Versailles.

THE ALLIES MEET AND DEBATE

(Pages 424–425)

***What* decisions were made at Versailles?**

Many nations sent delegates to the peace talks in Paris. The main leaders were **Woodrow Wilson** of the United States, **Georges Clemenceau** of France, and David Lloyd George of Britain. Germany and its allies and Russia were not present.

Wilson pushed for his peace plan called the **Fourteen Points.** He wanted to end secret treaties and alliances and give people **self-determination,** the right to form their own nation. He also hoped to set up a world organization that would police the actions of nations and prevent future wars.

Britain and especially France had different views. They had suffered greatly in the war. They wanted to punish Germany. After long debates, the leaders finally agreed on a peace settlement. It was called the **Treaty of Versailles** and was signed in June 1919.

The treaty called for a **League of Nations**—the world organization that Woodrow Wilson wanted. It would include 32 nations. The United States, Britain, France, Japan, and Italy would make up the leadership. Germany and Russia were left out of the League. The treaty took away German land in Europe and took away its colonies in Africa and the Pacific. Limits were placed on the size of Germany's armed forces.

Finally, Germany was given complete blame for the war. That meant it would have to make payments to the Allies for the damage caused.

1. How did the Treaty of Versailles affect Germany?

____

____

____

A TROUBLED TREATY

(**Pages** 425–427)

***Who* opposed the treaty?**

Germany's former colonies were given to the Allies to govern until they decided which were ready for independence. Poland, Czechoslovakia, and Yugoslavia were all declared independent. Finland, Estonia, Latvia, and Lithuania—once part of Russia—were made independent nations as well. The treaty also broke up the Ottoman Empire. The Ottomans kept control only of Turkey.

The treaty did not make a lasting peace. The United States Senate never approved the treaty or joined the League of Nations. Germans bitterly resented the treaty because it placed all the blame for the war on them. Colonial peoples in Africa and Asia were angry because the treaty did not make them independent. Japan and Italy were also upset by getting few territorial gains.

2. Which groups opposed the treaty and why?

____

____

____

Name ______________________ Class ______________ Date ______________

Section 4, *continued*

As you read this section, take notes to answer the questions about the peace settlement that left many nations feeling betrayed.

Wilson's goal of achieving a just peace differed from the peace objectives of France and Britain.	
1. What were the guiding principles of Wilson's Fourteen Points?	
2. What were the concerns and aims of France and Britain?	

After heated debate and compromise, the Treaty of Versailles is signed.	
3. In what ways did the treaty punish Germany?	
4. How did the treaty change the world map?	
5. How was Wilson's Fourteenth Point incorporated into the treaty?	

The legacy of Versailles was one of bitterness and loss.	
6. Why did the United States reject the treaty?	
7. How did this rejection affect the League of Nations?	
8. Why did many countries feel bitter and cheated as a result of the treaty?	

Section 1

Revolutions in Russia

Terms and Names

proletariat The workers

Bolsheviks Group of revolutionaries led by Lenin

Lenin Leader of the Bolsheviks and first ruler of the Soviet Union

Rasputin Eccentric monk assassinated because of his corrupt influence on the Russian royal family

provisional government Temporary government led by Alexander Kerensky

soviet Local governing council

Communist Party A political party practicing the ideas of Karl Marx and Lenin

Joseph Stalin Revolutionary leader who took control of the Communist Party after Lenin

Before You Read

In the last chapter, you read about World War I.

In this section, you will learn about the revolutions in Russia that occurred at the same time.

As You Read

Use a time line to record major events in the changing of Russian government between 1874 and 1922.

CZARS RESIST CHANGE (Page 433)

***How* did Alexander III rule?**

In 1881 Czar Alexander II was killed by radical students. When a new czar, Alexander III, took control of the Russian government, reforms stopped. He cracked down on anyone who seemed to threaten his government. He also mistreated all non-Russian peoples who lived within the Russian empire, especially Jews. Nicholas II, the son of Alexander III, continued his father's firm rule.

1. How did Alexander and Nicholas rule?

____

____

RUSSIA INDUSTRIALIZES (Page 434)

***What* changes did industrialization cause?**

Russia started a buildup of industry. It quickly became a leading producer of steel. Russia also built the Trans-Siberian Railway—the longest continuous rail line in the world.

Although there was progress, working conditions were poor, wages were low, and children were forced to work. Workers grew angry. Revolutionary groups wanted to overthrow the government. Some followed the teachings of Karl Marx. One group—the **Bolsheviks**—was led by **Lenin**. He fled Russia a few years later to await a better time to put forth his ideas.

2. Who were the Bolsheviks?

____

CRISES AT HOME AND ABROAD

(**Pages** 434–435)

***What* crises did Russia face?**

In early 1905, the Russian army killed hundreds of hungry workers who had peacefully gathered to ask for relief. Strikes spread in protest. Nicholas was forced to allow some reforms to take place. He approved the creation of the Duma, Russia's first parliament.

The suffering caused by World War I was the final blow against the czar's rule. As the war worsened, the czar lost control of Russia. Soldiers refused to fight, prices shot sky high, and people starved. Meanwhile, his wife fell under the influence of an odd monk named **Rasputin**. He spread corruption throughout the government.

3. What developments helped lead up to the revolution?

____

THE MARCH REVOLUTION

(**Page** 435–436)

***What* was the provisional government?**

In March 1917, the czar was forced to step down. A year later, he and his family were executed. A **provisional government** led by Alexander Kerensky was formed.

Kerensky hoped to keep Russia in the war. The decision cost him the support of soldiers who no longer wanted to fight. He also lost the support of workers and peasants who wanted an end to food shortages. Across the country, these forces formed local councils called **soviets.** In some cities, the soviets had more real power than the government. In the middle of all this, Lenin returned to Russia.

4. How did Kerensky lose support?

____

THE BOLSHEVIK REVOLUTION

(**Pages** 436–438)

***Who* led the Bolshevik Revolution?**

Lenin's slogan "Peace, Land, and Bread" was soon taken up by many people. In November 1917, armed workers took control of government offices. Kerensky's power came to an end.

To win the peasants' support, Lenin ordered all farmland be given to them. Workers were given control of the factories. Soon, Lenin agreed to a peace treaty with Germany. It gave away large amounts of Russian land, but it ended the war. Then, forces opposed to Lenin's revolution tried to defeat the Bolshevik army. The civil war lasted two years. The fighting and the famine that followed killed 15 million Russians. In the end, Lenin's Red Army won.

5. Who fought the civil war?

____

LENIN RESTORES ORDER; STALIN BECOMES DICTATOR (Page 438–439)

***How* did Lenin bring back order?**

In 1921, Lenin started a new plan to rebuild the Russian economy. It allowed for some private ownership of property. He also changed the government to form a new nation—the Soviet Union. It would be run by the leaders of the **Communist Party.** By the late 1920s, the Soviet economy had recovered. Farms and factories were producing as much as they had before World War I. After Lenin's death **Joseph Stalin** took power.

6. What changes did Lenin make?

____

As you read this section, take notes to answer questions about some factors in Russia that helped lead to revolution.

How did each of the following help to ignite the full-scale revolution?	
1. Policies of the czars	
2. Industrialization and economic growth	
3. The Russo-Japanese War	
4. "Bloody Sunday"	
5. World War I	
6. The March Revolution	

How did each of the following help the Bolsheviks gain and hold political control?	
7. November 1917 Revolution	
8. Civil war between the Red and White armies	
9. Organization of Russia into republics	

What role did each of the following play in the Russian Revolution?	
10. Karl Marx	
11. V. I. Lenin	
12. Leon Trotsky	

Case Study: Stalinist Russia

Terms and Names

totalitarianism Government that has total control over people's lives

Great Purge Arrest, exile, or killing of thousands of suspected enemies of the Communist Party

command economy Economy in which the government makes all the economic decisions

Five-Year Plans Plans to develop the Soviet Union's economy

collective farm Large, government-owned farm

Before You Read

In the last section, you learned about the factors leading to revolution in Russia.

In this section, you will read about the totalitarian government that resulted.

As You Read

Use a chart listing examples of methods of control used in the Soviet Union.

A GOVERNMENT OF TOTAL CONTROL (Pages 440–442)

***What* is totalitarianism?**

The term **totalitarianism** describes a government that takes control of almost all parts of people's lives. A very powerful leader leads this type of government. Usually the leader brings security to the nation. The government stays in power by using different ways to keep control.

The weapons of totalitarianism include using police terror. Police may spy on people, use brutal force, or even murder them. The government might also control schools and use them to mold students' minds. Another weapon is propaganda.

This is false information that is spread by the government to make people believe the government is working for their best interests. At other times the government will censor, that is block, certain information from becoming public.

Totalitarian rulers might also choose some people to persecute. The group may be blamed for things that go wrong in the country. Often these are people from a certain ethnic group or religion. They may be forced to live in certain areas or have rules that apply only to them.

1. What are two weapons of totalitarianism?

____

____

____

STALIN BUILDS A TOTALITARIAN STATE (Pages 442–443)

***How* did Stalin control the country?**

Stalin kept tight control on the Soviet Union. He did this by creating a powerful secret police. In the mid-1930s, he turned against enemies—both real and imagined—within the Communist Party. Thousands were arrested. Many were sent to exile or killed. This was known as the **Great Purge**.

Stalin also used propaganda to keep control. He controlled newspapers, radio, and other sources of information. He also used the arts to promote his ideas, Stalin's government also moved against religion. Churches were destroyed. Church leaders were killed or sent into exile.

2. Who died in the Great Purge?

____

____

STALIN SEIZES CONTROL OF THE ECONOMY (Pages 443–444)

***How* did Stalin change the economy?**

Stalin built a **command economy.** This is an economy in which the government makes all the decisions about economic life. He tried to make the economy fully industrial. All resources went to this effort. As a result, there were shortages of food, housing, and clothing for many years.

Stalin also began a farming revolution. The government took control of people's farms. It put them together into large, government-owned farms called **collective farms.** Wealthy peasants called kulaks resisted. Millions were killed, and millions more were exiled to Siberia. Stalin got farm output to rise by using these brutal methods.

3. How did Stalin's economic changes result in suffering?

____

____

DAILY LIFE UNDER STALIN; TOTAL CONTROL ACHIEVED (Pages 444–445)

***How* did Stalin change Soviet society?**

Stalin completely changed Soviet society. Women enjoyed equal rights. They filled all kinds of jobs on farms and in factories, They studied for careers that before had been closed to them. People in general were more educated.

By the mid-1930s Stalin was in complete control of all economic and political affairs in the Soviet Union. The Soviet Union had been transformed into a major political and economic world power.

4. What benefits did Stalin's rule bring to women?

____

____

As you read this section, fill in the web diagram with key characteristics of Stalinist Russia.

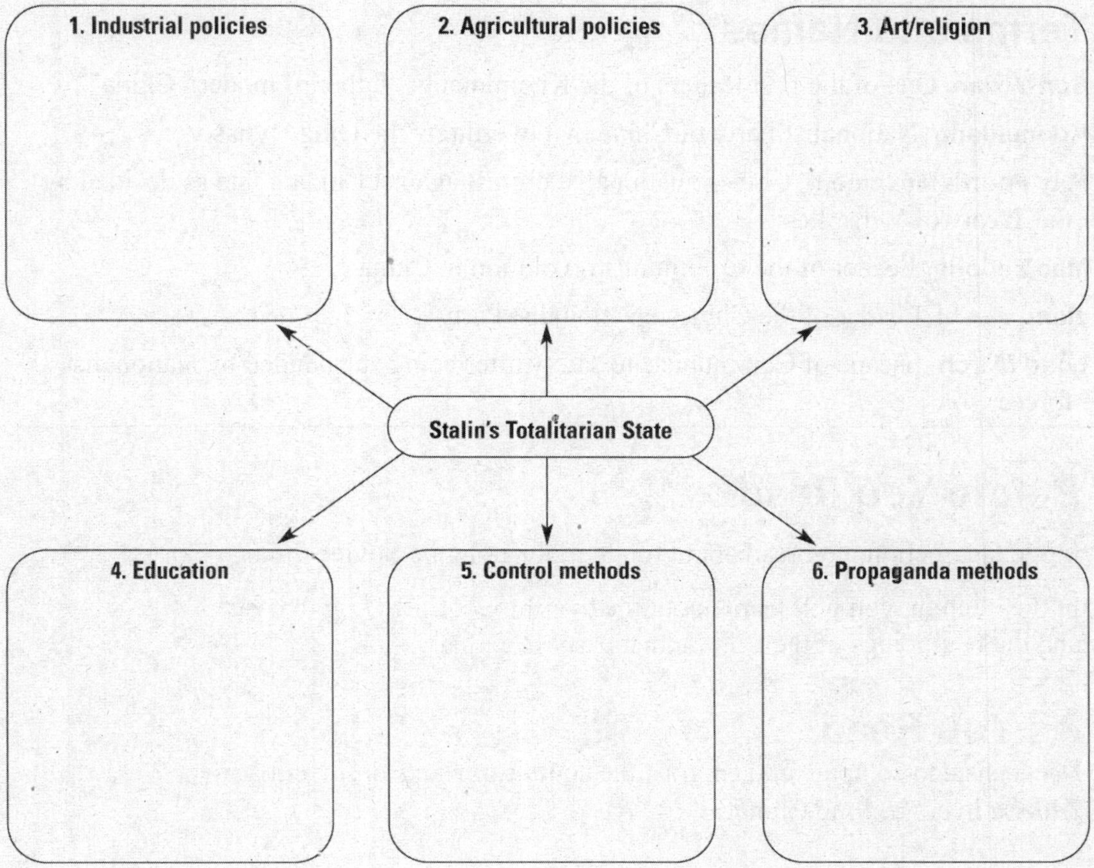

Section 3

Imperial China Collapses

Terms and Names

Sun Yixian One of the first leaders of the Kuomintang; "father of modern China"

Kuomintang Nationalist Party of China that overthrew the Qing Dynasty

May Fourth Movement Chinese nationalist protest against China's fate as decided by the Treaty of Versailles

Mao Zedong Leader of the Communist revolution in China

Jiang Jieshi Leader of the Chinese Nationalist Party

Long March Escape of Communists to safety after being surrounded by Nationalist forces

Before You Read

In the last section, you read about totalitarianism in the Soviet Union

In this section, you will learn about the overthrow of the Qing dynasty and the beginnings of the Communist party in China

As You Read

Use a chart to compare and contrast the actions of Jiang Jieshi and Mao Zedong in controlling China.

NATIONALISTS OVERTHROW QING DYNASTY (Pages 448–449)

***Who* was Sun Yixian?**

The early 20th century was a time of change in China. Many Chinese resented the great control that foreign nations had over their economy. Some wanted to modernize China. They hoped it could regain power.

One of the leaders of this push was **Sun Yixian**. His group was called the **Kuomintang**, or Nationalist Party. In 1912, he led a revolt that overthrew the Qing Dynasty. A republic was established, and he was made the president.

Sun wanted political and economic rights for all Chinese people. He also wanted an end to the foreign control of China. But Sun did not have the support of the military. Six weeks later, he turned over his presidency to Yuan Shikai, a powerful general. Yuan became a military dictator. After he died in 1916, civil war broke out. The people suffered terribly from famine and brutal attacks.

China's leaders hoped to win the support of the Allies during World War I. They declared war on Germany. When the war ended, though, they were disappointed. The Treaty of Versailles did not give China freedom from foreign influence. It only changed masters. The parts of China that had been controlled by Germany were handed over to Japan.

Angry Chinese protested during the **May Fourth Movement**. Protesters included a man named **Mao Zedong**.

He later became the leader of China's Communist revolution.

1. What did China's Nationalists want?

____

____

____

____

THE COMMUNIST PARTY IN CHINA

(Pages 449–450)

What happened to the Communist Party?

In the 1920s, revolutionaries began to look to Marxism and the Russian Revolution for a solution to China's problems. Meanwhile, Sun Yixian became disappointed in the Western democracies. They refused to support his struggling government. He decided to become allies with the newly formed Communist Party. Sun sought Soviet help, too. He died in 1925. **Jiang Jieshi** became leader of the Kuomintang.

At first, Jiang Jieshi joined with the Communists to try to defeat the warlords. These warlords ruled as much of the Chinese countryside as their armies could conquer. Together the Nationalists and Communists successfully fought the warlords.

Many in the Kuomintang were business people. They now feared Communist ideas about government control of economic life. In 1927, Jiang began fighting the Communists. The Communists were forced into hiding. In 1928, Jiang became president of China. Soon China was torn by a civil war between the remaining Communists and Jiang's forces.

2. What role did Jiang Jieshi play in creating the civil war?

____

____

____

____

CIVIL WAR RAGES IN CHINA

(Pages 450–452)

Who fought the civil war?

Jiang had promised democracy and political rights to all Chinese. But his government had become less democratic and more corrupt. Nothing was done to improve the life of the rural peasants. Many of them gave their support to the Chinese Communist Party.

Communist leader, Mao Zedong, built an army of peasants. In 1933, Jiang's army surrounded them. But the Communists got away. They began the famous **Long March** of 6,000 miles to the north. Thousands died. The Communists settled in caves in Northwest China.

At the same time, China had other problems. In 1931, Japan invaded the part of China called Manchuria. Japan took control there and six years later began invading other areas. With this new threat, Jiang and the Communists agreed to unite temporarily to fight the Japanese.

3. What finally united Communist and non-Communist forces?

____

____

____

____

As you read this section, note some of the cause-and-effect relationships in the struggle between nationalist and communist movements in China.

Causes	Actions/Events	Effects
	1. Sun's Revolutionary Alliance overthrows the Qing Dynasty.	
	2. Sun turns presidency over to Yuan Shikai.	
	3. The May Fourth Movement begins.	
	4. Nationalist forces move into Shanghai.	
	5. Communists begin the Long March.	
	6. Japan invades Manchuria.	

Section 4

Nationalism in India and Southwest Asia

Terms and Names

Rowlatt Acts Laws to prevent Indians from protesting British actions

Amritsar Massacre The slaughter of Indians by the British

Mohandas K. Gandhi Leader of the movement for Indian independence from Britain

civil disobedience Disobeying the law for the purpose of achieving some higher goal

Salt March A march to the sea to protest British salt tax

Mustafa Kemal Leader of Turkish nationalists who overthrew the last Ottoman sultan

Before You Read

In the last section, you read about nationalism and civil war in China.

In this section, you will learn about nationalism in India and Southwest Asia.

As You Read

Use a web diagram to identify the styles of government adopted by nations in this section.

INDIAN NATIONALISM GROWS

(**Pages** 453–454)

***Why* did feelings of nationalism increase?**

Many Indians grew angry at British domination of Indian life. Indian nationalism had been growing since the mid-1800s. Some Indians joined the Congress Party or the Muslim League. These were two groups that worked toward independence

More than one million Indians served in the British army in World War I. The British promised to make changes to the government of India. These changes would give the Indian people greater control of their own nation. After the war, though, returning Indian soldiers were once again treated as second-class citizens. Reforms were not made. When Indians protested, the British Parliament passed the **Rowlatt Acts** that allowed protesters to be jailed without a trial. Western-educated Indians believed this to be a violation of their rights.

About 10,000 Indians gathered at the city of Amritsar to protest this act in the spring of 1919. The British had also banned such public meetings. But the crowd was mostly unaware of that fact. British troops fired on the crowd. Several hundred protesters were killed. The **Amritsar Massacre** sparked further protests. Almost overnight millions of Indians changed from loyal British subjects to revolutionaries and nationalists.

1. What were three reasons for the increase of Indian nationalism?

____

____

GANDHI'S TACTICS OF NONVIOLENCE; GREAT BRITAIN GRANTS LIMITED SELF-RULE

(**Pages** 454–455)

What were Gandhi's ideas about nonviolence?

Mohandas K. Gandhi became the leader of India's protest movement. He had attended law school in England. He had a deeply religious approach to political activity. His teachings contained ideas from all of the major religions of the world, including Hinduism, Islam, and Christianity.

Gandhi organized a campaign of noncooperation with the British. It was based on passive resistance, or **civil disobedience,** to unjust laws. He asked Indians to stop buying British goods, attending British schools, paying British taxes, or voting in British-run elections. He also persuaded his followers to take these actions while not using violence. British jails filled with thousands of Indians who broke British laws in order to protest them.

Indians resented a British law that forced them to buy salt only from the government. Gandhi organized a huge march to the sea to make salt by evaporating sea water. This action was called the **Salt March.**

Soon afterward, some demonstrators planned another march. They went to the place where the British government made salt. They wanted to close this site down. The British violently broke up the march. A news story about the event was published everywhere. It helped Gandhi's independence movement gain worldwide support. In 1935, the British finally gave in. They passed a law that allowed local Indian self-government.

2. How did Indians use nonviolence to achieve their goals?

____

____

NATIONALISM SPREADS TO SOUTHWEST ASIA (Pages 456–457)

What countries in Southwest Asia experienced great changes?

Other changes took place in Southwest Asia. **Mustafa Kemal**, a military commander, led nationalists in overthrowing the last Ottoman sultan. Kemal became the leader of a new republic in Turkey. He modernized the society and the economy in Turkey.

Before World War I, both Britain and Russia had influence in the ancient country of Persia. Britain tried to take control of all of Persia after the war. This led to a nationalist revolt. In 1921, Reza Shah Pahlavi, a Persian army officer, seized power. He later changed his country's name to Iran. In both Turkey and Iran, women gained new rights.

In Arabia, different groups united to form one kingdom called Saudi Arabia.

Starting in the 1920s, Southwest Asia saw a major economic change and development. Western companies discovered large reserves of oil in several countries in this area. Oil brought huge sums of money to these countries. Western nations tried to gain power in the region so they could get some of this wealth.

3. What new countries were formed in Southwest Asia?

____

As you read this section, take notes to answer questions about nationalistic activity after World War I.

How did each of the following contribute to national independence for India?	
1. Formation of Congress Party and Muslim League	
2. World War I	
3. Rowlatt Acts	
4. Massacre at Amritsar	
5. Campaign of civil disobedience	
6. Salt March	

How did each country gain its independence?	
7. Turkey	
8. Persia	
9. Saudi Arabia	

Section 1

Postwar Uncertainty

Terms and Names

Albert Einstein Scientist who developed the theory of relativity

theory of relativity Idea that as moving objects approach the speed of light, space and time become relative

Sigmund Freud Physician who exposed the workings of the unconscious mind

existentialism Philosophy that says each person must make meaning in a world that has no universal meaning

Friedrich Nietzsche German philosopher who dismissed reason, democracy, and progress as empty ideas

surrealism Art movement in which a dreamlike world, outside of reality, is portrayed or evoked

jazz Lively, loose form of popular music developed in the United States

Charles Lindbergh First person to fly alone across the Atlantic

Before You Read

In the last chapter, you read about nationalism and revolution.

In this section, you will learn how new ideas changed old ways of thinking.

As You Read

Use a chart to identify two people who contributed to science, literature and philosophy, art and music, and technology.

A NEW REVOLUTION IN SCIENCE (Page 463)

How did Einstein and Freud challenge old ideas?

Two thinkers developed radical new ideas that challenged old ways of thinking. **Albert Einstein** completely changed physics with his ideas about space, time, matter, and energy. He said that as moving objects neared the speed of light, space and time became relative. That means they change. His idea is the **theory of relativity.**

Sigmund Freud changed the way people thought about the human mind. He said that much of human behavior was irrational—due to urges and desires buried in the unconscious mind of each person. At first, people did not want to accept Freud's ideas. Eventually, they gained wide influence.

1. What were Einstein's and Freud's new ideas?

____

____

LITERATURE IN THE 1920s
(**Pages** 464–465)
***How* did writers and philosophers of the 1920s reflect society's concerns?**

Many philosophers lost faith in reason and progress after they looked at the destruction caused by World War I. One group developed the idea known as existentialism. **Existentialism** argues that there is no universal meaning to the world. Each person must give life meaning through his or her own actions.

These thinkers had been influenced by **Friedrich Nietzsche.** Nietzsche was a German philosopher of the late 1800s. He said that reason, democracy, and progress were empty ideas. He urged people to adopt the values of pride and strength.

Some authors, like Franz Kafka, wrote about the horrors of modern life. His novels put people in threatening situations that they could not understand or escape.

2. What is existentialism?

____

REVOLUTION IN THE ARTS
(**Page** 465)
***How* was painting of this time different from traditional painting?**

Artists rebelled against traditional painting. They did not re-create realistic objects. Paul Klee used bold colors and distorted lines. Pablo Picasso founded a style called cubism that broke objects into geometric shapes. An art movement called **surrealism** showed a dreamlike existence outside reality.

Composers created a new style of music. Some, like Igor Stravinsky, used unusual rhythms or harsh, rather than pleasing, sounds. African-American musicians in the United States developed a lively, loose form of popular music called **jazz.**

3. What two new styles arose in the visual arts?

____

SOCIETY CHALLENGES CONVENTION (**Page** 466)
***How* did society change?**

Society changed after World War I as well. Young people experimented with modern values. Women set aside earlier forms of dress, wearing new styles that were looser and shorter. Many women also began to work in new careers.

4. In what ways was society more open?

____

TECHNOLOGICAL ADVANCES IMPROVE LIFE (**Pages** 466–467)
***What* new technology arose?**

Technology brought about changes to society as well. Improvements to the automobile helped make cars more desirable and affordable. More and more people bought cars. They began to move to suburbs.

Another change was the growth in air travel. American pilot **Charles Lindbergh** flew alone across the Atlantic Ocean in 1927. In 1932, Amelia Earhart became the first woman to make the flight alone.

The radio was developed and became popular. In the 1920s, large radio networks were built. Soon millions of people were entertained by radios in their homes. Millions more went to movie theaters to watch motion pictures.

5. What major changes came about in travel and entertainment?

____

As you read this section, take notes to answer questions about new ideas and lifestyles that developed during the 1920s.

How did the following challenge deeply rooted ideas and traditions?			
1. Theory of relativity	2. Freudian psychology	3. Existentialism	4. Surrealism

How did the following demonstrate the independent spirit of the times?	
5. Jazz	6. Women

How did the following change ways of life?			
7. Automobiles	8. Airplanes	9. Radio	10. Movies

Name ______________________ Class ______________ Date ______________

Section 2

A Worldwide Depression

Terms and Names

coalition government Temporary alliance of several political parties

Weimar Republic Government of Germany after World War I

Great Depression Severe economic downturn that followed the collapse of the U.S. stock market in 1929

Franklin D. Roosevelt President of the United States during the Depression

New Deal Roosevelt's program for creating jobs and improving the American economy

Before You Read

In the last section, you read about new ideas in the postwar world.

In this section, you will learn about economic crisis and worldwide depression.

As You Read

Use a web diagram to record the effects of the Great Depression in the United States.

POSTWAR EUROPE; THE WEIMAR REPUBLIC (Pages 470–472)

***What* problems did Europe face after the war?**

After the war, European countries were in bad political and economic shape. Even nations that had democratic governments for many years experienced problems. They had so many political parties that no one party could rule alone. Sometimes a **coalition government** had to be formed. This was an alliance of several political parties. In addition, governments lasted for such a short time that it was hard to develop policies.

The situation was the worst in Germany. The people felt little loyalty to the government. Germany's government, the **Weimar Republic**, was very weak. Prices rose sharply, and money lost its value. Later, American bank loans helped the German economy recover.

World nations also took steps to try to make sure there would be lasting peace. France and Germany promised never to attack one another. Most countries of the world signed a treaty in which they pledged not to go to war. There was no way to enforce the treaty, however.

1. Why was the postwar situation in Germany especially bad?

____

FINANCIAL COLLAPSE; THE GREAT DEPRESSION (Pages 472–474)

***Where* and how did the Great Depression begin?**

The economy of the United States enjoyed a boom in the 1920s. But this growth hid problems. Consumers were unable to buy all the goods produced.

When their purchases slowed, factories slowed production. Farmers faced falling food prices and slow sales. They were unable to repay loans and lost their farms. In 1929, stock prices in the United States plunged. The **Great Depression** had begun.

The depression affected other countries. Nations raised tariffs—taxes on goods imported from other countries—to keep import prices high. They hoped to increase sales by local companies. Unfortunately, trade between nations dropped, and unemployment shot up in many countries. The world suffered.

2. What caused the Great Depression?

____

____

THE WORLD CONFRONTS THE CRISIS (Pages 474–475)
***How* did various countries meet this crisis?**

Each country met the economic crisis in its own way. In Britain, a new multiparty government took over. It took steps that slowly improved the economy and cut unemployment.

In France, the political situation was worse. After several governments lost support, moderates and socialists combined to form a government. It passed laws to help workers, but companies raised prices to cover their labor costs. Unemployment remained high.

In Sweden, Norway, and Denmark, the governments played active roles in the economy. They taxed people with jobs to have money to pay benefits to people without jobs. The governments also created jobs by hiring out-of-work people to build roads and buildings.

In the United States, **Franklin D. Roosevelt** began a program called the **New Deal**. The government spent large amounts of money on constructing roads, dams, bridges, airports, and buildings. This effort created jobs for millions. Businesses and farmers also got help from the government. The American economy got better, but the recovery was slow.

3. How did the United States meet the crisis?

____

____

As you read about postwar Europe and the global depression, note one or more reasons for each of the following developments.

1. In new postwar democracies, there were frequent changes in government.	2. In Germany, the Weimar Republic was weak from the start.
3. Postwar Germany suffered from severe economic inflation.	4. The United States had a flawed economy.
5. On October 29, 1929, the U.S. stock market crashed.	6. A long depression followed the crash in the United States.
7. Collapse of the U.S. economy affected countries worldwide.	8. In Britain, the National Government rescued the economy.
9. In France, the Popular Front was formed as a coalition government.	10. Socialist governments in Scandinavian countries dealt with the economic crisis successfully.

Section 3

Fascism Rises in Europe

Terms and Names

fascism Political movement based on nationalism that gives power to a dictator and takes away individual rights

Benito Mussolini Fascist leader of Italy

Adolf Hitler Fascist leader of Germany

Nazism German brand of fascism

Mein Kampf Book by Hitler outlining his beliefs and goals for Germany

lebensraum Living space

Before You Read

In the last section, you read about the Great Depression.

In this section, you will learn about the rise of fascism in Europe during troubled economic times.

As You Read

Use a chart to compare Mussolini's rise to power and goals with Hitler's.

FASCISM'S RISE IN ITALY
(Pages 476–477)
***Why* did fascism arise in Italy?**

The economic crisis of the Great Depression led to the loss of democracy in some countries. In these nations, millions of people turned to strong rulers to try to solve their economic problems. Such leaders followed a set of beliefs called **fascism.** Fascist leaders were very nationalistic. They believed in authority and built powerful military forces. Fascist governments were controlled by one party, and that party was ruled by one leader. The leader was the nation's dictator. Fascist governments did not let their people have individual rights.

Fascism arose in Italy. It started there because people were angry that they did not get more territory in the treaty that ended World War I. Also, inflation and unemployment were big problems. **Benito Mussolini** came to power by promising to help the economy and build the armed forces. He used armed thugs to threaten political opponents. The king of Italy decided Mussolini was the best hope to save his dynasty and let him lead the government.

Mussolini became Il Duce, or the leader, of Italy. He outlawed all political parties except fascism. He tried to control the economy and outlawed strikes.

1. What did Mussolini promise the Italians?

____

____

____

HITLER RISES TO POWER IN GERMANY (Pages 477–478)

How did Hitler gain control of Germany?

Another Fascist came to power in Germany. **Adolf Hitler** was the leader of the Nazi party. The German brand of fascism was called **Nazism.** He tried to take control of the government of Germany in 1923, but the attempt failed. He was sent to prison. In prison, Hitler wrote a book that summarized his ideas. It was called ***Mein Kampf.*** Hitler believed that Germans were superior to all other people. He said that the Treaty of Versailles treated Germany unfairly. He also said that a crowded Germany needed more ***lebensraum,*** or living space. To get that space, he promised to conquer the lands of eastern Europe and Russia.

2. What were some of Hitler's beliefs?

____

____

____

HITLER BECOMES CHANCELLOR (Pages 478–480)

What did Hitler do when he became Germany's leader?

When the depression hit Germany, the country was in terrible shape. Hitler was named leader of the German government. Soon, he took the powers of a dictator. He became Germany's führer, or leader. Those who opposed him were arrested. His economic program gave work to millions but took away their rights to organize into unions or to strike. He took control of all areas of life. He burned books that went against Nazi ideas. He forced children to join Nazi groups.

Hitler also attacked Germany's Jews. Laws took away their rights. In November 1938, mobs attacked Jewish people and destroyed thousands of Jewish-owned buildings. This was the start of a process to eliminate the Jews from German life.

3. What changes did Hitler make?

____

____

____

____

OTHER COUNTRIES FALL TO DICTATORS (Page 480)

What other countries were ruled by dictators?

Fascist dictators took control in other countries as well, including Hungary, Poland, Yugoslavia, Albania, Bulgaria, and Romania. All had dictators or kings who ruled like dictators. Only Czechoslovakia remained as a democracy in eastern Europe.

Elsewhere in Europe, only in nations with strong democratic traditions—Britain, France and the Scandinavian countries—did democracy survive.

4. Why did democracy survive in some countries?

____

____

____

____

As you read about Fascist policies, note some of the causes and effects of the event identified.

Causes	Event	Effects
	1. Mussolini gains popularity.	
	2. King Victor Emmanuel III puts Mussolini in charge of the government.	
	3. Hitler is chosen leader of the Nazi party.	
	4. Hitler is tried for treason and sentenced to prison.	
	5. President Paul von Hindenburg names Hitler chancellor in 1933.	
	6. Hitler has books burned in huge bonfires.	
	7. Nazis pass laws depriving Jews of their rights.	

Aggressors Invade Nations

Terms and Names

appeasement Giving in to keep the peace

Axis Powers Germany, Italy, and Japan

Francisco Franco Spain's Fascist dictator

isolationism Belief that political ties with other countries should be avoided

Third Reich German empire

Munich Conference Meeting of world powers in 1938 that allowed Hitler to take part of Czechoslovakia

Before You Read

In the last section, you read about the rise of fascism.

In this section, you will learn about military actions that led to a second world war.

As You Read

Use a time line to trace the movement of Japan from democratic reform to military aggression.

JAPAN SEEKS AN EMPIRE (Pages 481–482)

***Why* did Japan wish to expand?**

Military leaders took control of Japan during the Great Depression. They wanted to solve the country's economic problems by foreign expansion.

In 1931, the Japanese army invaded Manchuria, a province of China. Manchuria was rich in coal and iron. These were valuable resources for the Japanese economy. Other countries spoke in protest in the League of Nations but did nothing else. Japan ignored the protests. In 1933, it pulled out of the League.

Four years later, Japan invaded China. The powerful Japanese army swept Chinese fighters aside. It killed tens of thousands of civilians and soldiers in the city of Nanjing. In spite of these losses, Chinese forces—both the nationalists of the government and Communist rebels—continued to resist Japan.

1. What territories did Japan invade?

____

____

EUROPEAN AGGRESSORS ON THE MARCH (Pages 482–483)

***What* European nations were aggressors?**

Italy's Mussolini also wanted to expand. He dreamed of an Italian empire in Africa. In 1935 he ordered the invasion of Ethiopia. His troops won an easy victory. Haile Selassie, the emperor of Ethiopia, pleaded with the League of Nations to help. The League did nothing.

By giving in to Mussolini in Africa, Britain and France hoped to keep the peace in Europe.

Hitler made moves also. He broke the Versailles Treaty by rebuilding Germany's army. In 1936, he sent troops into an area along the Rhine River between Germany and France that the treaty had forbidden the Germans to enter. The French and British again responded with **appeasement**—giving in to keep the peace.

The German movement into the Rhineland marked a turning point in the march toward war. Also in 1936, Hitler signed an alliance with Mussolini and with Japan. These three nations came to be called the **Axis Powers.**

In 1936, civil war broke out in Spain. The army, led by General **Francisco Franco,** revolted against a government run by liberals and socialists. Hitler and Mussolini sent aid to the army, which was backed by Spanish Fascists. The Soviet Union sent aid to the government. In early 1939, the government's resistance to the army collapsed. Francisco Franco became Spain's Fascist dictator.

2. What places did Germany and Italy invade?

____

____

____

DEMOCRATIC NATIONS TRY TO PRESERVE PEACE (Pages 484–485)

Why did the world's democracies fail to stop the aggression?

At this time, many Americans resisted accepting the nation's new role as a world leader. They believed that the United States should follow a policy of **isolationism**. Isolationism was the belief that political ties with other countries should be avoided. This, it was thought, would keep the country out of another foreign war.

In March 1938, Hitler moved his troops into Austria. He made it part of the **Third Reich**, or German Empire. This action broke the Versailles Treaty again. France and Britain once more did nothing.

Later that year, Hitler demanded that Czechoslovakia give up a part of its land to Germany. Czechoslovakia refused. The **Munich Conference** was held in September 1938 to solve the problem. At this meeting Germany, France, Britain, and Italy agreed to allow the Germans to take the land. In return, Hitler promised to respect the new borders of Czechoslovakia. A few months later, however, he took the entire country.

In the summer of 1939, Hitler made a similar demand of Poland. That nation also refused to give up land. Britain and France now said that they would protect Poland. But Hitler believed that they would not risk going to war. At the same time, he signed an agreement with Soviet dictator Joseph Stalin. The two countries promised never to attack one another.

The Axis Powers were moving unchecked at the end of the decade. The whole world was waiting to see what would happen next. It seemed that war would break out.

3. What happened at the Munich Conference?

____

____

____

As you read this section, take notes to answer the questions based on the time line.

Year	Event	Question
1931	**Japan invades Manchuria.**	1. Why did the Japanese invade Manchuria?
		2. Why did Britain and France take no action against Italian aggression?
1935	**Mussolini invades Ethiopia.**	
	U.S. Congress passes first of three Neutrality Acts.	3. Why did isolationists want these laws passed?
1936	**German troops move into the Rhineland.**	4. What were some effects of appeasing Hitler after his invasion of the Rhineland?
1937	**Japan invades China.**	5. What were the immediate results of this invasion?
	Hitler plans to absorb Austria and Czechoslovakia into the Third Reich.	
1938	**Munich Conference is held.**	6. Why was the Munich Conference unsuccessful?
1939	**Franco becomes Spanish dictator.**	7. How did other countries help Franco's Nationalist forces bring about the collapse of Republican resistance?
	Germany and Russia sign a nonaggression pact.	8. Why did Stalin sign an agreement with Fascist Germany, once a bitter enemy?

Name ______________________ Class ______________ Date ______________

World War II

Section 1

Hitler's Lightning War

Terms and Names

nonaggression pact Agreement that says countries will not attack or invade one another

blitzkrieg Warfare in which surprise air attacks are followed by massive attacks on land

Charles de Gaulle Leader of the French government-in-exile

Winston Churchill Leader of Britain

Battle of Britain Battle of British and German air forces fought over Britain during 1940–1941

Erwin Rommel German general who led troops in North Africa

Atlantic Charter Declaration of principles issued by Winston Churchill and Franklin D. Roosevelt in August 1941

Before You Read

In the last chapter, you read about actions that led up to World War II.

In this section, you will learn about the first years of the war in Europe.

As You Read

Use a chart to identify the effects of some of the early events of World War II.

GERMANY SPARKS A NEW WAR IN EUROPE (Pages 491–492)

***What* caused Britain and France to declare war?**

In 1939, Adolf Hitler decided to move on Poland. He had already conquered Austria and Czechoslovakia. When Hitler signed a **nonaggression pact** with Joseph Stalin of the Soviet Union, they agreed not to attack each other. Secretly, they also agreed to split Poland between them. This deal removed the threat of the Soviets attacking Germany from the east.

So, on September 1, the German army invaded Poland in a surprise attack. Using planes, tanks, and troops, it moved suddenly in a technique called **blitzkrieg,** or "lightning war." Britain and France declared war, but Poland fell.

On September 17, after secret agreement with Hitler, Stalin invaded eastern Poland. Stalin then began annexing the regions covered in a second part of the agreement. Lithuania, Latvia, and Estonia fell without a struggle. However, Finland fought back. In March 1940, Finland was forced to surrender.

For seven months after Poland fell to the Germans, Europe was calm. France and Britain got their armies ready. They waited for Hitler's next move.

1. Why did Poland fall to the Germans so quickly?

____

THE FALL OF FRANCE; THE BATTLE OF BRITAIN (Pages 492–494)

***What* happened when France and Britain were attacked?**

Suddenly in April 1940, Hitler's armies invaded Denmark and Norway. Within two months, they also captured Belgium, the Netherlands, Luxembourg, and France. Part of the French army, led by **Charles de Gaulle**, escaped to Britain to remain free and continue the fight. By then, Italy's Benito Mussolini had joined Hitler's side.

Great Britain—now led by **Winston Churchill**—stood alone. The German air force began bombing Britain. It wanted to weaken the country. Germany was getting prepared to invade Britain. But the British air force fought back. It was helped by the recently developed radar. This was an electronic tracking system that warned of coming attacks. Also, the British had broken the German army's secret code. The **Battle of Britain** lasted many months. Unable to break British defenses, Hitler called off the attacks in May 1941.

2. Why did Germany fail to win the Battle of Britain?

____

THE MEDITERRANEAN AND THE EASTERN FRONT (Pages 494–496)

***What* countries did Hitler invade?**

Hitler then turned his attention to the east and to the Mediterranean. Germany sent troops under General **Erwin Rommel** to North Africa to help Italy fight the British. In April 1941, German armies quickly took control of Yugoslavia and Greece. In June, Hitler began a surprise invasion of the Soviet Union. The Red Army was the largest in the world. But it was not well equipped or well trained. The Germans quickly pushed deep into Soviet territory. The Red Army was forced to retreat.

To keep supplies out of German hands, the Red Army destroyed everything left behind. The Germans were stopped from taking Leningrad in the north. They then turned on Moscow, the Soviet capital. A strong Soviet counterattack, combined with fierce Russian winter weather, forced the Germans back. Moscow had been saved, and the battle had cost the Germans 500,000 lives.

3. What happened when Germany invaded the Soviet Union?

____

THE UNITED STATES AIDS ITS ALLIES (Page 496)

***How* did the United States take sides?**

The United States watched these events. Many Americans did not want to join in the war. President Roosevelt wanted to help the Allies, however. He asked Congress to allow Britain and France to buy American weapons. Soon, American ships were escorting British ships carrying guns bought from the United States. By the fall of 1941, U.S. ships had orders to fire on German submarines that threatened the ships. The United States and Germany were fighting an undeclared naval war.

Roosevelt met secretly with Churchill in August of 1941. Although the United States was not officially in the war, the two leaders issued a statement called the **Atlantic Charter**. It supported free trade and the right of people to form their own government.

4. Name two ways in which the United States supported the Allies.

____

As you read about war in Europe and North Africa, answer the questions about the time line.

1939	
Aug.	**Hitler and Stalin sign a non-aggression pact.**
Sept.	**Hitler invades Poland.**
1940	
April	**Hitler invades Denmark and Norway.**
June	**France surrenders.**
Sept.	**German Luftwaffe begins bombing British cities.**
	Italy moves to seize Egypt and Suez Canal.
1941	
Feb.	**Hitler sends Rommel to help Italian troops seize Egypt and the Suez Canal.**
June	**Hitler invades the Soviet Union.**

1. What did each leader gain from the secret agreement?

2. What strategy did Hitler use to conquer Poland?

3. What was Hitler's plan for conquering France?

4. What happened at Dunkirk?

5. What was the outcome of the Battle of Britain?

6. What was the outcome of the fighting at Tobruk?

7. How did Hitler's invasion compare with Napoleon's invasion of Russia?

Japan's Pacific Campaign

Terms and Names

Isoroku Yamamoto Japanese admiral who decided that the U.S. fleet in Hawaii had to be destroyed

Pearl Harbor Navy base in Hawaii attacked by the Japanese

Battle of Midway Sea and air battle in which American forces defeated Japanese forces near Midway Island in the Pacific

Douglas MacArthur U.S. general who commanded Allied forces in the Pacific

Battle of Guadalcanal Six-month battle on the island of Guadalcanal in which American and Australian troops defeated Japanese defenders

Before You Read

In the last section, you read about the war against Hitler in Europe.

In this section, you will learn about the war against Japan in the Pacific.

As You Read

Use a chart to identify the effects of four major events of the war in the Pacific between 1941 and 1943.

SURPRISE ATTACK ON PEARL HARBOR (Pages 497–498)

***How* did the United States fight Japan before declaring war?**

The military leaders who ran the Japanese government also had plans to build an empire. Japan was overcrowded and did not have enough raw materials or oil.

The Japanese captured part of China in 1931. In 1937, they invaded the center of China. There they met strong resistance. Needing resources for this war, they decided to move into Southeast Asia.

The United States feared that Japanese control of this area would threaten U.S. holdings in the Pacific. Roosevelt gave military aid to China. He also cut off oil shipments to Japan.

Japanese Admiral **Isoroku Yamamoto** decided that the U.S. fleet in Hawaii had to be destroyed. On December 7, 1941, the Japanese navy began a surprise attack on the U.S. naval base at **Pearl Harbor** in Hawaii. In just two hours, Japanese planes sank or damaged a major part of the U. S. Pacific fleet—19 ships, including 8 battleships. The next day, Congress, at the request of President Roosevelt, declared war on Japan and its allies.

1. How did the United States respond to the Japanese attack on Pearl Harbor?

____

JAPANESE VICTORIES (Page 498)

***What* areas of Asia did the Japanese conquer between December 1941 and mid-1942?**

The Japanese attack on Pearl Harbor was just one of many sudden strikes. Japan also captured Guam, Wake Island, and the Philippines from the United States.

It took Indonesia from the Dutch and Hong Kong, Malaya, and Singapore from the British.

Japan then invaded Burma, located between India and China. Japan wanted to stop China from receiving supplies through Burma. Burma fell in May 1942. By that time, Japan had conquered more than 1 million square miles of land with about 150 million people.

Before these conquests, the Japanese had tried to win the support of Asians. They used the anti-colonial slogan "Asia for the Asians." After their victory, the Japanese made it clear that they had come as conquerers.

2. What countries lost territory to Japan early in the war?

____

____

____

____

THE ALLIES STRIKE BACK; AN ALLIED OFFENSIVE (Pages 500–501)

How did the Allies strike back?

The Japanese seemed unbeatable after a string of victories. But the Allies wanted to strike back in the Pacific. In April 1942, the United States sent planes to drop bombs on Tokyo. The attack raised the morale of Americans. In May 1942, the Allies suffered heavy losses at the Battle of the Coral Sea. Still, they were able to stop the Japanese advance and save Australia.

The next month, the U.S. Navy scored an important victory near Midway Island in the central Pacific. In the **Battle of Midway**, Japan lost four aircraft carriers, the most important naval weapon in the war. The victory turned the tide of war against Japan.

The United States now went on the attack. General **Douglas MacArthur** did not want to invade the Japanese-held islands that were most strongly defended. He wanted to attack weaker ones. The first attack came on Guadalcanal, in the Solomon Islands in August. The Japanese were building an air base there. It took six months of fighting for U.S. and Australian troops to drive the Japanese off the island in the **Battle of Guadalcanal**. The Japanese abandoned the island in February 1943.

3. Name three Allied victories against Japan.

____

____

____

____

As you read this section, answer the questions about the war in the Pacific.

a. What happened?

b. What is the significance of the battle or attack?

1. Bombing of Pearl Harbor	a. b.
2. Fall of Southeast Asian colonies	a. b.
3. Doolittle's raid on Japan	a. b.
4. Battle of the Coral Sea	a. b.
5. Battle of Midway	a. b.
6. Battle of Guadalcanal	a. b.

The Holocaust

Terms and Names

Aryans Germanic peoples

Holocaust Systematic mass killing of Jews and other groups considered inferior by Nazis

Kristallnacht "Night of Broken Glass," when Nazis attacked Jews throughout Germany

ghettos Neighborhoods in which European Jews were forced to live

"Final Solution" Hitler's plan to murder as many Jews as possible

genocide Systematic murder of an entire people

Before You Read

In the last section, you read about the battles in the Pacific.

In this section, you will read about Hitler's "final solution" in Europe.

As You Read

Use a web diagram to identify examples of Nazi persecution.

THE HOLOCAUST BEGINS

(**Pages** 502–503)

***What* was the Holocaust?**

Part of Hitler's new order for Europe included getting rid of "inferior" people. Hitler believed that the **Aryans**, or German peoples, were a "master race." He had a deep-seated hatred of people who were not German. He particularly hated Jews. This led to the **Holocaust**, the murder of millions of Jews and other civilians.

During the 1930s, Hitler passed laws that took away the rights of German Jews. One night in November 1938, Nazi mobs attacked Jews throughout Germany. They destroyed homes and businesses and killed or beat many people. This night became known as ***Kristallnacht***, or "Night of Broken Glass."

Kristallnacht was a major step-up in the Nazi policy of persecuting the Jews. The future for the Jews in Germany looked grim. Thousands of Jews tried to leave Germany. Other countries accepted a large number but were unwilling to take all those who wished to leave.

Hitler ordered all Jews in Germany and his conquered lands to live in certain parts of cities called **ghettos**. The Nazis then sealed off the ghettos with barbed wire and stone walls. They wanted the Jews inside to starve or die of disease. Even under these horrible conditions, the Jews hung on.

1. How did the Holocaust begin?

____

____

____

____

THE "FINAL SOLUTION"

(**Pages** 503–505)

***What* was the "Final Solution"?**

Hitler soon got tired of waiting for the Jews to starve or die of disease in the ghettos. He decided to take more direct action. He was going to kill as many Jews as possible.

Hitler's plan was the "**Final Solution**" to what the Nazis called the "Jewish problem." It was **genocide**, the systematic murder of an entire people. The Nazis also wanted to wipe out many other people to protect the "purity" of the Aryan race. These people included Roma (gypsies), Poles, Russians, and those who were mentally or physically disabled. The Germans paid the most attention to Jews, however.

Thousands of Jews were shot to death by "killing squads." Millions were gathered and placed in concentration camps. These prisons used the inmates as slave workers. Many in the camps died of starvation or disease.

Starting in 1942, the Nazis built "death camps." At these camps, thousands of Jews were gassed to death in huge gas chambers. In the end, six million Jews were murdered by the Nazis. Fewer than four million European Jews survived.

2. How was the "Final Solution" carried out?

____

____

____

____

As you read about the Holocaust, use the following questions to help summarize information in this section.

1. Who? Who were the victims of the Holocaust? Who were members of the "master race"?	
2. What? What were the Nuremberg Laws? What happened on the night of November 9, 1938? What was Hitler's "final solution"?	
3. Where? Where did German Jews try to migrate to find safety from Nazi terror? Where were Jews forced to live in German-controlled cities? Where were the concentration camps?	
4. Why? Why did Hitler believe that Jews and other "subhumans" had to be exterminated? Why did the Germans build extermination camps?	
5. When? When did the final stage of the Final Solution begin?	
6. How? How did non-Jewish people try to save Jews from the horrors of Nazism? How many Jews died in the Holocaust?	

Section 4

The Allied Victory

Terms and Names

Dwight D. Eisenhower American general who helped drive the Germans out of Africa

Battle of Stalingrad Battle during which the Red Army forced the Germans out of Stalingrad

D-Day Huge Allied invasion mounted to retake France from the Germans

Battle of the Bulge Final large-scale attack by German troops that was forced back by the Allies

kamikaze Japanese suicide pilots

Before You Read

In the last section, you read about the Holocaust in Europe.

In this section, you will learn how the war was fought and brought to an end around the world.

As You Read

Use a chart to identify the outcomes of several major World War II battles.

THE TIDE TURNS ON TWO FRONTS (Pages 506–507)

***Where* did the tide of war turn in favor of the Allies?**

In 1942, Roosevelt, Churchill, and Stalin planned the Allies' strategy. Stalin wanted Britain and the United States to open a second front against Germany to relieve the pressure on his armies. Stalin wanted the attack in France. Roosevelt and Churchill agreed to a second front but chose to attack German General Erwin Rommel in North Africa.

In late 1942, the British army led by General Bernard Montgomery drove the Germans out of Egypt and back to the west. Meanwhile, American troops under the command of General **Dwight D. Eisenhower** landed behind the Germans and began moving east. The Germans were finally forced out of Africa in May 1943.

At the same time, the Soviets gained a major victory as well. German troops had invaded the Soviet city of Stalingrad in 1942. The Red Army forced the Germans to surrender in February 1943, ending the **Battle of Stalingrad.**

American and British soldiers next invaded Italy and captured Sicily in August 1943. Mussolini was driven from power and the new Italian government surrendered. But Hitler did not want to give up Italy. His army fought there until 1945.

1. What major victories did the Allies win?

____

____

THE ALLIED HOME FRONTS

(**Pages** 507–509)

***What* problems did people face at home?**

While the Allies continued to fight, people at home suffered. Some British and Soviet citizens died. In the United States, citizens faced shortages. Goods such as food, tires, gasoline, and clothing were in short supply. The government rationed, or limited, these items so there would be enough for the military.

Some Americans were even imprisoned. Bitter feelings against the Japanese became widespread. As a result, mistrust of Japanese Americans grew. The U.S. government took thousands of Japanese Americans who lived on the West Coast and moved them to relocation camps in the western United States. Two-thirds of these people were American citizens.

2. What happened to Japanese Americans?

____

VICTORY IN EUROPE

(**Pages** 509–511)

***What* were the final battles in Europe?**

In early 1944, the Allies built a massive force to retake France. In June, an invasion of thousands of ships, planes, and soldiers was launched. It was called **D-Day.** The invasion force suffered heavy losses but gained a foothold in northern France. A month later, Allied forces began to pour through German lines. In August, they marched in triumph into Paris. By September, they had driven the Germans out of France, Belgium, Luxembourg, and much of the Netherlands.

At the same time, the Soviets were pushing the Germans back in eastern Europe. In late 1944, Hitler ordered his army to make one final, large-scale attack in the west. In the **Battle of the Bulge**, it punched through Allied lines until an Allied counterattack forced it back to Germany. By late April 1945, Soviet troops surrounded Berlin, Hitler's headquarters. Five days later, he killed himself. A week later, the Germans surrendered. Roosevelt did not live to see this victory, however. He had died in early April. Harry Truman was now president.

3. Name three events that led directly to Germany's surrender.

____

VICTORY IN THE PACIFIC

(**Pages** 511–513)

***What* led to victory in the Pacific?**

In the Pacific, the Allies began to move toward Japan in 1943. They landed troops in the Philippines in the fall of 1944. In the Battle of Leyte Gulf, in October 1944, the Japanese navy was crushed.

As American troops moved closer to Japan, they faced attacks by **kamikaze.** These Japanese suicide pilots sank Allied ships by crashing their bomb-filled planes into them. In March 1945, U.S. Marines captured the island of Iwo Jima, a strategic Japanese stronghold. By June, they had won control of Okinawa, an island just 350 miles from Japan.

Japan was the next stop. But the U.S. military feared that an invasion of Japan would cost half a million Allied lives. In August, President Truman ordered that an atomic bomb be dropped on the city of Hiroshima. A second bomb was dropped on Nagasaki three days later. Tens of thousands of Japanese died. Japan surrendered in September.

4. Name two events that led directly to Japan's surrender.

____

Name ______________________ Class ______________ Date ______________

Section 4, *continued*

As you read this section, note how each of the following events or campaigns contributed to the Allies' victory in World War II.

1. Battle of El Alamein	2. Operation Torch

3. Battle of Stalingrad	4. Invasion of Italy

5. Propaganda campaigns on home fronts	6. D-Day invasion

7. Battle of the Bulge	8. Battle of Leyte Gulf

9. Battle of Okinawa	10. Bombing of Hiroshima and Nagasaki

Europe and Japan in Ruins

Terms and Names

Nuremberg Trials Trials of Nazi leaders charged with crimes against humanity, held in Nuremberg, Germany

demilitarization Breaking down armed forces

democratization Process of creating a government elected by the people

Before You Read

In the last section, you read about how the war ended.

In this section, you will learn about the war's effects on Europe and Japan.

As You Read

Use a Venn diagram to compare and contrast the aftermath of World War II in Europe and Japan.

DEVASTATION IN EUROPE (Pages 514–515)

***How* did the war change Europe?**

The war had left Europe in ruins. Almost 40 million people were dead. Hundreds of cities were reduced to rubble by constant bombing and shelling. The ground war had destroyed much of the countryside. Displaced persons from many nations were trying to get back home. Often there was no water, no electricity, and little food. Hunger was constant.

Agriculture had been disrupted. Most able-bodied men had served in the military, and the women had worked in war production. Few had remained to plant the fields. With factories destroyed or damaged, most people had no earnings to buy the food that was available. Also the small harvests did not reach the cities because the transportation system had been destroyed. Suffering continued for many years in Europe.

1. What conditions existed in Europe after World War II?

____

POSTWAR GOVERNMENTS AND POLITICS (Pages 515–516)

***Who* did the Europeans blame for the war?**

Europeans often blamed their leaders for the war and its aftermath. Once Germany was defeated, some prewar governments—like those in Belgium, Holland, Denmark, and Norway—returned quickly. In Germany, Italy, and France, the old fascist governments had disappeared. At first, the Communist parties grew strong in France and Italy. People who opposed Communism grew alarmed. They voted leaders from other parties into power. Communism lost its appeal when the economies of these lands improved.

During efforts to rebuild Europe, the Allies held the **Nuremberg Trials** in the German city of Nuremberg. There, captured Nazi leaders were charged with crimes against humanity. They were found guilty, and some were executed.

2. What were the Nuremberg Trials?

____

____

POSTWAR JAPAN; OCCUPATION BRINGS DEEP CHANGES

(**Pages** 516–517)

What changes were made in Japan?

The defeat suffered by Japan in World War II had devastated that country. Two million lives had been lost. The country's major cities were in ruins.

The U.S. Army occupied Japan under the command of General MacArthur. He began a process of **demilitarization**, breaking down the Japanese armed forces. MacArthur also paid attention to **democratization,** or creating a government elected by the people. His first step was to write a new constitution. It gave all power to the Japanese people, who voted for members of a parliament that would rule the land. All Japanese over age 20—including women—were given the right to vote. In 1951, other nations finally signed a formal peace with Japan. A few months later, U.S. military occupation ended.

3. How did the government of Japan change?

____

____

As you read this section, fill out the chart by writing notes to describe conditions in postwar Europe and Japan.

Postwar Europe:	
1. Note three ways war affected the land and people of Europe.	
2. Note three political problems postwar governments faced.	
3. Note one way the Allies dealt with the Holocaust.	

Postwar Japan:	
4. Note two effects of Allied bombing raids on Japan.	
5. Note three ways U.S. occupation changed Japan.	
6. Note three provisions in Japan's new constitution.	

Name ______________________ Class ______________ Date ______________

Cold War: Superpowers Face Off

Terms and Names

United Nations World organization formed to prevent war

iron curtain Division between Eastern and Western Europe during the Cold War

containment Policy aimed at preventing the spread of communism

Truman Doctrine Policy of giving aid to countries threatened by communism

Marshall Plan Plan to give aid to European countries to help them recover

Cold War State of tension and mistrust between the United States and the Soviet Union

NATO Military alliance including the United States, Canada, and Western Europe

Warsaw Pact Military alliance between the Soviet Union and Eastern Europe

brinkmanship Willingness on the part of the superpower to go to the edge of war

Before You Read

In the last section, you learned about the end of the Second World War.

In this section, you will learn about the international tensions that followed the war.

As You Read

Use a time line to organize early Cold War events.

ALLIES BECOME ENEMIES

(Pages 531–532)

***What* caused the Cold War?**

The United States and the Soviet Union were allies during World War II. In February 1945, they agreed to divide Germany into separate zones. Each zone was occupied by the soldiers of one of the Allies. The Allies also helped form the **United Nations** (UN) in 1945 The UN pledged to prevent war.

The United States and the Soviet Union had important differences after the war. The United States suffered few casualties and was the richest nation in the world. The Soviet Union suffered enormous loss of life and damage to its cities.

There were also striking political differences. The United States wanted to encourage democracy. The Soviet Union wanted to set up Communist governments. These differences caused tensions between the two countries.

1. How did U.S. goals and Soviet goals differ after World War II?

____

EASTERN EUROPE'S IRON CURTAIN (Page 533)

***How* did the Soviet Union gain control of Eastern Europe?**

At the end of World War II, Soviet forces occupied lands along its western border. After the war, Stalin made sure Communist governments were in place in these lands: Albania, Bulgaria, Hungary, Czechoslovakia, Romania, Poland, and Yugoslavia. This divided Europe between East and West. Winston Churchill called this division the **"iron curtain."**

2. What countries were separated from the West by the iron curtain?

____

UNITED STATES TRIES TO CONTAIN SOVIETS (Pages 533–535)

***HOW* did the United States respond to communism?**

Truman began a policy of **containment**—blocking the Soviets from spreading communism. Under the **Truman Doctrine**, the United States helped nations that were threatened by communism. The United States also adopted the **Marshall Plan** in 1947. This plan gave food and other aid to European countries to help them recover.

In 1948, the Soviets and Americans clashed over Germany. France, Britain, and the United States agreed to pull their troops out of Germany. They let the three zones that they occupied unite. But the Soviets refused to leave their zone. Then they cut off all highway and train traffic into Berlin, which was deep within the Soviet zone. The United States and Britain responded with the Berlin airlift. They flew supplies into the city for 11 months. Finally, the Soviets lifted the blockade.

3. What was the Berlin airlift?

____

COLD WAR DIVIDES THE WORLD (Pages 535–536)

***Why* did tensions between the superpowers increase?**

The struggle between the United States and the Soviet Union was called the **Cold War**. Many countries supported one superpower or the other.

The United States, Canada, and several countries in Western Europe formed the North Atlantic Treaty Organization (**NATO**). NATO was a military alliance. Each nation promised to defend any other member that was attacked. The Soviets and the countries of Eastern Europe made a similar agreement. It was called the **Warsaw Pact**.

In 1949, the Soviet Union announced that it had developed an atomic bomb. Three years later, both superpowers had an even more deadly weapon—the hydrogen bomb. Soon both nations were involved in an arms race. They produced more and more nuclear weapons and developed new ways to deliver them. Both sides were willing to go to the brink, or edge, of war. This became known as **brinkmanship**.

In 1957, the Soviet Union launched *Sputnik*, the world's first human-made satellite. Americans felt that the Soviets were far ahead in science and technology. The United States then began spending huge amounts of money to improve science education.

The U-2 incident brought more tension. The United States sent planes, called U-2 planes, to spy over Soviet territory. One was shot down in 1960.

4. What are three developments or events that increased tensions during the Cold War?

____

As you read this section, take notes to explain how each of the following actions or policies led to the Cold War between the United States and the Soviet Union.

1. Meeting at Potsdam, Germany	2. Policy of containment
3. Truman Doctrine	4. Marshall Plan
5. Blockade of Berlin	6. Formation of North Atlantic Treaty Organization (NATO)
7. Policy of brinkmanship	8. Launching of *Sputnik I*

Name ______________________ Class ______________ Date ______________

Communists Take Power in China

Terms and Names

Mao Zedong Communist leader who defeated the Nationalists and led the People's Republic of China

Jiang Jieshi Nationalist leader who set up a new government in Taiwan

commune Large farm setup in China in which many families work the land and live together

Red Guards Young Chinese students who carried out the Cultural Revolution

Cultural Revolution Uprising in China between 1966 and 1976 that aimed to establish a society of peasants and workers in which all were equal

Before You Read

In the last section, you read about tensions between the superpowers.

In this section, you will read about civil war and the rise of communism in China.

As You Read

Use a chart to identify the causes and effects of the Communist Revolution in China.

COMMUNISTS VS. NATIONALISTS (Pages 538–539)

***Who* fought the civil war?**

Nationalists and Communists fought for control of China in the 1930s. During World War II, they joined forces to fight against the Japanese. The Communists, led by **Mao Zedong,** organized an army of peasants in northwestern China. From there they fought the Japanese in the northeast.

The Nationalists, led by **Jiang Jieshi,** controlled southwestern China. The Nationalists were protected from the Japanese by mountains. The United States sent the Nationalists large amounts of money and supplies, but corrupt officers took much of it. The Nationalists built a large army, but they only fought a few battles against the Japanese.

After the Japanese surrendered, the Communists and Nationalists resumed their civil war. The war lasted from 1946 to 1949. The Communists won because their troops were well trained in guerrilla war. They also enjoyed the backing of the peasants to whom they had promised land. In 1949, Jiang Jieshi and other Nationalist leaders fled to the island of Taiwan.

1. What two groups fought the civil war, and who led them?

____

____

____

____

____

THE TWO CHINAS AFFECT THE COLD WAR (Pages 539–540)

How did the two Chinas participate in the Cold War?

The United States helped the Nationalists set up a new government. The Nationalists called their land the Republic of China. Meanwhile, the Soviets helped Mao Zedong and his government, the People's Republic of China.

The Chinese and the Soviets promised to help defend each other if either country were attacked. The United States responded by trying to halt Soviet expansion in Asia. Communist China also tried to expand its power. The Chinese invaded Mongolia, Tibet, and India.

2. How did the superpowers take sides with the two Chinas?

____

____

____

____

____

THE COMMUNISTS TRANSFORM CHINA (Pages 540–541)

How did Mao change China?

Mao set out to rebuild China. He seized land and gave it to the peasants. But he also forced the peasants—in groups of 200 to 300 households—to join collective farms, or **communes**. On these farms, the land belonged to the group. Mao also took control of China's industries. Under Mao's plan, production of industrial products went up.

With this success, Mao launched the "Great Leap Forward." He wanted to make the communes larger and more productive. The plan failed. People did not like strong government control. The government did not plan effectively. Between 1958 and 1961, famine killed millions.

In 1966, Mao tried to revive the revolution. He encouraged young people to revive the revolution. Students formed groups called **Red Guards.** This was the beginning of the **Cultural Revolution.** The Red Guards struck at teachers, scientists, and artists. They shut down schools and sent intellectuals to the country to work on farms. They killed thousands of people who resisted. China was in chaos. Factories shut down and farm production dropped. Eventually, Mao put an end to the Cultural Revolution.

3. What are three changes Mao made?

____

____

____

____

____

As you read about the civil war in China and the creation of two Chinas, take notes to answer the questions.

1. **Who?** Who was Mao Zedong? Who was Jiang Jieshi?	
2. **When?** When did the civil war in China resume? When did the civil war end?	
3. **What?** What advantages did Nationalist forces have? What advantages did Communist forces have?	
4. **Where?** Where is Nationalist China located? Where is the People's Republic of China located?	
5. **How?** How did the superpowers react to the existence of two Chinas? How did Mao transform the economy of China?	
6. **Why?** Why did the Great Leap Forward fail? Why did Mao launch the Cultural Revolution?	

Section 3

Wars in Korea and Vietnam

Terms and Names

38th parallel Line that separated North Korea and South Korea

Douglas MacArthur Leader of United Nations forces during the Korean War

Ho Chi Minh Vietnamese nationalist who drove the French out of Vietnam and who led North Vietnam

domino theory Theory that nations were like a row of dominoes: if one fell to communism, the others would fall, too

Vietcong Communist rebels in South Vietnam who were supported by North Vietnam.

Ngo Dinh Diem Leader of the anti-Communist government of South Vietnam

Vietnamization Nixon's plan for gradually withdrawing U.S. troops from Vietnam and replacing them with South Vietnamese troops

Khmer Rouge Communist rebels who set up a brutal government in Cambodia

Before You Read

In the last section, you read about the civil war in China.

In this section, you will read about wars in Korea and Vietnam.

As You Read

Use a diagram to compare and contrast the Korean and Vietnam wars.

WAR IN KOREA (Pages 542–544)

***How* was Korea divided?**

When World War II ended, Korea became a divided nation. North of the **38th parallel,** a line that crosses Korea at 38 degrees north latitude, the Japanese surrendered to the Soviets. South of that line, the Japanese surrendered to the Allies.

As in Germany, two nations developed. The Soviet Union supported a Communist government in North Korea. The United States supported a non-Communist government in South Korea. On June 25, 1950, North Korea invaded South Korea. President Truman fought this move with help from the UN. The United States and other countries sent troops to assist South Korea. At first, the North Korean army captured almost all of South Korea.

Then the UN army made a bold counter attack. The attack was led by General **Douglas MacArthur**. In 1953, the two Koreas agreed to a cease-fire. The earlier boundary splitting North and South Korea remained the same.

North Korea had a Communist government. It had a large, strong army and tight government control, but it also had many economic problems. For more than 30 years, dictators ruled South Korea. But its economy grew, in part because it received U.S. aid. Free elections were held in South Korea after a new constitution was adopted in 1987.

1. How did the Korean War change the way Korea was divided?

____

____

WAR BREAKS OUT IN VIETNAM; THE UNITED STATES GET INVOLVED; POSTWAR SOUTHEAST ASIA (Pages 544–547)

***How* did the United States get involved in Vietnam?**

A nationalist named **Ho Chi Minh** drove the French out of Vietnam. This worried the United States because Ho had turned to the Communists for help. Many Americans thought if one country became Communist, others would also, like a row of dominoes. This idea is known as the **domino theory**. A peace conference split Vietnam in two, with Ho taking charge of North Vietnam. The country had a Communist government. Communist rebels—the **Vietcong**—stayed active in the South.

The non-Communist government of the South had been set up by the United States and France. Its leader was **Ngo Dinh Diem**. When his government was threatened by Communists, the United States began to send troops. When they could not win the war on the ground, they tried bombing. Many people in the United States came to oppose the war.

In the late 1960s, President Richard Nixon began a plan called **Vietnamization**. This plan called for a gradual pullout of U.S. troops. At the same time, the South Vietnamese increased their combat role. The last American troops left in 1973. Two years later, North Vietnam overran the South and made Vietnam one country again. Today, Vietnam remains Communist but is looking for other nations to invest in its economy.

Fighting in Vietnam spilled over into Vietnam's neighbor, Cambodia. Rebels there were known as the **Khmer Rouge**. They set up a brutal Communist government. The Khmer Rouge killed 2 million people. In 1978, the Vietnamese invaded the country. They overthrew the Khmer Rouge. Vietnam withdrew in 1989. In 1993, Cambodia held free elections for the first time.

2. What happened in Vietnam after the United States withdrew?

____

____

As you read this section, fill out the chart below to help you better understand the causes and outcomes of wars in Asia.

War in Korea

Causes	Outcomes
1. Why did the UN send an international force to Korea?	2. What was the legacy of the war for North Korea and South Korea?

French War in Vietnam

Causes	Outcomes
3. Why did war break out between the Vietnamese nationalists and the French?	4. What was the outcome of the war for France and for Vietnam?

U.S. War in Vietnam

Causes	Outcomes
5. How did the United States get involved in Vietnam?	6. Why did the United States withdraw its troops from Vietnam?

Section 4

The Cold War Divides the World

Terms and Names

Third World Developing nations in Africa, Asia, and Latin America

nonaligned nations Countries that did not take sides with either the United States or the Soviet Union

Fidel Castro Communist leader of Cuba

Anastasio Somoza Nicaraguan dictator

Daniel Ortega Leader of Communist rebels in Nicaragua

Ayatollah Ruholla Khomeini Muslim leader who overthrew the Shah of Iran

Before You Read

In the last section, you read about wars in Korea and Vietnam.

In this section, you will learn about Cold War struggles in other parts of the world.

As You Read

Use a chart to list main points about Third World confrontations.

FIGHTING FOR THE THIRD WORLD (Pages 548–549)

***How* were developing nations affected by the Cold War?**

After World War II, the world's nations were grouped into three "worlds." The First World included the United States and its allies. The Second World consisted of Communist nations led by the Soviet Union. The **Third World** was composed of developing nations in Africa, Asia, and Latin America.

Many Third World nations had serious problems. These problems were often due to a long history of colonialism. Some Third World nations faced political unrest that threatened the peace. Other problems included poverty and a lack of education and technology. Some of these countries tried to stay neutral in the Cold War. They met to form what they called a "third force." It consisted of **nonaligned nations,** or countries that did not take sides between the Soviets and Americans. Others actively sought American or Soviet aid.

1. What problems did Third World nations face?

____

____

____

____

____

CONFRONTATIONS IN LATIN AMERICA (Pages 550–551)

What happened in Latin America?

In Cuba, the United States supported a dictator in the 1950s. In 1959, a young lawyer, **Fidel Castro**, led a successful revolt. Castro received aid from the Soviet Union. In 1962, the Soviets and Americans almost went to war over nuclear missiles that the Soviets placed in Cuba. The Soviets finally pulled the missiles out. Over time, the Cuban economy became more dependent on Soviet aid. When the Soviet Union collapsed in 1991, this aid stopped. It was a serious blow to Cuba's economy.

The United States had also backed a dictator, **Anastasio Somoza,** in Nicaragua. Somoza's government fell to Communist rebels in 1979. The rebels were led by **Daniel Ortega.** When the new government began helping leftist rebels in nearby El Salvador, the United States struck back. It began to support Nicaraguan rebels that wanted to overthrow the Communists. The civil war in Nicaragua lasted more than a decade. Finally, the different sides agreed to hold free elections.

2. Where did Communists gain power in Latin America?

____

____

____

____

____

CONFRONTATIONS IN THE MIDDLE EAST (Pages 552–553)

What happened in Iran and Afghanistan?

The Middle East often saw conflict between those who wanted a more modern, Western-style society and those who wanted to follow traditional Islam. Such a struggle took place in Iran. In the 1950s, a group tried to take control of the government from Iran's ruler, **Shah Mohammed Reza Pahlavi.** The United States helped the Shah defeat them.

Over time, the Shah tried to weaken the influence of Islam in Iran. A Muslim leader, the **Ayatollah Ruholla Khomeini,** led a successful revolt. In 1979, the Shah was forced to leave the country. Khomeini made Islamic law the law of the land. He followed a foreign policy that was strongly against the United States. He also led his country in a long war against its neighbor, Iraq.

The Soviets gained influence in Afghanistan after 1950. In the 1970s, Islamic rebels threatened the country's Communist government. The Soviets sent in troops to support the government. The United States felt its Middle East oil supplies were in danger and supported the rebels. In 1989, after a costly occupation, Soviet troops left Afghanistan.

3. How did Khomeini change Iran?

____

____

____

____

____

As you read about conflict between the superpowers over Latin America and the Middle East, answer the questions about events listed in the time line.

Year	Event	Question
1959	**Fidel Castro leads a revolution in Cuba.**	1. How did revolution affect Cuba?
1961	**Castro turns back Cuban invasion at Bay of Pigs.**	2. Why did the United States support the invasion?
1962	**United States demands that Soviets withdraw missiles from Cuba.**	3. How was the Cuban missile crisis resolved?
1979	**Communist Sandinista rebels overthrow dictatorship in Nicaragua.**	4. What were the consequences of civil war for Nicaragua?
1981	**Iran releases U.S. hostages.**	5. Why did the Ayatollah Khomeini hate the United States?
1988	**UN ceasefire ends hostilities between Iran and Iraq.**	6. What part did the United States play in this Muslim war?
1989	**Soviet Union withdraws its forces from Afghanistan.**	7. How was the Soviet involvement in Afghanistan similar to U.S. involvement in Vietnam?

Name ______________________ Class ______________ Date ____________

The Cold War Thaws

Terms and Names

Nikita Khrushchev Leader of the Soviet Union after Stalin

Leonid Brezhnev Soviet leader after Khrushchev

John F. Kennedy President of the United States from 1961 to 1963

Lyndon Johnson President of the United States from 1963 to 1969

détente Policy to decrease tensions between the superpowers

Richard M. Nixon President of the United States from 1969 to 1974

SALT Talks to limit nuclear arms in the United States and the Soviet Union

Ronald Reagan President of the United States from 1981 to 1989

Before You Read

In the last section, you read about Cold War struggles around the world.

In this section, you will read about the major events of the Cold War from the 1950s to the 1980s.

As You Read

Use an outline to organize main ideas and details about the Cold War thaw.

SOVIET POLICY IN EASTERN EUROPE AND CHINA (Pages 554–556)

***How* did the Soviets keep control over Eastern Europe?**

Nikita Khrushchev became the Soviet leader after Stalin died in 1953. Krushchev began a process of "destalinization." This meant getting rid of Stalin's memory. Krushchev also believed that the Soviet Union should have "peaceful competition" with the capitalist nations.

In Eastern Europe, many people still resented Soviet rule. Eastern Europeans took part in protest movements against Soviet control. In 1956, protesters and the army overthrew the Communist government of Hungary. Khrushchev sent Soviet tanks to put the Communists back in power. In 1964, Leonid Brezhnev replaced Krushchev. When Czechoslovakians began to reform their Communist government in 1968, Brezhnev sent in tanks to stop them.

The Soviets did not have the same control over their larger neighbor, China. Although the Soviet Union and China enjoyed friendly relations at first, they gradually grew apart. The split became so wide that the Soviet Union and China sometimes fought along their border. The two nations now have a peaceful relationship.

1. In what two European countries did the Soviets put down revolts against Soviet control?

____

____

____

____

____

FROM BRINKMANSHIP TO DÉTENTE; THE COLLAPSE OF DÉTENTE (Pages 556–557)

***Did* tensions between the United States and the Soviet Union change?**

Tensions between the Soviets and the United States had been very high during the presidency of **John F. Kennedy**. They remained high during the presidency of **Lyndon Johnson**. The war in Vietnam helped keep relations tense.

In the early 1970s, the United States began to follow a policy called **détente** under President **Richard M. Nixon.** Détente was a policy of lowering tensions between the superpowers. Nixon made visits to both Communist China and the Soviet Union. In 1972, he and Brezhnev held meetings called the Strategic Arms Limitations Talks (**SALT**).They signed a treaty to limit the number of nuclear missiles each country could have.

The United States retreated from détente when the Soviet Union invaded Afghanistan in 1979. In 1981, **Ronald Reagan,** a fierce anti-Communist, became president. He proposed a costly anti-missile defense system to protect America against Soviet missiles. It was never put into effect. But it remained a symbol of U.S. anti-Communist feelings.

The Soviets grew angry over American support for the rebels fighting against the Communists in Nicaragua. Tensions between the United States and the Soviet Union increased until 1985 when a new leader came to power in the Soviet Union.

2. Name two actions or events that got in the way of détente.

____

____

____

____

____

As you read this section, take notes to answer the questions.

How did each country try to resist Soviet rule?		
1. Hungary	2. Czechoslovakia	3. China

What was the foreign policy of each U.S. president?			
4. John F. Kennedy	5. Lyndon Johnson	6. Richard Nixon	7. Ronald Reagan

What was the objective of each of the following?		
8. détente	9. SALT I Treaty	10. "Star Wars"

Section 1

The Indian Subcontinent Achieves Freedom

Terms and Names

Congress Party Group consisting mostly of Hindus that led a campaign for India's independence

Muhammed Ali Jinnah Leader of the Muslim League

Muslim League Muslim group that led a campaign for India's independence

partition Division of India into two nations

Jawaharlal Nehru First prime minister of India

Indira Gandhi Daughter of Nehru who followed him as prime minister

Benazir Bhutto Former prime minister of Pakistan

Before You Read

In the last chapter, you read about the Cold War.

In this section, you will read about changes in India, Pakistan, and Sri Lanka.

As You Read

Use a time line to take notes on prominent Indian prime ministers from independence through the current day.

A MOVEMENT TOWARD INDEPENDENCE (Page 563)

***What* led to the movement for independence?**

Many Asians served in the armies of the colonial powers during World War II. The fight against the Nazis deepened Asians' desire for independence. Japanese victories over European powers early in the war made Asians believe that the colonial rulers could be defeated. In Europe, people began to doubt that it was right for nations to have colonies.

1. Name two things that increased Asian hopes for independence.

____

FREEDOM BRINGS TURMOIL (Pages 564–565)

***What* divisions existed between Indian political groups?**

In the 1920s, Mohandas Gandhi led a movement for Indian independence. Two groups worked in this effort. The Indian National Congress, also called the **Congress Party**, said that it represented all of India. Most of its members were Hindu. **Muhammad Ali Jinnah** formed the **Muslim** League in 1906. He said that the Congress Party did not care for the rights of Indian Muslims. The British encouraged the division of Hindus and Muslims. This division helped the British keep control of the country.

After World War II, Britain was ready for India to be independent. But the British did not know which people in India would take power. Riots broke out between the Hindus and Muslims throughout India.

Gandhi tried to end the violence. A Hindu extremist assassinated him for protecting Muslims. Lord Louis Mountbatten, the last British viceroy of India, also tried to stop the violence. He finally accepted the idea that **partition,** or the division of India into two nations, was necessary.

The British Parliament passed a law granting independence in July 1947. It created the separate Hindu and Muslim nations of India and Pakistan. The law gave people only one month to decide which country they wanted to live in and to move there. As millions of people began to move, more violence broke out.

2. What happened when the separate nations of India and Pakistan were created?

____

MODERN INDIA (Pages 565–567)

What problems has modern India faced?

Jawaharlal Nehru became the first prime minister of India. He led the country for 17 years.

India and Pakistan went to war over the state of Kashmir. Kashmir bordered both countries. It had a Hindu ruler and a large Muslim population. Conflict over Kashmir continues today.

Nehru tried to reform Indian society. He hoped to improve the status of the lower castes and of women. Shortly after he died in 1964, his daughter, **Indira Gandhi,** became prime minister. She took steps to increase food production. In 1984, she ordered an attack on Sikh rebels. A few months later, she was killed by Sikhs. She was followed by her son Rajiv Gandhi. He was later assassinated. Separatist movements continue to disrupt Indian society.

3. Why does conflict continue in Kashmir?

____

PAKISTAN COPES WITH FREEDOM; BANGLADESH AND SRI LANKA STRUGGLE (Pages 567–569)

How have new political divisions led to violence?

Pakistan has faced a great deal of violence, too. When Pakistan was first formed, it had east and west parts that were separated by India. In a bloody fight in 1971, the eastern part won its independence. The new nation took the name Bangladesh. Power struggles have caused problems in the western part since then. Its leaders have included Ali Bhutto and his daughter, **Benazir Bhutto.** She was elected prime minister twice.

Ceylon, an island on the southeastern coast of India, won its independence in 1947 as well. In 1972 it was renamed Sri Lanka. In 2009, a Hindu minority on the island—the Tamils—lost a civil war to form a separate nation.

4. Why has violence occurred in Pakistan?

____

Name ______________________ Class ______________ Date ______________

As you read this section, take notes to answer the questions about the time line.

Year	Event
1920	Mohandas Gandhi launches first nonviolent campaign for independence.
1940	Muslim League proposes partition of India at Lahore Conference.
1947	India and Pakistan become independent.
1949	UN arranges cease-fire between India and Pakistan in Kashmir.
1964	Jawaharlal Nehru dies.
1971	The nation of Bangladesh is formed.
1980	Indira Gandhi is reelected India's prime minister.
1987	Leaders of India and Sri Lanka reach an accord.

1. What were the major concerns of the Muslim League?

2. What problems had to be resolved in the months prior to independence?

3. What were the terms of the cease-fire?

4. How did Nehru contribute to India's modernization and democracy?

5. What events led to the creation of this new nation?

6. What major problem did Indira Gandhi face?

7. What was the cause of turmoil in Sri Lanka?

Southeast Asian Nations Gain Independence

Terms and Names

Ferdinand Marcos Leader of the Philippines who was elected but ruled as a dictator

Corazón Aquino Woman who defeated Marcos in the elections of 1986

Aung San Suu Kyi Daughter of Aung San; winner of Nobel Prize for her fight for democracy in Burma

Sukarno Leader of Indonesian independence movement; first president of Indonesia

Suharto Leader who turned Indonesia into a police state

Before You Read

In the last section, you read about independence and conflict in India.

In this section, you will read about independence and the challenges of self-rule in Southeast Asia.

As You Read

Use a chart to summarize the major challenges that Southeast Asian countries faced after independence.

THE PHILIPPINES ACHIEVES INDEPENDENCE (Pages 570–572)

***What* happened in the Philippines after it gained independence?**

In 1946, the United States gave the Philippines independence. The United States also promised money to help the Filipinos rebuild their economy. To win the aid, however, the Filipinos had to agree to a trade deal. For the next few decades, the United States kept naval and air bases on the islands. Many Filipinos wanted the bases closed. In 1991, the United States left the bases.

From 1966 to 1986, **Ferdinand Marcos** led the country. He was elected president but after a few years ruled as a dictator. He then harshly put down dissent and stole millions of dollars from the country. When he lost an election to **Corazón Aquino** in 1986, he refused to leave office. A large public outcry forced him to step down.

1. Who was Ferdinand Marcos?

____

____

BRITISH COLONIES GAIN INDEPENDENCE (Pages 572–573)

***Which* Southeast Asian British colonies won independence?**

Burma was the first British colony in Southeast Asia to become independent. Nationalist leader Aung San helped drive the British out of Burma in 1948. Burma changed its name to Myanmar in 1989. Since 1962, generals have ruled the country.

Myanmar has been torn by conflict often. **Aung San Suu Kyi** won the Nobel Peace Prize in 1991 for her opposition to this military rule.

After World War II, the British moved back into the Malay peninsula. They tried to form a country there. But ethnic conflict between Malays and Chinese who lived in the area stopped them. In 1957, independence was given to Malaya, Singapore, and parts of two distant islands.

Singapore later declared independence as a city-state. Singapore is one of the busiest ports in the world. It is also a banking center. Its economy creates a high standard of living.

2. What happened in Burma after it gained independence?

____

____

____

INDONESIA GAINS INDEPENDENCE FROM THE DUTCH (Pages 574–575)

***What* challenges did Indonesia face?**

Sukarno led an independence movement in Indonesia while Japan held that country. After World War II, he quickly declared an independent Indonesia. The Dutch at first tried to regain control over their former colony. But in 1949 they recognized Indonesia's independence.

Indonesia is spread out. It has 13,600 islands and includes people from 300 different groups that speak 250 different languages. It has been difficult for leaders to unite the nation. In 1967, a general named **Suharto** took control. He ruled until 1998. Many criticized him for taking over the island of East Timor and for corruption in his government. In the late 1990s Indonesia faced severe economic problems.

3. Why has governing Indonesia proven difficult?

____

____

____

As you read about Southeast Asia, answer the questions that follow.

1. What was the Bell Act?	
a. Why did the Filipinos object to this act?	b. Why did they agree to sign it?

2. Why did the United States demand a long lease on its military and naval bases in the Philippines?

3. Why does the Philippine constitution restrict the president to a single term of office?

4. What role did each play in recent Burmese history?	
a. General Ne Win	b. National League for Democracy

5. What is the current political status of these former British colonies?		
a. Singapore	b. Malaya	c. Sarawak and Sabah

6. What factors finally forced Indonesian dictator Suharto to step down?

Section 3

New Nations in Africa

Terms and Names

Negritude movement African movement after World War II to celebrate African culture, heritage, and values

Kwame Nkrumah Leader in the Gold Coast independence movement

Jomo Kenyatta Nationalist who helped lead Kenya to independence

Mobutu Sese Seko Ruler who took control of the Congo in 1965 and renamed it Zaire

Ahmed Ben Bella Leader of the FLN who became the first president and prime minister of Algeria

Before You Read

In the last section, you read about the struggle for self-rule in Southeast Asian colonies.

In this section, you will read about new nations in Africa.

As You Read

Use a chart to list an idea, an event, or a leader important to Ghana, Kenya, Zaire, Algeria, and Angola.

ACHIEVING INDEPENDENCE

(**Pages** 578–579)

***Why* did independence movements increase after World War II?**

During World War II, Africans fought as soldiers along with Europeans. After the war, Africans wanted independence. Many Africans took part in the **Negritude movement.** The purpose of this movement was to celebrate African culture, heritage, and values.

1. What was the Negritude movement?

____

____

GHANA LEADS THE WAY; FIGHTING FOR FREEDOM

(**Pages** 579–581)

***What* challenges did newly independent nations face?**

The British gave Africans a greater part in the colonial government of its Gold Coast colony. **Kwame Nkrumah** led a movement to push Britain to act more quickly. The effort succeeded. In 1957 the Gold Coast colony became independent. The new nation took the name Ghana.

Nkrumah had big plans for building the economy of Ghana. But these plans were very expensive. Opposition grew. Finally, the army seized power in1966. Ghana has been ruled by a military dictator since 1981.

The strong leadership of nationalist **Jomo Kenyatta** helped Kenya achieve independence in 1963. An uprising of Africans called Mau Mau also helped. Mau Mau aimed at frightening the British settlers to leave. Kenyatta became president of the new nation. He tried to unite the many different people in his country. Kenya has faced violence and a weak economy in the 1990s.

A bloody conflict for independence took place in Algeria. About 1 million French settlers lived there. They were unwilling to give up their property or their control of the colonial government.

Violence broke out in 1945 and continued for many years. In 1954, the Algerian National Liberation Front, or FLN, announced its intention to fight for independence. In 1962, the French finally granted independence to Algeria.

Ahmed Ben Bella, a leader of the FLN, was the first prime minister and then the first president of Algeria. From 1965 until 1988, Algerians tried to modernize their country. These efforts failed.

An Islamic party won elections in 1991. But the government rejected the vote. Fighting between Islamic militants and the government continued through the 1990s.

2. What problems did the new nations of Ghana and Kenya face?

____

____

____

CIVIL WAR IN CONGO AND ANGOLA (Pages 581–582)

What happened in the Congo after independence?

The Congo won its independence from Belgium in 1960. But the new nation was not well prepared for self-rule. The Congo quickly fell into civil war.

In 1965, **Mobutu Sese Seko** took control. He renamed the country Zaire and ruled until 1997. Zaire had rich mineral resources. But Mobutu's harsh and corrupt rule made the country poor. He was overthrown in a coup in 1997. The country's name was changed back to the Congo.

The colonies of Portugal were the last to gain their independence. Portugal did nothing to prepare the people of Angola for self-rule. Three Angolan groups emerged in the 1960s that were determined to control the new government.

In the 1970s, the army of Portugal revolted against its government over the war in Angola. The troops left Angola without putting any group in charge. Angolans fought a long civil war. The war ended in 1989. But no strong government has formed yet.

3. How did Mobutu rule the Congo?

____

____

____

As you read this section, write notes about each African nation. Describe how each nation gained independence and the reforms and problems that followed independence.

1. Ghana	Nkrumah's reforms:	Problems:
Tactics used by Nkrumah:		

2. Kenya	Kenyatta's reforms:	Problems:
Tactics used by Mau Mau:		

3. Zaire	Mobutu's rule:	Problems:
How independence gained:		

4. Algeria	Ben Bella's program:	Problems:
How independence gained:		

5. Angola	Causes of civil war:	Other problems:
How independence gained:		

Name ______________________ Class ______________ Date ______________

Conflicts in the Middle East

Terms and Names

Anwar Sadat Egyptian leader who signed a peace agreement with Israel

Golda Meir Israeli prime minister at the time of the 1973 Arab–Israeli war

Camp David Accords Agreement in which Egypt recognized Israel as a nation and Israel gave the Sinai Peninsula back to Egypt

Oslo Peace Accords Agreement aimed at giving Palestinians self-rule

PLO Palestine Liberation Organization

Yasir Arafat Leader of the PLO

intifada Sustained rebellion by Palestinians

Before You Read

In the last section, you read about conflicts in the new nations of Africa.

In this section, you will learn about conflicts in the Middle East.

As You Read

Use a chart to list some important political and military events that occurred following the Suez Crisis.

ISRAEL BECOMES A STATE
(Pages 583–584)

***How* did Israel come into being?**

The movement to settle Jews in the region of Palestine began in the late 1800s and early 1900s. These Jews desired to create a state in their ancient homeland. But Muslims had lived there since the 7th century.

After World War I, Britain took control of the area. The British found that Jews and Muslims did not live together peacefully. In 1917, Britain announced it would support the establishment of a Jewish national homeland in Palestine. This statement is known as the Balfour Declaration.

After World War II, the British left the area. The United Nations proposed that the Palestine Mandate be divided into two states: one for the Palestinian Arabs; the other for the Jews.

Arab countries voted against the plan. Many countries backed the idea of a separate Jewish state. They wanted to help make up for the suffering Jews had experienced in World War II. On May 14, 1948, the Jewish people declared the existence of the State of Israel.

1. Why did the creation of Israel cause conflict?

____

ISRAEL AND THE ARAB STATES IN CONFLICT (Pages 584–585)

***How* did Arab states respond to the creation of Israel?**

On May 15, 1948, six Arab nations invaded Israel. Israel won the war in a few months with strong support from the United States. This war was the first of many Arab-Israeli wars.

Another war was started by the Suez Crisis. The crisis began in 1956 when a group of Egyptian army officers seized control of the government of Egypt from Britain. The British and French had kept control of the Suez Canal. Gamal Abdel Nasser, the new leader of Egypt, attacked the canal. The Israeli army helped the British and French keep control. The peace settlement that followed gave the canal to Egypt anyway.

The Six-Day War broke out in 1967 when Egypt and other nations threatened Israel. Israel defeated Egypt, Iran, Jordan, and Syria in just a week. Israel's success brought new areas under its control.

The next war, in 1973, began when Egypt, led by **Anwar Sadat,** and its allies launched a surprise attack. At first, Arab forces won some of the territory lost in 1967. Israel, led by its prime minister, **Golda Meir,** fought back and won control of much of the territory it had lost.

2. What did the Suez Crisis and Six-Day War have in common?

____

____

EFFORTS AT PEACE

(**Pages** 586–587)

What happened at Camp David?

In 1978, Egyptian leader Sadat signed a peace agreement with Israeli prime minister Menachem Begin. In this agreement, Israel gave the Sinai Peninsula back to Egypt. In return, Egypt recognized Israel as a nation. Egypt was the first Islamic country to give this recognition. This agreement became known as the **Camp David Accords.** It was followed by the first peace treaty between Israel and an Arab country. This angered many Arabs. Sadat was assassinated in 1981.

3. What is significant about the Camp David Accords?

____

____

PEACE SLIPS AWAY

(**Pages** 588–589)

How have Palestinians responded to living in Israel?

Despite many efforts, Israel and the Palestinians have not made peace. Many Palestinians living in Israel dislike Israeli rule. They want a nation of their own.

The Palestine Liberation Organization (**PLO**), led by **Yasir Arafat,** became a leading group in the struggle for self-rule. During the 1970s and 1980s, the military arm of the PLO made many attacks on Israel. Israel responded by invading Lebanon to attack bases of the PLO. In the late 1980s, many Palestinians in Israel began a revolt called the **intifada.**

In the early 1990s, the two sides took steps toward peace. Israel agreed to give Palestinians control of an area called the Gaza Strip and of the town of Jericho. The agreement was known as the **Oslo Peace Accords.** The Israeli leader who signed this agreement, Yitzhak Rabin, was assassinated in 1995. He was killed by a Jewish extremist who opposed giving in to the Palestinians. A second intifada occurred in 2000. Then, in 2003, the two sides began working on a new peace plan pushed by U.S. leaders.

4. What is the state of Israeli-Arab relations today?

____

____

As you read this section, fill in the chart to describe cause-and-effect relationships in the Middle East.

Causes	Actions	Effects
	1. Britain issues the Balfour Declaration.	
	2. Independent Israel is created.	
	3. The 1956 Arab-Israeli war breaks out.	
	4. The 1967 Six-Day War begins.	
	5. The 1973 Yom Kippur war begins.	
	6. Sadat and Begin sign the Camp David Accords.	
	7. Rabin and Arafat issue a Declaration of Principles.	

Central Asia Struggles

Terms and Names

Transcaucasian Republics The nations of Armenia, Azerbaijan, and Georgia

Central Asian Republics The nations of Uzbekistan, Turkmenistan, Tajikistan, Kazakhstan, and Kyrgyzstan

mujahideen A group that fought against the Soviet-supported government in Afghanistan

Taliban A conservative Islamic group that controlled most of Afghanistan from 1998 to 2001

Before You Read

In the last section, you read about conflicts in the Middle East.

In this section, you will learn how the nations of Central Asia have struggled to achieve freedom.

As You Read

Use an outline to organize the section's main ideas and details.

FREEDOM BRINGS NEW CHALLENGES (Pages 590–591)

What challenges have the countries of Central Asia faced?

In 1991 the Soviet Union broke apart. As a result, the republics that it had conquered became fifteen independent states. These states include nine countries in Central Asia. One group of Central Asia States is known as the **Transcaucasian Republics.** The other group of states is called the **Central Asian Republics.**

Since independence, the countries of Central Asia have faced economic problems. These countries are some of the poorest in the world. They were helped economically by the Soviet Union. When they gained independence, they had a hard time standing on their own. In addition, economic practices during the Soviet era created problems. For example, the Soviets made certain areas of Central Asia grow only one crop, such as cotton. Growing a single crop hurt the nations of Central Asia. They did not develop a balanced economy.

Central Asia is home to many different peoples. Some of these people have a history of hatred toward each other. When the Soviets ruled the region, they controlled these hatreds. However, after the Soviet Union broke apart, various groups began to fight. Some of these fights became regional wars.

1. Why have countries in Central Asia faced economic problems?

____

____

____

AFGHANISTAN AND THE WORLD

(**Pages** 591–593)

***How* has Afghanistan struggled for freedom?**

Afghanistan had a long history of struggle. During the 1800s, both Russia and Britain wanted to control Afghanistan. Russia wanted to get to the Indian Ocean through Afghanistan. Britain wanted to protect the northern borders of its Indian Empire. Britain fought three wars with the Afghanis. Eventually, Britain left the country in 1919.

In 1919, Afghanistan became an independent nation. It set up a monarchy, or rule by a king. In 1964, the country created a constitution. This constitution set up a more democratic style of government. However, the democratic system failed to grow.

In 1973, military leaders put an end to the democratic government. Five years later, a group took control of the country. This group was supported by the Soviet Union. Many Afghanis were against this group.

The Soviet-supported government had strong enemies. Many of these enemies formed a rebel group known as the **mujahideen,** or holy warriors. The mujahideen fought strongly against the Soviet-supported government. The Soviet Union wanted to defeat the rebels in Afghanistan. To get this done, Soviet troops invaded Afghanistan in 1979. The Soviets greatly outnumbered the rebels. Despite this, the rebels were tough to beat. The two groups fought for 10 years. Eventually, the Soviet troops left the country.

After the Soviets left, various Afghan rebel troops began fighting each other for control of the country. By 1998, an Islamic group known as the **Taliban** controlled most of Afghanistan. Another rebel group, the Northern Alliance, held the northwest corner of the country.

The Taliban had an unusual understanding of the Islamic religion. Many other Muslims disagreed with this understanding. The Taliban believed that they should control nearly every part of Afghan life. Women were forbidden to go to school or hold jobs. The Taliban did not allow watching television and movies or listening to modern music. Punishment for disobeying the rules included whipping and execution.

The Taliban allowed terrorist groups to train in Afghanistan. They allowed terrorist leaders, such as Osama bin Laden, to stay in their country. Bin Laden led a terrorist group called al-Qaeda. Many believe this group has carried out attacks on the West. For example, Al-Qaeda is believed to have done the attacks on the World Trade Center. Those attacks happened in New York on September 11, 2001.

After the September 11 attacks, the U.S. government told the Taliban to turn over bin Laden. The Taliban refused. Then the United States took military action. In October 2001, U.S. forces began bombing Taliban air defense, airfields, and command centers. Al-Qaeda training camps were also bombed. On the ground, the United States helped anti-Taliban forces, such as the Northern Alliance. By December, the United States had driven the Taliban from power.

The Afghanis then created a new government. Hamid Karzai was the leader of this government.

2. What are some of the ways that the Taliban controlled Afghan society?

____

____

As you read about the struggles of Central Asia, take notes to answer the following questions.

Freedom in Central Asia brings new challenges	
1. Since gaining independence, why have the nations of Central Asia struggled economically?	
2. Why have many regional wars been fought in Central Asia?	

Afghanistan Struggles for Freedom	
3. During the 1800s, why did Britain want to gain control over Afghanistan? Why did Russia want control over this region?	
4. Why did the Soviet Union invade Afghanistan in 1979?	

Rise and Fall of the Taliban	
5. How did rule by the Taliban affect Afghanistan?	
6. How did the United States help to defeat the Taliban?	

Name ______________________ Class ______________ Date ______________

Democracy

Case Study: Latin American Democracies

Terms and Names

Brasília Capital city of Brazil

land reform Breaking up large estates in order to give land to the landless

standard of living Quality of life as judged by the amount of goods people have

recession Decrease in the size of the economy

PRI Institutional Revolutionary Party, which has controlled Mexico for most of the century

Before You Read

In the last section, you read about conflicts in the Middle East.

In this section, you will read about the struggles for democracy in Latin America.

As You Read

Use a chart to take notes on the steps Brazil, Mexico, and Argentina have taken toward democracy.

DEMOCRACY AS A GOAL

(**Pages** 599–600)

***How* does democracy work?**

For democracy to work, several conditions must exist. There must be free and fair elections. There must also be more than one political party. The people of the country should have a good education. Then they can make informed choices. They should share a common culture. All must accept the idea that everyone has equal rights. Finally, there must be rule by law, not by power. Many nations in Latin America have had difficulty achieving democracy because all these factors are not present.

1. Name at least four factors needed to make democracy work.

____

____

DICTATORS AND DEMOCRACY

(**Pages** 600–602)

***What* challenges has Brazil faced?**

After independence in 1822, Brazil started out as a monarchy. After 1930, a dictator ruled. But in 1956, Juscelino Kubitschek was elected president. He tried to improve the economy. He built a new capital city, **Brasília.** He supported **land reform.** Land reform aimed at breaking up large estates and giving land to the peasants.

Landowners opposed land reform. They backed a group of army leaders who took power in 1964. The military ruled Brazil for 20 years. The country's economy grew. But the people had few rights. Eventually, their **standard of living** also fell. This means the quality of life, judged by the amount of goods people have, went down. By the 1980s a **recession**—a decrease in the size of the economy—hurt Brazil.

2. What changes did land reform bring in Brazil?

____

____

____

____

____

ONE-PARTY RULE (Pages 602–604)

What party has controlled Mexico for most of the century?

Mexico has had a stable government since the 1920s. One political party—now called the Institutional Revolutionary Party (**PRI**)—has been in power during this period. This party has controlled the local, state, and national governments.

At times, the PRI acted harshly to stop any dissent. For example, in 1968 the government killed many people who took part in a demonstration for economic reform.

The PRI recently opened up the political system to candidates from other parties. In 1997, two opposition parties won many seats in the national legislature. They ended PRI control of that congress. Then, in 2000, Mexican voters ended 71 years of PRI rule by electing Vicente Fox as president.

3. How has the PRI controlled Mexico?

____

____

____

____

____

POLITICAL AND ECONOMIC DISORDER (Pages 604–605)

How has democracy grown in Argentina?

Argentina has also struggled toward democracy. In the 1940s and 1950s, Juan Perón was a popular dictator. He put in place many programs to benefit the masses. But in 1955, the army overthrew him. The army controlled the government for many years. Army leaders ruled harshly. They killed many people who opposed them.

In 1982, the army suffered a stinging defeat in a war with Britain. The generals agreed to step down. Since 1983, Argentina has been led by freely elected leaders. However, it has experienced a growing economic crisis.

4. What happened after Perón was overthrown?

____

____

____

____

____

As you read this section, fill in the chart by writing notes in the appropriate spaces.

Making Democracy Work	
1. Note four practices that are common in a democracy.	
2. Note three conditions that contribute to democratic progress in a nation.	

Steering Brazil Toward Democracy	
3. Note three actions Brazilian leaders took to stabilize Brazil's economy.	
4. Note one democratic practice in Brazil today.	

Ending One-Party Rule in Mexico	
5. Note two crises that threatened democratic stability in Mexico.	
6. Note one way that the election of 2000 advanced democracy in Mexico.	

Ending Repression in Argentina	
7. Note three ways military rule affected Argentina.	
8. Note one democratic practice in Argentina today.	

The Challenge of Democracy in Africa

Terms and Names

federal system System in which power is shared between state governments and a central authority

martial law Military rule

dissident Person against government policy

apartheid Strict separation of blacks and whites

Nelson Mandela Leader of the African National Congress who was imprisoned

Before You Read

In the last section, you read about challenges to democracy in South America and Mexico.

In this section, you will read about struggles for democracy in Africa.

As You Read

Use a Venn diagram to compare political events in Nigeria and South Africa.

COLONIAL RULE LIMITS DEMOCRACY (Page 606)

***What* problems did colonial rule create?**

African nations have had a hard time setting up democratic governments because of the effects of colonial rule. European powers made borders in Africa that paid no attention to ethnic groupings. They put people who disliked each other in the same area. This practice caused conflict.

Also, the European nations never built up the economies of their colonies. Most of the colonies lacked a middle class or skilled workers. Both are needed for a strong democracy. When Britain and France gave their African colonies independence, they gave them democratic governments. But problems soon arose between rival groups.

1. Name three things that have slowed democracy in Africa.

____

____

____

____

CIVIL WAR IN NIGERIA; NIGERIA'S NATION-BUILDING (Pages 607–609)

***What* happened after Nigeria gained independence?**

In 1960, Nigeria became independent from Britain. It adopted a federal system.

In a **federal system,** power is shared between state governments and a central authority. But conflict broke out in just a few years. The people of one ethnic group—the Igbo—tried to break away from Nigeria in 1967. The Igbo lost in a three-year civil war.

A period of **martial law,** or military rule, followed the war. In 1979 Nigeria got an elected government. Some army officers said the government was corrupt, The officers overthrew the government in 1983. Once in power, they treated the people from other ethnic groups harshly. They jailed **dissidents,** opponents of government policy. The military rulers allowed elections in 1993. But they did not accept the results of the elections and continued to rule the land.

2. What happened after Nigeria's civil war?

____

____

____

SOUTH AFRICA UNDER APARTHEID (Page 609)

What was apartheid?

In South Africa, the conflict was between races. A white minority ruled a black majority. In 1948, the whites put in place a policy called **apartheid**—the strict separation of blacks and whites. Black South Africans were denied many basic rights. Some joined together in a group called the African National Congress (ANC) to fight for their rights. The white government cracked down on the ANC. They put many ANC leaders in prison. **Nelson Mandela,** the leader of the ANC, was one of the people imprisoned.

3. Why was the African National Congress formed?

____

____

____

____

STRUGGLE FOR DEMOCRACY (Pages 610–611)

How did apartheid end?

By the late 1980s, several riots had taken place. Blacks angrily struck back against apartheid. People in other nations also opposed apartheid. They boycotted, or would not buy, goods produced in South Africa. They hoped the boycott would persuade the South African government to end apartheid.

In 1990, President F. W. de Klerk took that step. He made the ANC legal and released ANC leader Nelson Mandela from prison. The South African parliament passed a law ending apartheid. In April 1994, all South Africans—even blacks—were able to vote in an election for a new leader. The ANC and Mandela won easily. In 1996, the new government approved a new constitution. It gave equal rights to all South Africans.

4. Why did F. W. de Klerk end apartheid?

____

____

____

____

As you read about Nigeria and South Africa, note the consequences of each of the policies or actions listed.

Policies/Actions		Consequences
1. In drawing up colonial boundaries in Africa, the colonial powers ignored ethnic and cultural divisions.	→	
2. The colonial powers developed plantations and mines but few factories in Africa.	→	
3. Civil war breaks out in ethnically divided Nigeria.	→	
4. The military overthrows Nigeria's civilian government.	→	
5. The National Party gains power in South Africa.	→	
6. Riots break out in the black township of Soweto.	→	
7. South Africans elect F. W. de Klerk president.	→	
8. President de Klerk agrees to hold universal elections.	→	

The Collapse of the Soviet Union

Terms and Names

Politburo Ruling committee of the Communist Party

Mikhail Gorbachev Leader of the Soviet Union from 1985 to 1991

glasnost Gorbachev's policy of openness

perestroika Gorbachev's policy aimed at reforming the Soviet economy

Boris Yeltsin Political opponent of Gorbachev who became president of Russia

CIS Commonwealth of Independent States, a loose federation of former Soviet territories

"shock therapy" Yeltsin's plan for changing the Soviet economy

Before You Read

In the last section, you read about political conflicts in Africa.

In this section, you will read about the fall of the Soviet Union and the rise of Russia.

As You Read

Use a time line to record significant events in the Soviet Union and Russia.

GORBACHEV MOVES TOWARD DEMOCRACY (Page 612)

***How* did Gorbachev open up Soviet society?**

During the 1960s and 1970s, the leaders of the Soviet Union kept tight control on society. Leonid Brezhnev and the **Politburo**—the ruling committee of the Communist Party—crushed all political dissent. In 1985, Communist Party leaders named **Mikhail Gorbachev** as the leader of the Soviet Union. He was the youngest Soviet leader since Joseph Stalin. He was expected to make minor reforms. But his reforms led to a revolution.

Gorbachev felt that Soviet society could not improve without the free flow of ideas. He started a policy called **glasnost,** or openness. He opened churches. He let political prisoners out of prison. He allowed banned books to be published.

1. What was the Glasnost policy?

____

REFORMING THE ECONOMY AND POLITICS (Page 613)

***What* changes did Gorbachev make in the Soviet economy and politics?**

Gorbachev began a policy called **perestroika,** or economic restructuring. It tried to improve the Soviet economy by lifting the tight control on all managers and workers.

In 1987, Gorbachev opened up the political system. He allowed the people to elect representatives to a legislature.

Finally, Gorbachev changed Soviet foreign policy. He moved to end the arms race against the United States.

2. What was the policy of perestroika?

____

THE SOVIET UNION FACES TURMOIL (Pages 614–616)

What problems did the Soviet Union face?

People from many different ethnic groups in the Soviet Union began calling for the right to have their own nation. In 1990, Lithuania declared independence. Gorbachev sent troops. They fired on a crowd and killed 14 people. This action and the slow pace of reform cost Gorbachev support among the Soviet people.

Many people began to support **Boris Yeltsin.** Old-time Communists were becoming angry at Gorbachev. They thought his changes made the Soviet Union weaker. In August 1991, they tried to take control of the government. When the army refused to back the coup leaders, they gave up.

To strike back, the parliament voted to ban the party from any political activity. Meanwhile, more republics in the Soviet Union declared their independence. Russia and the 14 other republics each became independent states. Most of the republics then agreed to form the Commonwealth of Independent States, or **CIS,** a loose federation of former Soviet territories. By the end of 1991, the Soviet Union had ceased to exist.

3. Name three events that led up to the collapse of the Soviet Union.

____

RUSSIA UNDER BORIS YELTSIN (Page 616)

What happened when Gorbachev lost power?

After the coup failed, Gorbachev lost all power. Yeltsin became the most powerful Russian leader. As president of Russia, he faced many problems. He tried to change the economy. His economic plan was known as **"shock therapy."** This move toward capitalism caused suffering.

In addition, rebels in the small republic of Chechnya declared their independence from Russia. Yeltsin refused to allow it. He sent thousands of troops to put down the Chechen rebels. As a bloody war raged, Yeltsin resigned and named Vladimir Putin as president.

4. What decisions did Yeltsin make about the economy?

____

RUSSIA UNDER VLADIMIR PUTIN (Page 617)

How did Putin handle the situation in Chechnya?

Putin dealt harshly with the rebellion in Chechnya but the rebellion dragged on for years. Chechen rebels seized a theater in Moscow and more than 100 people died.

Economic troubles continued as Russia dealt with social upheaval caused by years of change and reform. Social problems included homeless children, domestic violence, and unemployment, as well as declines in population, standard of living, and life expectancy.

5. What were some of the signs of social distress in Russia?

____

As you read this section, explain how Communist leaders responded to each problem or crisis.

Problems/Crises		Responses
1. Soviet society had stopped growing as a result of totalitarian policies banning political dissent.	→	
2. The Soviet economy was inefficient and unproductive.	→	
3. The Soviet-U.S. arms race had become too costly.	→	
4. In August 1991, hard-liners staged a coup against Gorbachev.	→	
5. The Soviet Union broke up.	→	
6. The Russian economy under Boris Yeltsin was ailing.	→	
7. In 1991, Chechnya declared its independence.	→	

Changes in Central and Eastern Europe

Terms and Names

Solidarity Polish workers' movement

Lech Walesa Leader of Solidarity

reunification Uniting of East and West Germany into one nation

ethnic cleansing Policy of murder and brutality aimed at ridding a country of a particular ethnic group

Before You Read

In the last section, you read about the collapse of the Soviet Union.

In this section, you will read about the fall of communism and other changes in Central and Eastern Europe.

As You Read

Use a chart to record reasons that nations in Central and Eastern Europe broke apart.

POLAND AND HUNGARY REFORM (Pages 618–619)

How did Poland and Hungary change?

Gorbachev urged Communist leaders in Eastern Europe to change their policies but many of them resisted. Despite resistance from the old Communist leaders, the people of Eastern Europe wanted reform. Protest movements began to build.

In Poland, years of economic problems troubled the people. Polish workers organized a union called **Solidarity.** Solidarity went on strike to get the government to recognize the union.

The government gave in to Solidarity's demands. But later, the government banned the union and threw **Lech Walesa,** the union's leader, in jail. This caused unrest. Finally, the government was forced to allow elections. The Polish people voted overwhelmingly against the Communists and for Solidarity. However, the Polish people became frustrated with how slow and painful the road to economic recovery and capitalism was. In 1995, they voted Walesa out of office and replaced him with Aleksander Kwasniewski as president.

Inspired by the Poles, leaders in Hungary started a reform movement. The reformers took over the Communist party. Then the party voted itself out of existence. In 1999, Hungary joined NATO as a full member.

1. What caused frustration and change in Poland?

____

____

GERMANY REUNIFIES

(**Pages** 619–620)

***What* changes occurred in Germany?**

Thousands of people across East Germany demanded free elections. Soon, the Berlin Wall, which divided East and West Berlin, was torn down. By the end of 1989, the Communist party was out of power.

The next year **reunification** occurred. The two parts of Germany, East and West, were one nation again. But the new nation had many problems. The biggest problem was the weak economy in the east.

2. What happened after the Berlin Wall fell?

____

DEMOCRACY SPREADS IN CZECHOSLOVAKIA (Page 621)

***What* happened in Czechoslovakia?**

In Czechoslovakia, calls for reform took place. When the government cracked down on protesters, thousands of Czechs poured into the streets. One day hundreds of thousands of people gathered to protest in the nation's capital. The Communists agreed to give up power.

Reformers launched an economic reform program that caused a sharp rise in unemployment that especially hurt Slovakia, the republic occupying the eastern third of the country. In 1993, the country split into two separate nations: the Czech Republic and Slovakia. The economies of both slowly improved.

3. How did the government of Czechoslovakia change?

____

OVERTHROW IN ROMANIA

(**Pages** 621–622)

***What* happened in Romania?**

In Romania, Nicolae Ceausescu, the Communist dictator, ordered the army to shoot at protesters. This caused larger protests. The army then joined the people and fought against the secret police loyal to Ceausescu. He was captured and executed in 1989. General elections quickly followed and the new government reformed the economy. The government made economic reforms to introduce capitalism.

4. How did the government of Romania change?

____

THE BREAKUP OF YUGOSLAVIA

(**Pages** 622–624)

***What* happened in Yugoslavia?**

Yugoslavia was made up of many different ethnic groups. In the early 1990s, they began fighting. When Serbia tried to control the government, two other republics—Slovenia and Croatia—declared independence. Slovenia beat back a Serbian invasion. But Serbia and Croatia fought a bloody war.

In 1992, Bosnia-Herzegovina also declared independence. Serbs who lived in that region opposed the move. Using aid from Serbia, they fought a brutal civil war against the Bosnian Muslims. The Serbs used murder and other forms of brutality against the Muslims. This **ethnic cleansing** was intended to rid Bosnia of its Muslims. The United Nations helped create a peace agreement.

In 1998, the Balkan region experienced violence again in Kosovo, a province in southern Serbia, which Serbian forces invaded in order to suppress an independence movement. A NATO bombing campaign forced Serbian leaders to withdraw their forces.

5. Who fought in the civil war in Yugoslavia?

____

As you read about changes in Central and Eastern Europe, take notes to answer the questions.

Poland and Hungary Reform	
1. Why did the Poles choose a former Communist leader over Lech Walesa in the 1995 election?	
2. What were some of the reforms introduced in Hungary?	

Germany Reunifies	
3. Why did huge demonstrations break out throughout East Germany?	

Democracy Spreads in Czechoslovakia	
4. Why did Czechoslovakia break up?	

Overthrow in Romania	
5. What brought about Ceausescu's downfall in Romania?	

China: Reform and Reaction

Terms and Names

Zhou Enlai Chinese leader who worked with President Nixon to improve U.S.–Chinese relations

Deng Xiaoping Chinese leader after Zhou Enlai

Four Modernizations Goals of Deng Xiaoping that called for progress in agriculture, industry, defense, and science and technology

Tiananmen Square Square in the capital of Beijing; scene of a student demonstration and massacre

Hong Kong Island that became part of China again in 1997

Before You Read

In the last section, you read about the collapse of communism and other changes in Central and Eastern Europe.

In this section, you will learn about the recent history of China.

As You Read

Use a diagram to list events leading up to the demonstration in Tiananmen Square.

THE LEGACY OF MAO (Pages 625–626)

How did Mao change China?

Mao Zedong had tried to build a China on the ideas of equality, revolutionary spirit, and hard work. But his policies failed to create a strong economy. He reduced incentives for higher production. The Great Leap Forward helped cause an economic disaster.

During Mao's rule, China had little role in world affairs. **Zhou Enlai**, another Chinese leader, worried about this. He worked with U.S. President Richard Nixon to improve U.S.–Chinese relations.

1. How successful were Mao's economic programs?

____

____

CHINA AND THE WEST (Page 626)

How did Deng Xiaoping change China?

After Mao and Zhou died in 1976, moderates took control of the government. The most powerful leader was **Deng Xiaoping.** He tried to modernize the economy. Deng had goals known as the **Four Modernizations.** These called for progress in agriculture, industry, defense, and science and technology. He ended farming communes and allowed farmers to sell part of their produce for a profit. Farm production increased greatly.

Deng made similar changes to industry. People's incomes began to rise. They began to purchase appliances and other goods that were once scarce.

2. What were the results of Deng Xiaoping's changes?

____

____

____

MASSACRE IN TIANANMEN SQUARE (Pages 627–628)

What caused the protest at Tiananmen Square?

Deng's new plan caused problems. The gap between rich and poor grew wider, which caused unrest. Western political ideas spread throughout the country. In 1989, thousands of Chinese students gathered in **Tiananmen Square** in the capital of Beijing. They called for democracy and freedom. Deng responded by sending army troops and tanks to put down the rally. Thousands were killed or wounded. China has continued to stamp out protests since then.

3. What happened to the protesters at Tiananmen Square?

____

____

____

CHINA ENTERS THE NEW MILLENNIUM (Pages 628–629)

What happened to Hong Kong?

Another major issue for China was the status of **Hong Kong.** The island became part of China again in 1997 when the British gave it back after 155 years of colonial rule. China promised to respect Hong Kong's freedom for 50 years. But many worried that China would take away Hong Kong's freedoms.

4. Why do people worry about Hong Kong's new rule?

____

____

____

CHINA BEYOND 2000 (Page 629)

What is the connection between political and economic reform in China?

Liberal economic reforms in China did not immediately lead to political reforms. China has been successful in reducing poverty, in part because it has been cautious in privatizing the economy. China managed to maintain economic growth in the early 21st century.

As economic and social conditions in China improve, the political situation may improve as well. An important sign of China's engagement with the world was its successful campaign to be chosen as the site for the 2008 Summer Olympics.

5. Which came first in China—political or economic reform?

____

____

____

As you read about Communist China, fill in the chart by noting the goals and outcomes of each action listed.

Goals	Actions	Outcomes
	1. Mao begins the Cultural Revolution.	
	2. Zhou Enlai invites the American table tennis team to tour China.	
	3. Deng Xiaoping launches a bold program of economic reforms.	
	4. Students stage an uprising in Tiananmen Square.	
	5. Britain hands Hong Kong over to China.	

Section 1

The Impact of Science and Technology

Terms and Names

International Space Station Project, involving 16 nations, to build a huge laboratory in space

Internet Worldwide computer network

genetic engineering Use of genes to develop new products and cures

cloning Process of creating identical copies of DNA for research and other purposes

green revolution Attempt to increase food resources worldwide

Before You Read

In the last section, you read about struggles for democracy in China.

In this section, you will learn about recent changes in science and technology.

As You Read

Use a chart to list the effects of scientific and technological developments.

EXPLORING THE SOLAR SYSTEM AND BEYOND (Pages 637–638)

***How* did competition give way to cooperation in space?**

From the 1950s to the 1970s, the United States and Soviet Union took their Cold War rivalry to space. Each nation tried to be the first to reach the moon and beyond.

In the 1970s, the two nations began to cooperate in space exploration. In 1975, United States and Soviet spacecraft docked, or joined together, in space. Later, American and Soviet space missions included scientists from other countries. In the late 1990s, the United States, Russia, and 14 other nations began working together to build the **International Space Station.**

Some space missions did not include human crew members. Unmanned flights sent back pictures and information about other planets.

In 1990, the United States and European countries sent the Hubble Space Telescope into orbit around the earth. This satellite sent back unprecedented images of objects in space.

1. Give three examples of international cooperation in space.

____

____

____

____

EXPANDING GLOBAL COMMUNICATIONS

(**Pages** 638–639)

How has technology changed communications?

Every day satellites are used to track the weather around the world. They are also used to search for minerals on the planet. Satellites allow television broadcasts to carry events live around the world.

Another advance in technology has been the computer. Computers have become more powerful since they were first invented. At the same time, they have gotten smaller in size. Consumer goods such as microwave ovens, telephones, and cars often include computer chips to keep them running.

Millions of people around the world use personal computers at work or at home. Many of these people are connected through the **Internet,** a worldwide computer network. The Internet allows people to get a great deal of information more quickly and easily than ever before. The Internet also allows people to communicate with one another.

2. How have computers changed everyday living?

____

____

____

____

TRANSFORMING HUMAN LIFE

(**Pages** 639–640)

How has new technology changed medicine?

New technology has changed medicine. Lasers allow doctors to perform surgery to fix problems in delicate areas, such as in the eye or the brain. New methods for making images of the body help doctors locate problems.

Research into genes has helped unlock the secrets of some diseases. **Genetic engineering** enables scientists to use genes in new ways. For example, scientists can develop plants with special traits. **Cloning** is part of genetic engineering. It is the creation of identical copies of DNA. Cloning can be used to produce plants and animals that are identical to the existing plants and animals. The application of this new understanding of genes has led to many developments in agriculture.

Scientists have made other advances in farming. In the **green revolution,** scientists have developed new strains of food crops to help farmers grow more food.

3. Why is genetic engineering an important development?

____

____

____

____

As you read this section, fill out the chart by listing examples of technological progress in each of the following areas.

1. Space exploration	2. Astronomy	3. Communications
4. Health and medicine	**5. Genetics**	**6. Agriculture**

Section 2

Global Economic Development

Terms and Names

developed nation Industrialized nation

emerging nation Nation that is still developing industry

global economy Economy linking the economies of many nations

free trade Absence of barriers that can block trade between countries

ozone layer Layer of atmosphere that blocks dangerous rays from the sun

sustainable growth Economic growth that meets current needs but conserves resources for the future

Before You Read

In the last section, you read about changes in science and technology.

In this section, you will read about the new global economy.

As You Read

Use a web diagram to identify the forces that have shaped the global economy.

TECHNOLOGY REVOLUTIONIZES THE WORLD'S ECONOMY

(Pages 641–642)

***How* have the economies of the developed nations changed?**

Technology has changed the world's economies. In the 1950s, scientists found new ways to make plastics, which came to be widely used. In recent years, industries have begun using robots to make products. These changes have required workers to have more and different skills than before.

In industrialized nations, or **developed nations,** there are more jobs in service and information industries. Manufacturing jobs began to grow more quickly in the **emerging nations** where wages are lower.

1. What types of jobs are on the increase in developed nations?

____

____

____

____

ECONOMIC GLOBALIZATION

(Pages 642–643)

***Why* is free trade important in a global economy?**

A **global economy** continued to develop in the 1980s. Telephone and computer links connect banks and other financial companies around the world. Multinational corporations operate in many countries.

After World War II, many leaders believed that world economies would grow best if there were **free trade.** This means there would be no barriers to block goods from one country entering another country. Many steps have been taken to put free trade in practice. In 1951, some nations in Europe joined together to create free trade. That group, now called the European Union (EU), has grown to become a powerful trading bloc.

The United States, Canada, and Mexico agreed to the North American Free Trade Agreement (NAFTA) in 1994. Another free trade zone was set up in Latin America. Similar groups are being put together in Africa and Asia.

In recent years, there has been considerable disagreement on the impact of the globalization of the economy. Supporters suggest that open, competitive markets and the free flow of goods, services, technology, and investments benefit all nations. Opponents charge that globalization has been a disaster for the poorest countries. Many, they suggest, are worse off today than they were in the past.

2. Name three steps that have been taken in the direction of free trade.

____

____

IMPACT OF GLOBAL DEVELOPMENT (Pages 645–646)

***How* has the development of the global economy affected the use of energy and other resources?**

Economic growth needs many resources. Manufacturing and trade both use huge amounts of energy. Oil has been a major source of this energy. Whenever the flow of oil has been threatened, the world's economies have suffered shocks.

In 1990, Iraq invaded Kuwait. This threatened the flow of Kuwaiti oil. Soon, the countries of the United Nations went to war against Iraq. This was known as the Gulf War.

Economic growth has also caused environmental problems. Burning coal and oil has polluted the air. It has also caused acid rain and contributed to global warming. The release of some chemicals into the air has weakened Earth's **ozone layer.** This layer of atmosphere blocks dangerous rays from the sun.

One new idea about growth involves sustainable development. **Sustainable growth** requires meeting current needs while conserving future resources.

3. What environmental problems have resulted from economic growth?

____

____

As you read about global economics, complete the chart by filling in the cause or effect.

Causes		Effects
1.	→	Manufacturing jobs moved out of developed nations to emerging nations.
2. Multinational companies developed worldwide; computer linkages made business transactions easier and faster.	→	
3.	→	The United States, Canada, and Mexico signed NAFTA.
4. Activities essential for industry and trade require the use of much energy.	→	
5. Manufacturing processes release chemicals called chlorofluorocarbons.	→	
6.	→	Many plants and animals are becoming extinct.

Global Security Issues

Terms and Names

proliferation spread

Universal Declaration of Human Rights 1948 United Nations statement of specific rights that all people should have

political dissent Difference of opinion over political issues

gender inequality Difference between men and women in terms of wealth and status

AIDS Acquired immune deficiency syndrome, a disease that attacks the immune system, leaving sufferers open to deadly infections

refugees People who leave their country to move to another to find safety

Before You Read

In the last section, you read about the growth of the global economy.

In this section, you will read about challenges to global security.

As You Read

Use a chart to list methods employed to increase global security.

ISSUES OF WAR AND PEACE

(**Pages** 648–649)

***How** have nations worked together for global security?*

After World War II, nations joined together to pursue global security. The United Nations (UN) was formed at the end of World War II to promote world peace. It now has more than 180 member nations. The UN provides a place for countries—or groups within countries—to share their views.

The UN can also send troops as a peacekeeping force. These soldiers—who come from member nations—try to stop violence from breaking out.

Another approach to world peace has been to limit weapons of mass destruction. These include nuclear weapons, chemical weapons, and biological weapons. In 1968, many nations signed a Nuclear Non-Proliferation Treaty. The nations that signed the treaty agreed to prevent the **proliferation,** or spread, of nuclear weapons. In the 1990s, the United States and Russia agreed to destroy many of their nuclear weapons. In another treaty, many nations promised not to develop chemical or biological weapons.

Ethnic and religious differences are the sources of many world conflicts. Some of these conflicts have roots that reach back decades or even centuries. Governments and many international organizations, including the UN, are trying to find peaceful solutions to these conflicts.

1. Name two specific approaches toward collective security.

____

HUMAN RIGHTS ISSUES (Page 650)

What efforts have been made to ensure human rights?

In 1948, the UN approved the **Universal Declaration of Human Rights.** This declaration gives a list of rights that all people should have. In 1975, many nations signed the Helsinki Accords that also support human rights. Many groups around the world watch to see how well nations do in protecting these rights for their people.

Despite the efforts of human rights organizations, violations of fundamental rights continue to occur around the world. One type of violation occurs when governments try to stamp out **political dissent.** In many countries, individuals and groups have been persecuted for holding political views that differ from those of the government.

In the past, women suffered considerable discrimination. However, a heightened awareness of human rights encouraged women to work to improve their lives. They pushed for new laws that gave them greater equality. Since the 1970s, women have made notable gains, especially in the areas of education and work. Even so, **gender inequality** still is an issue.

2. Name two events that have been important in the worldwide struggle for human rights.

____

HEALTH ISSUES (Page 651)

What is the greatest challenge to global health?

Recently, the enjoyment of a decent standard of health has become recognized as a basic human right. However, for many people across the world, poor health is still the norm. Perhaps the greatest global challenge to the attainment of good health is **AIDS,** or acquired immune deficiency syndrome. AIDS is a worldwide problem. However, Sub-Saharan Africa has suffered most from the epidemic. The disease has had devastating impact on the populations and economies of many countries in this region.

3. Which area of the world has been hardest hit by the AIDS epidemic?

____

POPULATION MOVEMENT (Page 652)

What are some of the causes of the global movement of people?

In recent years, millions of people have moved from one country to another. Some people are **refugees,** who leave to escape natural disasters or harsh treatment at home. Others leave for more positive reasons—the chance of a better life for themselves and their children.

While people have a right to leave, every country does not have to accept them. Sometimes these people have to live in crowded refugee camps. They suffer hunger and disease. They can also cause political problems for the country where they are held. However, immigrants also can bring many benefits to their new home.

4. What problems can result from the global movement of people?

____

As you read this section, fill out the charts by writing answers in the appropriate boxes.

How do the following help to ensure collective security?	
1. Military alliances	
2. United Nations	
3. Nuclear Non-Proliferation Treaty	

How have the following threatened global security?	
4. Ethnic and religious rivalries	
5. Health issues	

How have the following promoted the cause of human rights?	
6. Universal Declaration of Human Rights	
7. Women's rights movement	
8. Migration	

Name ______________________ Class ______________ Date ______________

Terrorism

Case Study: September 11, 2001

Terms and Names

terrorism Use of violence against people or property to force changes in societies or governments

cyberterrorism Attacks on information systems for political reasons

Department of Homeland Security Department of the U.S. government that organizes the fight against terrorism in the United States

USA Patriot Act Antiterrorism law that allowed the government certain rights to help chase and capture terrorists

Before You Read

In the last section, you read about global security issues.

In this section, you will learn about terrorism and its effect on today's world.

As You Read

Use a chart to take notes on the September 11 and other terrorist attacks.

WHAT IS TERRORISM?

(Pages 653–654)

***What* motivates terrorists and what methods do they use?**

Terrorism is the use of violence against people or property to force changes in societies or governments. The reasons for modern terrorism are many. Reasons include gaining independence, getting rid of foreigners, and changing society. In the late 20th century, another type of terrorist appeared. These terrorists wanted to destroy what they believed were the forces of evil.

Terrorists use violence to try to achieve their goals. Terrorists often use bombs and bullets. Some terrorist groups have used biological and chemical weapons. Attacks on information systems such as computer networks are called **cyberterrorism.** These attacks are done for political reasons.

1. What types of weapons do terrorists use?

____

TERRORISM AROUND THE WORLD

(Pages 654–655)

***How* has terrorism affected the world?**

In the Middle East, Palestinians and Israelis have argued for decades about land ownership. This argument has resulted in many terrorist acts. Often a Palestinian group does an act of terrorism. In response, the Israelis strike back. In Northern Ireland, the Irish Republican Army (IRA) carried out terrorist acts for many years. The IRA wanted the British to give up control over Northern Ireland.

Many terrorist groups, such as Aum Shinrikyo, are found in East Asia. In Africa, civil unrest and regional wars cause most terrorist acts. Narcoterrorism often happens in Latin America. Narcoterrorism is terrorism connected with the trade of illegal drugs.

2. What has caused most of the terrorist activity in Africa?

____

ATTACK ON THE UNITED STATES

(**Pages** 656–657)

How has terrorism affected the United States?

On the morning of September 11, 2001, 19 Arab terrorists hijacked four airliners. The hijackers crashed two of the jets into the twin towers of the World Trade Center in New York City. The third jet destroyed part of the Pentagon in Washington, D.C. The fourth plane crashed in an empty field in Pennsylvania.

As a result of the attacks, the twin towers fell to the ground within two hours. About 3,000 people died in all the attacks. The dead included more than 340 New York City firefighters and 60 police officers.

Before September 11, many Americans thought that terrorism was something that happened in other countries. After September 11, many Americans became afraid that terrorist attacks could happen to them.

A few days after September 11, letters containing the disease anthrax were mailed. The letters were sent to people in the news media and to members of Congress. Five people died from inhaling the anthrax in these letters. Officials did not find a link between the anthrax letters and the September 11 attacks.

3. How did the September 11 attacks affect the way Americans looked at life?

____

THE UNITED STATES RESPONDS

(**Pages** 657–658)

How has the United States fought back against terrorism?

After September 11, the United States asked for an international effort to fight terrorism. U.S. officials suspected that Osama bin Laden directed the September 11 attacks. Bin Laden was the leader of a terrorist group called al-Qaeda.

The U.S. government created the **Department of Homeland Security** in 2002. Its job was to organize the fight against terrorism in the United States.

U.S. officials began to search for al-Qaeda terrorists in the United States. In addition, U.S. officials arrested and questioned many Arabs and other Muslims. Critics said that arresting people because of nationality or religion was unfair. They said that some of the arrested people probably did not commit a crime.

The **USA Patriot Act** became law. This law allowed the government several powers to help capture terrorists.

The Federal Aviation Administration (FAA) ordered airlines to put bars on cockpit doors. These bars would help stop hijackers from getting control of planes. National Guard troops began to guard airports. Trained security officers called sky marshals were put on planes. The Aviation and Transportation Security Act was passed. It put the federal government in charge of airport security.

4. How was aviation security increased?

____

As you read about terrorism, take notes to answer the questions.

1. Who? Who is Osama bin Laden? Who are sky marshals?	
2. When? When were the U.S. embassies in Kenya and Tanzania bombed? When did terrorists crash two airliners into the twin towers of the World Trade Center?	
3. What? What is cyberterrorism? What is the Department of Homeland Security?	
4. Where? Where did terrorists strike in Munich, Germany in 1972? Where did cult members release a deadly nerve gas in 1995?	
5. How? How has the United States increased aviation security? How was part of the Pentagon destroyed?	
6. Why? Why did the Irish Republican Army (IRA) engage in terrorist attacks? Why are some people critical of the USA Patriot Act?	

Section 5

Cultures Blend in a Global Age

Terms and Names

popular culture Cultural elements—such as sports, music, movies, and clothing—that reflect a group's common background

materialism Placing high value on owning things

Before You Read

In the last section, you read about terrorism.

In this section, you will learn about the global blending of cultures.

As You Read

Use a web diagram to identify areas of popular culture that have become international in scope.

CULTURAL EXCHANGE ACCELERATES (Pages 659–660)

***What* has speeded up the sharing of cultures?**

Changes in technology have made it possible for people to share their cultures with one another. Television is one of the main forces in this trend. It allows people to see things that happen around the world. Movies and radio also have had an impact in bringing the world's people together.

As a result of these mass media, the world's popular culture now includes elements from many different cultures. **Popular culture** includes music, sports, clothing styles, food, and hobbies. American television shows have become popular around the world. Broadcasts of some sporting events can reach millions of people in all corners of the globe. Music has also become international.

1. Name three aspects of culture that have become international.

____

____

WORLD CULTURE BLENDS MANY INFLUENCES (Pages 661–662)

***What* countries have most influenced cultural blending?**

Cultural blending occurs when parts of different cultures are combined. In recent times, the United States and Europe have been a major force in this blending. One reason is that Western nations dominate the mass media.

The political power of the West has also spread Western culture to other regions. For example, English is a major world language. About 500 million people speak English as their first or second language. More people speak Mandarin Chinese. But English speakers are more widely spread throughout the world. Western clothes can be seen throughout the world.

Western ideas have also influenced world thought. The Western idea of **materialism**—placing high value on owning things—has also spread. Some ideas have also traveled from East to West. The worlds of art and literature have become more international in recent years.

2. What Western aspects of culture have spread throughout the world?

____

____

____

FUTURE CHALLENGES AND HOPES (Pages 662–663)

How has the world responded to cultural blending?

Some people think the spread of international culture is a problem. They worry that their own culture will be swallowed up by other cultures. Some countries have adopted policies that reserve television broadcast time for national programming. In other countries, television programmers take Western programs and rework them according to their own culture. In some areas, people have returned to old traditions in order to keep them alive.

The people of the world are becoming more and more dependent on each another. All through human history, people have faced challenges to their survival. In the 21st century, those challenges will be faced by people who are in increasing contact with one another. They have a great stake in living together in harmony.

3. What problems or challenges can cultural blending bring?

____

____

____

As you read this section, take notes to answer questions about the sharing and blending of cultures.

Cultural exchanges are taking place at a faster pace than ever before.	
1. How has technology affected the sharing and blending of cultures?	
2. Why is mass media such a powerful force in spreading popular culture throughout the world?	

Western culture has greatly influenced cultures in many parts of the world.	
3. Why does the West play such a dominant role in shaping world culture?	
4. What is one significant difference between Western cultural beliefs and many non-Western cultural ideas?	

Global interdependence has ushered in change and challenges.	
5. Why do many people view with alarm the development of a global popular culture heavily influenced by Western ways?	
6. How have different countries responded to the impact of cultural intrusion?	